Roman's Journey

Roman Halter

———

ROMAN'S JOURNEY

with a preface by
Sir Martin Gilbert

Portobello
BOOKS

Published by Portobello Books Ltd 2007

Portobello Books Ltd
Eardley House
4 Uxbridge Street
Notting Hill Gate
London w8 7sy, UK

A CIP catalogue record is available from
the British Library

9 8 7 6 5 4 3 2

ISBN 1 84627 032 4
13-digit ISBN 978 1 84627 032 1
www.portobellobooks.com

Designed by Lindsay Nash

Typeset in New Caledonia by
Avon DataSet Ltd, Bidford on Avon,
Warwickshire

Printed and bound in Great Britain by
William Clowes Ltd, Beccles, Suffolk

Contents

Acknowledgements

When most people see the words 'I would like to thank', they stop reading, but… My great debt is to the main editor, my daughter Aloma Halter, whose sensitivity and acuity have given my book its shape and direction. Since her work also happens to be writing, editing and translating – trimming down a manuscript from several parallel versions, written over two decades, and from an unwieldy eight hundred pages to something manageable, was well within her field of competence. However, dealing with the degree of pain that must have been involved in the close and repeated reading of material on the destruction of so many family members, grandparents, uncles and aunts and young cousins; this was uncharted territory. So I particularly appreciate the fact that she took on this project when her own two daughters were very young.

At a certain stage, and to maintain the necessary degree of objectivity, Aloma co-opted a friend, another Jerusalemite, the writer and translator Betsy Rosenberg, whose experience and superb editing prised away the wheat from the chaff, bringing this book to the stage where it could be published. Her work was generously funded by the Sigrid Rausing Trust. I am so glad to have this opportunity to express my heartfelt thanks to Sigrid Rausing – both for her support of the manuscript at the editing stage, and later in her capacity as co-founder of Portobello Books – for without her unwavering support, this project might not have come into being.

During the early stages of this manuscript, Celia Brookes of Surrey and Yvonne Marcus of Jerusalem contributed their typing skills. For the many Polish and Russian names in the book, I would like to thank another friend of Aloma's, Karin Pozimski, for her expertise in Slavic languages and her readiness to give the manuscript her skills.

It has been a privilege to work with the team at Portobello Books – their creativity, kindness and patience have been prodigious. Here I would like to express my appreciation for my publisher, Philip Gwyn Jones, and my editor, Laura Barber, whose careful editorial guidance of this project, together with Mandy Kirkby's discerning editorial eye and attention to detail, have brought this book to completion.

My deep thanks are owed to Sir Martin Gilbert – my friend Martin – for his Preface.

Since this is a book about a lost family, it is vastly fitting that my thanks also end on a family note. In this context I would like to mention my son, Ardyn Halter, an artist and stained-glass window designer, who has been my colleague on many joint projects – several of them related to Holocaust memorials. Ardyn read all my handwritten pages in *all* the versions, giving me invaluable advice, which I too frequently ignored. Ardyn also supported Aloma's work throughout the initial editing process.

With the completion of the book, my appreciation goes to my daughter Aviva Halter-Hurn, an artist and book illustrator, with whom I often collaborate on projects – whether the making of Royal Coats of Arms or stained-glass windows.

And finally I would like to thank my wife, Susan Halter, champion swimmer and life partner, with whom I rebuilt my family. Susie has always encouraged me, and her patience in living for so many years with my telling and retelling of my Holocaust experiences, has been exceeded only by her inimitable zest for life, which has added so much to my own.

Preface by Sir Martin Gilbert

Roman Halter is an artist, with a gift not only for painting but for words. His memoirs reflect a deep sensitivity to his life and times, which during the Second World War were perilous in the extreme. His memoirs show just how implacable the Nazi enemy could be. It is important that he has now chosen, more than fifty years after the end of the war, to set down his recollections. They are vivid and in many places extremely harrowing. No one who reads them from cover to cover, lingering over the episodes that are the most dramatic and savage, will have any doubt that the fate of the Jewish people at the hands of the Nazis was intended to be total destruction.

It has always been essential, in studying the Holocaust, to recognize the nature of German life before the war, in all its variety and vibrancy. Roman Halter's account of his childhood is no mere preface, but a portrait-in-the-round of a lost era.

Pre-war Poland was home to more than three million Jews. In these pages it is the small town of Chodecz, with its eight hundred Jews, that is brought to life. It was a life that the Nazis were to destroy utterly.

The slow but relentless encroachment of German rule after the German invasion of Poland in September 1939 is powerfully described. Evil appeared in gradations, starting when Roman Halter and his family were evicted from their home. The rest of the story, of the descent into hell, is described in measured, unambiguous tones. These events impressed themselves on the young boy's mind with fierce clarity. His eyewitness testimony is a record that will live on as a memorial to those who were murdered – his family and friends, and all the six million Jews – and as a warning of man's capacity for evil. That capacity to kill and destroy human life did not die when the Second World War came to an end in 1945.

The full panoply of evil is here, whether it is mass murder in a ravine near his home town of Chodecz itself – which Roman Halter witnessed – or the grim circumstances of the Lodz ghetto, or Auschwitz, or Stutthof concentration camp, or slave labour in Dresden, or life in hiding with a courageous German couple, the husband of whom was killed after the war by his neighbours for hiding Jews. It is a disturbing picture. It is also one that needs to be read in every generation, so that no person need ever be in doubt as to the fate of individuals and whole peoples when prejudice, racism and extremism come to power.

To my wife Susie, and to my children Aloma,
Ardyn and Aviva, and my grandchildren Maia,
Shirin, Koram, Zak, Hazel, Dara and Netta.

Chodecz – Early Days

One Sunday afternoon in June 1933, my mother and my Aunt Sabina took me and my Cousin Misio swimming in the lake. Aunt Sabina held Misio, who was a year and a half younger than me, by the back of his swimming trunks and my mother did the same with me. Both of us were told to do a kind of doggy paddle and we imagined that we could swim. It was a new and marvellous experience going round in circles on the surface of the water. When we got home, we couldn't stop talking about it.

That evening at dinner, my brother Iccio, who was then fifteen years old, told me that being held by the trunks was not considered 'swimming'. That, if I wanted to, as his birthday treat to me (I would be six in July), he would teach me to swim properly. Mother consented without really giving it much thought. My father thought it was a good idea, and I was over-joyed with Iccio's offer and wanted to know when it would be.

'Next Sunday, we'll leave home by 9.30 and we will be back well before lunch.'

Two people we knew in the village, Mr Lewandowski and Mr Wojski, had fishing rights on the lake. Iccio paid Mr Wojski to hire his boat for two hours, and received the keys to the padlock and the oars, which he carried down to the lake. Draped diagonally across my shoulder, I had a rope, and under my arm I carried a towel and swimming trunks. I marched purposefully towards the water behind Iccio.

Peasants were making their way from the villages to the church in Chodecz. They carried their shoes slung across their shoulders, or hung by their laces around their necks. They would put them on in the marketplace just before entering the church. If we asked them why they went barefoot, this would be their reply: 'Feet are old and cost nothing; shoes are new and cost a lot; only a fool would wear them all the way to the church.'

It was a lovely Sunday. The sun shone. It was hot and the lake was calm. Iccio rowed us to the middle of the lake, told me to undress, put the rope around my waist, lifted me up and threw me into the water. I found myself going down and down. I wanted to shout, but instead I began to swallow water and I was choking. I felt a tug around my waist, and after what seemed like an eternity, I came to the surface, coughing and spluttering.

I wanted to tell him that I had had enough. I wanted to shout, to plead with him, but no word came out and instead I coughed and coughed.

'Do doggy paddle, you donkey! The way you told us at dinner, the way mother showed you. And kick with your legs at the same time... go on, stop coughing and do as I tell you.'

I looked at him pleadingly, still stuttering.

'Go on, we can only keep this boat till midday, and we're losing precious time while you frolic about,' he said sternly.

I didn't want to go down to the green, muddy depths again. Anything, absolutely anything but that! So I did what Iccio told me, I kicked with my legs and beat the water with my arms like a windmill.

'Hey, I have an idea!' said Iccio, and he pulled me into the boat. 'Put the towel around yourself, cough yourself out, and just sit there. I will tie the rope to one of the oars and lower and raise you that way; when you start going down, I will turn the oar one way and wind you up. If I see that you do well, I'll unwind you and give you more rope. It's going to be more scientific that way.'

Scientific was one of Iccio's favourite words.

I sat there with the towel around me, completely stunned, not even able to cry. Water was coming out of my mouth and my nose. I still coughed intermittently and felt that I wanted to vomit. I wanted to tell my brother that I had had enough and wanted to go home now...

But Iccio worked fast. In no time at all, he had one end of the rope tied to the tip of the oar. Then he coiled it around the middle of my body, picked me up again, and threw me into the lake. Having had a little rest, I kicked and beat my arms more vigorously than before, trying both to stay afloat and to reach the side of the boat.

'You're doing well. Carry on and try to swim away from the boat, and not towards it!'

'I have... no... strength left...' I said between gulps of air. 'Iccio, please...'

Iccio turned the oar like one turns the handle at a well, and I felt myself being lifted above the surface, my arms and legs still moving. 'Rest, don't move. Breathe in and out and try not to cough.'

I looked at him pleadingly and he understood my look and said: 'Five more gos and then you'll sit in the boat and I will swim and show you how it ought to be done.'

On the way home, he said: 'I suppose you'll now go straight to Mother and Father and complain about me mistreating you?'

I had, in fact, already been forming a most dramatic account of this experience...

'No, why should I?' I said coolly.

Just before we entered our house, Iccio got hold of me and said sternly, 'I don't want a cowardly display from you over lunch. You understand me? What I did was for your own good. Old ways of teaching important things like swimming are a lot of nonsense. In order to learn well and quickly, you need to adopt a new and *revolutionary* approach.'

As he talked, I had been sure that he would say 'scientific approach', but instead, he said 'revolutionary'. Both were terms he had picked up from Uncle Ignac, Aunt Sabina's husband. Aunt Sabina was my mother's sister.

Uncle Ignac was a socialist. On his desk stood a cast-bronze paperweight with a picture of an ugly bearded man on it and the words 'Karl Marx' written beneath. Iccio, who had not been accepted for high school in Wloclawek because it had already exceeded its quota of Jews, had decided to further his education by going to the library in Chodecz every day, and there, with the guidance of Uncle Ignac, he read books on socialism. The communist books were not kept in the library, but circulated privately. Iccio read as much as he could, and he had made himself a large breast pocket on his jacket so that he could always carry a book around with him.

At lunch, when Mother asked me how my swimming lesson had gone, I simply said 'All right.'

Iccio was very pleased with himself and told everyone at the table how his 'scientific' and 'revolutionary' methods achieved stupendous results. He described the whole episode from his point of view. Of course, I was on the point of saying something, but I bit my tongue instead and kept quiet. Mother got the picture and was quite horror-struck. She took me straight into the bedroom, and had a look to see whether my appendix incision scar hadn't opened afresh. My operation had only been three months ago.

'Go and finish your lunch, and afterwards we'll go and see Doctor Baron.'

Father was angry with Iccio and said in his stern voice that in future he was forbidden to use his 'scientific' and 'revolutionary' methods on me, my sisters or anyone else, not even the dogs.

We ate in silence for a while, and then confidence began to return to Iccio, for he said to Mother: 'Wait, you'll see when you take him swimming next Sunday that this frog-spawn here has suddenly become a tadpole. His progress…' And here he paused and looked around the table. '… has undergone a dramatic leap forward.'

Pleased with himself and encouraged by the giggles of my elder sister Zosia, he added, 'Just remind him to kick his legs and move his arms before you put him in deep water.'

The doctor pronounced me well, and the following Sunday I swam around my mother without her having to hold me by my swimming trunks.

Dr Baron, our Jewish physician, was always called the 'new' doctor after the old doctor had been forcibly retired, and it was the 'new' doctor who had diagnosed acute appendicitis in the early spring and had me whisked off to Torun, our nearest big city, to be operated on.

The old doctor would probably never have recognized such a thing as an appendix; he used to prescribe cod-liver oil for all internal and external pains around the abdomen. This was the major cause of death of most of the people he had dispatched to the next world, including the mayor. The previous year, in 1932, our mayor, a clever young German Pole had come down with acute appendicitis, which our old doctor misdiagnosed, inadvertently killing him.

My operation at hospital in Torun was only marginally more successful than the treatment meted out by our old doctor – though I didn't die right there on the operating table, I hovered between life and death for three months.

After I was brought back to the ward from the operating theatre, the man who had cut me open presented me with a bottle full of liquid in which my appendix was floating – I suppose as evidence that he had found it and managed to cut it out.

The incision, which was two of my fingers in length, would not heal. It was infected and kept extruding pus. I had a temperature day after day. My parents couldn't afford to keep me in Torun and brought me home. My grandfather, my cousin Misio, my mother and other members of my family, took it in turns to sit with me for hours on end. During those three months, I learned to read and to write a little. My grandfather told me stories from the Bible… Then, one day, I suddenly had no temperature, my scar had healed and I was well again.

Our new doctor told my mother that the person operating can only effect ten per cent of the cure for the patient, but that 'thanks to God, and with His help, this little patient has done ninety per cent for himself.'

•

In September that year, when I was fully recovered, I began school.

Unlike the high school, our local Szkola Powszechna was a 'public school', that is, everyone could attend and there was no Jewish quota. It was medium-sized, with about 550 pupils. The teachers, whom everyone looked up to, lived in a block of flats next to the school building.

It was compulsory for every child to attend from the age of seven. I was six when my mother took me – all nicely dressed – to the headmistress, who was in her school office together with another teacher who was called Mrs Wisniewska, in charge of the pupil intake that year. I knew both of them by sight.

My mother talked about me being a 'handful' at home and said that I was tall for my age, and that after my appendix operation, I had been ordered to remain in bed for three months, and during that time had done a fair amount of reading.

As my mother talked, I studied Mrs Wisniewska's kind face. I thought it was a lovely face and fell in love with it instantly. I no longer heard the rest of the talk. I imagined Mrs Wisniewska and I being the only two people in Chodecz, living by the lake, where every day I would catch big bream, carp and pike, and bring them to her...

And as I was with her by the lake, deep in my fantasy, Mrs Wisniewska gently and almost tenderly touched my head and said to my mother that all my lovely curls would have to come off, that I would be a naked lamb like all the other boys. Before my mother could answer, I found myself speaking rapidly: 'Oh, I don't mind, I would like to have my curls cut off. I only have them because my mother likes me to have them, and whenever she combs them for me and that's often – because she doesn't think that I brush them well enough – they hurt a lot and what's more, other boys tease me and call me "curly girlie" and I hate it when they do it…'

At that moment my mother exchanged glances with the other two, put her hand on my shoulder and squeezed it gently to indicate to me that my turn to speak would come, and I should behave and keep quiet. I was about to tell Mrs Wisniewska how I hated the white buttons on the sides of my velvet trousers and how I wanted to look like all the other boys… but Mrs Wisniewska was now handing me a book and asking me to read aloud from it. I read two pages of large print and would have liked to have gone on, for the story was beginning to get interesting, when the headmistress said, 'That's enough, thank you. Do you also know how to count?'

'Oh yes,' I replied, 'I can count all our chickens, ducks, geese, turkeys and pigeons… The pigeons actually belong to me because I feed them every day.'

Then Mrs Wisniewska said, 'Do you know how to bow like a nice Polish officer and a gentleman?' Her own husband was an officer in the Polish army.

And I said, 'No. No one in our house taught me, not even my grandfather!'

My mother looked at me, slightly surprised.

'Well, I will teach you now,' she said. 'You stand up straight, put your hands down by your sides, then smartly click your heels together, dipping your head downward at the same time, and then, fairly loudly, you say "Goodbye". Now, you do this to each one of us, including your mother, and when you have done this, you leave us and go home, for we still want to talk with your mother. Begin with me now.'

When I clicked my heels together to Mrs Wisniewska, I did it so hard that the bones of my ankles crashed together and I hobbled home in considerable pain.

My grandfather was interested in my interview and said that if I were accepted, he would need to rearrange my Bible study programme and *heder* (these were extra classes for boys to learn the Torah, Talmud and other subjects) and that things would change for me now. And then, when I showed him my bruised ankles and told him what Mrs Wisniewska had taught me, he replied that it's usually painful for a Jew to learn the ways of a Polish officer and gentleman. I pondered over this later on.

A few days afterwards, my curls were cut off by my Uncle Ignac, who in the past had had a barber's shop. My mother gathered them up. She wanted to keep some to send to my grandmother.

When I was one year old, my mother's mother, Grandmother Makower, had gone to live in Jerusalem. Her son Reuven, my mother's brother and an outstanding young Torah scholar, a leading disciple of my father's cousin, Rabbi Alter from Gur, had gone there a few years previously with his wife, where they swiftly had four small children. Tragically, Reuven became ill and died, leaving his wife struggling to bring up the family. She needed help to cope and my grandmother went out to assist. My mother's other sister, Jadzia, was also living out there. It was always the intention of my grandfather to join them eventually. In the meantime, he lived with us. My paternal grandparents were long dead.

When Uncle Ignac showed me the mirror, I found that apart from the small fringe, I was quite bare on top. I had a very short crewcut and my ears stuck out a lot. I looked quite strange to myself. That evening, after my bath in the wooden tub, I lay in bed thinking of what my father said at lunch, that I 'should do only the things at school which he, my mother and the whole family would be proud of.' I pondered over my grandfather's words – that things would change for me now. I thought about the new haircut and the loss of my curls, and the way I looked now; but I thought the longest about Mrs Wisniewska and it was with her in my mind that I said the *Shema*, and went to sleep.

'Sit down, children, keep quiet and listen to me very carefully. My name is Mrs Wisniewska, and you will call me Mrs Wisniewska, and not Teacher, or Ma'am, or anything else. I will be your main teacher. You will also have other teachers to teach you music, gym, drawing and gardening. But I will be with you for many years. That is, with those children who do well and pass to the next class every year. Those children will be known as Mrs Wisniewska's children. So it's important that you listen carefully, work hard and do all the homework that you will be given, and behave yourself in and out of school. I want to be proud of you all!'

Mrs Wisniewska went on to tell us these important things and we, in Class 1a – thirty-six boys and girls in all – the boys with shorn heads and their ears sticking out, sat there very quietly, listening to everything that she told us. The girls, neatly combed and brushed, and in their school uniforms, looked unblinkingly at Mrs Wisniewska. I sat in front, staring at her admiringly as she spoke... and I thought: she'll be my teacher... how wonderful!

On that first day, I finished before lunchtime and went to find Zosia, who was in a higher class at the same school. She was supposed to take me home. Zosia, whose name came from *Zisa*, 'sweet', never lost an opportunity to put me down. Now she gave me a telling off, so I ran home without her.

We sat down to eat. My father was ready, but Zosia had still not arrived. I had gone with her at 7.30 a.m. that morning, and Mother had expressly told her: 'This is Romek's first day at school, and I want you to collect him and bring him back home with you.'

'Did you see Zosia before you came running home?'

'Yes, I did,' I replied casually.

'What did she say to you?' answered my mother.

'She told me that you should have sent me to a stable to be educated with horses because I'm a donkey and unfit for school.'

Everyone around the table looked at me. Father asked me, 'Do you know why she said that?'

Mother enquired, 'Is that all she said?'

I couldn't answer both questions at the same time, and decided to crown them with a longish silence. Then, after a while, I said, 'She told me to leave her alone, and go home myself; she said she didn't want to be seen with me – ever!'

'Let's start lunch,' Father said.

In between soup and the main course, I began telling everyone at the table about how we had all had to change into slippers and that my locker number was '7', and I didn't even have a chance of getting into my story about wonderful Mrs Wisniewska, when Emma Hoffmann, a neighbour and friend of Zosia's, knocked, and without waiting to be asked to come in, just entered the room and said breathlessly that Zosia was outside crying, that no harm had come to her, but she had been horribly humiliated by Romek. She pointed her muff, in which she had her left hand, fiercely in my direction. 'Would you like me to tell you what happened because I was there, and I'm Zosia's friend? I can give you an impartial account of the incident.'

'Zosia's friend,' I muttered under my breath. I could see that she had the whole thing prepared in her mind, and couldn't wait to give the family her résumé of it.

'No thanks, Emma dear,' said my mother. 'You'd better go

home quickly to your parents – otherwise they'll be wondering what happened to you on the first day of term. Just tell Zosia to come in straight away.'

In our house there was a rule that if any of the children were late for lunch, they had to wait until we all finished eating, and then they would be given whatever was left over in the kitchen afterwards.

Zosia came in, her face all weepy, and her eyes, although moist from tears, were blazing and defiant. Father asked her to explain why she was late.

She pointed at me, and said passionately, 'It's all because of him. He humiliated me today, and if you have such an ox...' (So I was no longer a donkey but an ox!) '... for a son, don't send him to school; just let him out into the meadows to graze.'

I took advantage of the pause and asked Mother if I could have another helping of the main course, adding in an angelic voice, 'Since Zosia will not be allowed to have lunch, may I please have some more of her food?'

Mother gave me one of her sterner looks. Father asked Zosia to go wash her face with cold water, and then come back immediately and tell us about the incident at school. The cold water seemed to help, and Zosia returned more collected and less puffy. She began by taking a deep breath that sounded like a sigh.

'Well, when Mrs Wisniewska came to my class at eleven, to take us for poetry, she said: "I must tell you what happened this morning when I was with my new intake class, 1a." We all listened because it's interesting to find out things about the little ones,' said my grown-up sister of twelve.

'Yes, come on, let's hear it,' said Mother.

Zosia took a deep breath. 'Mrs Wisniewska always tests the intelligence of new intakes by asking them simple questions. She did this to class 1a this morning by saying, "Children, who can tell me what is the most important thing on a person's head?" Hands flew up, and this ox here also raised his hand. Mrs Wisniewska chose this ox…'

'Now, now,' said my mother, 'you know his name.'

Zosia took another breath. 'Mrs Wisniewska asked him…' – and she pointed at me – '"All right, Romek, you tell me." And he said, "Lice!" And everyone laughed, and it was just horrible, because they all looked at me. Then Mrs Wisniewska asked, "Why lice?" and so *he* replied, "Because so few people have them!" Surely you can all understand what a horribly humiliating time I'm in for at school now that *he's* in the school too.' And she burst into tears again.

Everyone turned to me. I looked down at my empty plate.

My father said, 'Is that all?'

My father, Mordechai, was a timber merchant and he also owned agricultural land and sold coal and building materials. The timber yard and my father's office were part of our house. One of his good friends and best customers was Emma Hoffmann's father who, like my father, was in his late fifties. They both served on the town council in the early 1930s.

Mr Hoffmann was a joiner-carpenter whose speciality was making coffins. Although there were other coffin-makers in Chodecz, they were all Polish Roman Catholics, whereas Hoffmann was a *Volksdeutsch*, a German Pole, and his coffins were the best for miles around. Polish peasants with a lot of life still left in them would come to Mr Hoffmann, consult with him, and then start saving up their money to ensure that when their time came, they would be laid to rest in a hardwood coffin made by a master craftsman, and Mr Hoffmann contributed not a little to their conviction that they could do no better. He would discuss the type of wood, the thickness of the sides, the style, the decorations, the soft padding inside for comfort, the dowels on the lids, or small interlocking wedges, among numerous other details. Mrs Hoffmann would serve tea during these discussions, and if she found out that the weekly payment was for an oak coffin with all the trimmings, there would be a glass or two of vodka to clinch the deal.

Sometimes, on Sunday afternoons, when the shop was closed (as it was from Friday afternoon to Monday morning), Mr Hoffmann would come to Father's lumber yard to pick out wood for his coffins, and Stanislaw Podlawski, Father's foreman and estate manager, would deliver it to him the next day. Stanislaw Podlawski had started working for Father in 1925, two years before I was born, when he left the estate of a Polish nobleman with whom he had quarrelled. Father and Podlawski got on well. He liked Podlawski's dignity, trusted him implicitly and often consulted him about farming and livestock.

When Father was not too busy, he and Hoffmann would settle down in the office for a game of chess and I would often be allowed to watch them play. As they moved their pieces around the board they would converse in German which to my ears sounded like distorted Yiddish, the language I spoke with my grandfather.

When their chess game was over, Mrs Lewandowska, who worked in our home and had been my wet-nurse, would bring in the coffee and they would share a few tumblers of *wisniak* – a home-brewed alcoholic cherry cordial. If Mrs Lewandowska wasn't there, I would be the one to bring in the refreshments.

'Ask your mother for a piece of her delicious cake,' Father would say in his confidential tone. On Sundays, as Mr Hoffmann knew, there was always a chance of getting a piece of Mother's delicious, home-baked Shabbat cake. He would invariably turn up just when my mother was serving tea from the samovar, or handing out slices of cake. His timing was perfect. Mother would enquire after the health of Mrs Hoffmann and Emma; and he would compliment her wonderful baking.

Once, his mouth full of my mother's poppyseed cake, he told us how he had courted his wife, his 'dear, dear Lotte', by carving her a beautiful wooden angel in Kolo, where he was apprenticed. She still had the angel hanging by her bed.

I made a mental note that one day, I should pop in and ask if I could see the carved angel. That might also present a good opportunity to sample some of Mrs Hoffmann's cooking. But

this second idea seemed less practical, for if I were to eat something there – in their completely non-Kosher household – and
should my father find out about it, the food would hardly be
worth the punishment… or would it? No matter how much I
tried to dislodge it, my mind presented visions of succulently
fried pork, which in our house it was forbidden even to talk
about. I saw Mrs Hoffmann, holding the carved angel in one
hand, and in the other the plate of fried pork and onions…

Grandfather, who was sometimes with us at the table,
became rather absent-minded when Mr Hoffmann was there.
He hardly approved of eating and drinking with a *goy*, an eater
of pork, at the same table. He once said so to my mother and
father, who replied that times were changing and he must be
more understanding and tolerant. Grandfather was not per-
suaded. He would hardly look at Mr Hoffmann, though he felt
that to get up and leave would be rude to the visitor and con-
trary to the wishes of my parents. He would drink his tea and
probably think about the Torah portion which had been read in
the synagogue the previous day. Mr Hoffmann, however, would
sense my grandfather's vibrations towards him, and made a
point of addressing him personally, and in German. Although
my grandfather spoke Polish fairly well, Mr Hoffmann thought
that German would endear him most to my grandfather. But
the subject which he chose on such occasions would never be to
my grandfather's taste. 'If only, dear sir,' he would begin,
looking at my grandfather with half a smile, 'I could bring you
some of my wife's cooking to sample, then you could judge for

yourself, dear sir, and agree with me that my superlatives about her culinary powers are indeed rather modest. Or what I would like even better would be to invite you to our home to partake in a meal with us, but I know that you are a Hebrew...'

Hoffmann avoided the word *Jude*, for as early as 1933, it already had an offensive ring to it. 'And as an Orthodox person, you would not wish to eat *treife* in a *goyishe* home... am I right, dear sir?'

Treife was food that wasn't kosher.

'You are quite right, Mr Hoffmann,' said Grandfather. 'And if you will excuse me, I will go and say my prayers,' he said, rising, and leaving us.

'So, it's time for *mincha*?' Mr Hoffmann enquired loudly. He knew some Yiddish and a lot about Jewish ways of life.

'We'd better go and look over the oak boards before it gets dark, Mr Halter,' he would say, giving my father a big wink, and again thanking my mother for her cake and warm hospitality, waving to us all with the fingers of his left hand, and transferring their moving motion to the handkerchief in his breast pocket, and if at that moment he caught my eye, he would give me a wink too, as if to indicate that he and I, despite my being very young at the time, understood one another perfectly.

Some Sundays he would bring Emma with him. Emma liked coming to our house because she thought we all liked her, and she was right in thinking that, though possibly I was the only exception. Why, I didn't really know myself. But I was six and

she was twelve, and my feelings to her were of little conse-
quence; Emma believed she could handle me with ease. She
and my sister Zosia were in the same class at school; they were
close friends and had lots to talk about when they were together – things I wasn't allowed to hear.

Emma's left hand was always hidden away inside a beautifully embroidered muff. Both her left hand and left foot were
deformed from birth. She was very sensitive about her deform-
ities and would howl and weep when children called her a
'cripple drag foot'. Then she would run to her father, weeping
bitterly. Mr Hoffmann, even more than Mrs Hoffmann, would
cuddle and hug his darling Emma and wipe away her tears with
his big white pocket handkerchief. Then he would resolutely
go to see the headmistress about it. The headmistress would
announce in hall that any child behaving in such a manner
would be punished appropriately. And every child in the school
knew what 'appropriately' meant.

Often, if Mr Hoffmann knew who the culprits were, he
would deal with them himself, one by one. He would stop at
nothing to protect and defend his Emma.

My mother, fearing that I might be tempted to join in with
those children who shouted abusive and hurtful words at
Emma, took preventative measures and gave me a good talking
to, during which she warned me: 'Never, never call her those
horrid, hurtful words such as "cripple hand, drag foot" –
or indeed any other words which refer to her left hand and her
left foot.'

I knew my mother well, and understood her warning. The fear of being given a good hiding by Mother or being caught by Mr Hoffmann, who would flog me hard with his belt, or both, made me bite my tongue and remain 'good' whenever that impulse prompted me, yet there was something within me that wanted to say words which would hurt Emma. Try as I might to pay no attention to it, her crippled hand continued to fascinate me. I wanted to see it, to look at it closely. Sometimes I would go to Aunt Sabina's house to play with Cousin Misio, knowing that on certain days Emma would be there in the afternoons, taking singing lessons.

My aunt and uncle, Sabina and Ignac Gora, owned a grocery store but were very musical. When they got married, they decided that they would use Aunt Sabina's dowry money to convert my uncle's barber's shop into a grocery store, specializing in good tea and soaps and other things. They also had a corner of the shop ingeniously sliced off and converted into a music room, which had a glass partition and was separated from the rest of the living space. Here, they occasionally gave lessons.

Emma had a tremulous voice, which I liked. As she was in full flow, I would creep up very quietly to the glass screen, pull the curtain slightly apart, and strain myself to see her left hand. Misio, who had true pitch and an infinitely better ear, said that she warbled too much. After her lesson, he would imitate the sound she had made on his violin.

Misio was younger than me, but he was my hero – he could

beat both Mr Hoffmann and my father at chess when he was still under five. He was Aunt Sabina and Uncle Ignac's only child, and a very serious little boy for his age. He had inherited my aunt and uncle's gift for music. Uncle Ignac conducted the fire brigade orchestra and could play a number of instruments. Misio had been taught the violin by his father and now, at the age of five, he could play it well. Uncle also taught him chess and Misio taught me in turn. During the three months when I was recovering from my appendix operation, Misio sat by my bed, and we would play chess for hours, or look at books or photo albums. My father, who was always busy, might come in for a few minutes to watch us play. He himself was a good chess player, and was keen that I should learn to play the game well. He would assess different positions, smile, tap us both gently on the head, and then leave the room without saying a word. Misio at first gave me his Queen and later, when I improved, his Castle, as a handicap.

Uncle Ignac had not enjoyed the barber's shop he had run before marrying Aunt Sabina: scrupulously clean himself, he hated cutting other people's hair because their dirt, and sometimes their lice, disgusted him. He never came to the communal *mikva* on a Thursday – it was not clean enough for him. Whenever I slept at their house, I would witness their washing ritual in the morning. Misio and I were washed by Aunt Sabina in the evening, before going to bed. Uncle Ignac had his water heated for him in the morning, on the stove, for they had no bathroom or bath. When the water was warm, it would be poured into a large wooden tub, which was placed on the kitchen floor. Uncle Ignac would stand in the tub and soap himself with his special brush, which had a long handle. Then he would dip his sponge into a bowl of clean water, and rinse himself with it. When he had finished, Aunt Sabina would close the kitchen door, and very quickly wash herself. For them, this was a daily routine.

The Eszners were our neighbours and Karol Eszner was my best friend. Like the Hoffmanns, the Eszners were 'German' Poles, just as we were 'Jewish' Poles. They were separated from us by the timber fence my father had put up between their property and ours. Father would stack his tree trunks and logs against this fence. I liked to clamber up the logs where, from the top, I could overlook the Eszners' property and call out to my friend Karol. We were both in the same local school, but he was a class above me, as he was exactly two years older than me. Our birthdays were a week apart. We would often walk to school together talking all the way. He was the best at drawing and writing in his class and I was best at drawing in my class. Karol was the youngest of four sons and a daughter and I was the seventh and youngest in my family. My parents were selective about my playmates, but even though Karol was a German Pole, he seemed well-bred and friendly enough and he never called me anti-Semitic names, so they were not averse to our spending time together. Karol would come over and ask permission to sketch our two horses, and then we would go out to the stable, careful not to get too close to the horses for fear that they would kick us.

My father's family was originally called Federhalters, 'feather holders' or scribes – mainly Torah scribes. Then the family split into sections. The very orthodox part of the family became 'Ha Alters' – and the head of that group was Rabbi Yitzhak Meir Alter, the founder of the Gur Hasidic Dynasty, and my father's cousin.

My father's father had been married three times (his first two wives had died in childbirth), and so, to support his large family – he had close to twenty children – he became a timber merchant, which brought in more money than being a scribe.

Other branches of the family called themselves Halterrehts – which meant 'legal scribes' – meaning that they did most of the basic work of lawyers, for it was very difficult, if not impossible for a Jew to qualify as a solicitor because of the *Numerus Clausus* barring Jews from qualifying professionally.

From my paternal grandfather's twenty or so children, three were born to his third wife: my Aunt Sarah, who married and went to live in Switzerland, my father, and then my Uncle David, who lived in Izbica Kujawska, about ten miles away from Chodecz. There was a little over a year between the siblings.

When he was a young man, my father worked for the family business and had lived in a timber hut in a part of a forest which his father had bought. There, he supervised the cutting down of the trees, the loading and marking for transport to my grand-father's sawmill in Izbica Kujawska. He cooked and looked after himself, kept a horse, and fished for carp in the lake, sending some home to his family for Shabbat. He grew strong and fit. His father sent him books to read and study: his Russian, Hebrew, German, Polish and Yiddish were all fluent.

In 1898 my father was conscripted into the Russian Czarist army; everyone in the family wept. Very often Jews, who were usually physically weak and frightened, would not survive the preliminary training in the army. The physically strong and clever ones would be seconded to serve as managers for a Russian officer on his estate when their military service came to an end. They would be sent to some godforsaken part of Russia, never to be heard of again. So it was a no-win situation.

He served in the Czar's army in the Caucasus. His major appointed him 'chief supplies officer', with the specific task of making the major rich. My father understood the major, and during this period, he not only made him very rich, but he also established himself. When the time came to be demobbed, the major signed the papers, but asked him to return after a month. The major was in a bit of a drunken state when he signed the papers, embracing my father and saying 'I need you, and you need me.'

On his return to Izbica Kujawska, my father left all his newly-acquired wealth with his father — and, with his brother David, decided to join his three half-brothers for a year or so in England. That was in 1902. His half-brothers had left for abroad some time earlier, but hadn't had the money to sail to the USA, just enough to reach Liverpool. My father arrived in Liverpool and discovered that two of them had gone to live in the East End of London. The third one was a Torah scribe and a synagogue beadle, and as poor as a synagogue mouse. My father helped him financially.

When my grandfather wrote to inform him that the Russian major was no longer looking for him (Father was meant to return to help him on his estate), he came back to Poland, but before doing so, he helped one of his half-brothers sail from Liverpool to Canada.

On his return to Poland, my father married and settled in Izbica Kujawska. Then he moved to a pretty and smaller place where he could set up on his own... a picturesque little town which had a lake, little hills and good forests – Chodecz. There, he started his own timber business. He had five children – Szlamek, Sala, Peccio, Iccio, Ruzia – with his first wife, who died giving birth to their sixth child in 1919. The child also died. After the year of mourning had elapsed, he needed a wife from the 'right' family to look after the five children. The rabbi from Gur, my father's cousin, came to his help; he knew the Makower family from Kolo, who also needed help because the principal breadwinner, my grandfather, Makower senior, had suddenly lost his position. Makower senior had been the capable and respected manager of a large estate near Kolo. The owner of the estate, a Polish aristocrat, gambled his fortune and estate away in a card game one day, and Makower senior lost his position and livelihood – without pay or compensation. He was simply kicked out. This family consisted of the father, mother, one son and three daughters. One of the daughters, Salomea – my mother – was chosen to marry my father. They married in 1920; she was twenty years younger than him. The condition of the marriage was that my father would take in the father and mother of the new bride, and support them until their son Reuven (who had gone to Jerusalem with his wife) was able to do so himself.

The ensuing decade was a happy one. Between 1920 and 1930 were good years for my father: the children of his first wife grew to independence and started families of their own; my sister Zosia was born in 1921 and I followed in 1927; his timber business thrived, with a particularly good government commission for a large timber consignment one year, which enabled him to come home and put 7,000 zloty under his wife's pillow…

My eldest half-brother Szlamek was a manager of a sawmill in Wloclawek, some twenty miles from Chodecz. He was married to Eva, and they had a little boy called David. We called him Danus. Szlamek and Eva were rather an unusual couple. While he was well over six foot tall, she was barely five foot.

My father never liked short women. My mother was tall – even our maid, Mrs Lewandowska, was tall. This utterly idiosyncratic prejudice caused him to take an instant and irrational dislike to Eva even before he met her, from the moment that he saw her photograph. The real reason may have been that my father's first wife had been chosen for him by his own father, and he probably assumed that he would do the same for his first-born, Szlamek. But Szlamek broke with this Jewish custom: he simply came home one day and told my father that he had fallen in love with Eva Wislicka, who was attractive, fast thinking and bright, and worked as the chief cashier at a large department store in Wloclawek, and showed him a photograph of the two of them together. However, when my father saw his son standing next to this diminutive person, he became unspeakably angry, even refusing to go to the wedding.

In my father's office there were glass-fronted shelves on the wall which could be slid open or locked. There he kept his precious books and manuscripts. The coins that he also collected were displayed like medals in another, shallow cabinet which hung on the right behind the desk. We children could see the medals through the glass but to see the beautifully illustrated manuscripts, father had to unlock the cabinet and show them to us. The Haggadahs had coloured pictures. At Pesach my father would choose one of his Haggadahs and show it to us children after the reading; the actual reading was done from a less precious book. Seeing the lovely coloured illustrations was a special treat for me. None of us was allowed to touch the paper. My father would put on thin gloves, which he kept for handling the manuscripts and turning the pages carefully. As the youngest, I sat on his lap. My favourite of all the colours was the gold leaf.

'It's real gold,' he used to say and without knowing why, I would repeat 'read gold!' which would make my father laugh.

My sister Zosia would invariably be irritated by my remarks and to put me down, would add, 'And real flowers… go on state the obvious.'

However, back in 1930, the fate of the Haggadahs had hung in the balance. Our home and the timber property had been set on fire. I remember being woken up by my mother and being bundled up into blankets and taken to Aunt Sabina's place in the middle of the night. It is one of my earliest memories.

Father suspected the aristocrat whom Podlawski had previously worked for of starting the fire deliberately. This aristocrat had never forgiven Father for hiring Podlawski, whom he considered his property, like the horses and cows and other workers on his land.

My father could not get the insurance for the fire damage. Unfortunately, Jews were outdone by insurance companies and it was difficult to take such cases to court because the judges themselves were partial and anti-Jewish. To restart his business he thought that he might need to sell his illustrated Haggadahs and other precious things.

'Most were entrusted to me by my grandfather and I am their custodian' was the phrase he used when telling the story of the fire, and about having to start from scratch, and everything that was lost in that 'terrible' night.

When I grew a little older, I began to hope that I would one day be asked to look after the Haggadahs and be their custodian as Szlamek was not that interested in manuscripts. At one point, the family had been sure that Peccio, another of my half-brothers, would be the person that my father would choose to be custodian. However, it was not to be. From stories I heard at the table, I pieced the following together: Peccio had been chosen to work as a scribe on the advice and the recommendation of my father's cousin (we had umpteen cousins in Poland!), the renowned rabbi from Gur. This to my father was as important as if the matter were predestined. Father believed totally in everything the rabbi told him.

Loaded with presents, he used to go to see him once a year and stay there for two or three days. When father took Peccio one year to see the great rabbi, Peccio made a nice impression on him and he thought that the lad had humour, read Hebrew fluently, had a nice sparkle in his eyes and could draw well with his pen which he had made himself, and that his fingers were long and dextrous. So he gave Father a note to give to his friend, the rabbi from Kolo, recommending Peccio to study calligraphy with his son, a renowned calligraphy teacher. Peccio was supposed to be there for a long time but he only stayed for three months. Father tried to persuade him to change his mind and stay longer, in accordance with the wishes of the great rabbi from Gur, who had singled him out. But Peccio wouldn't budge. He was tired of calligraphy; and was brought home.

After a couple of days he ran away. He ran to my mother's cousins, the Makowers in Kolo, with whom he was happy. He was brought home again by my father and lay on his bed for days, reading. He read mainly Polish adventure stories. One day he was gone again. This time he didn't return to the Makowers. About a week passed and the police came to say that Peccio Halter had been arrested in the southern part of Poland travelling on a train without a ticket. My father went to bail him out and brought him home. Shortly afterwards the Makowers from Kolo invited him to live with them. They liked Peccio's freckled face, his smiling eyes.

The Makowers had two shops; one sold hats for ladies and the other, cloth. Peccio worked in the fabric shop, writing postcards to us in his beautiful hand. Although my father didn't approve of what Peccio was doing, he collected and kept his cards. Peccio was like an adopted son to the Makowers and worked there and lived with them for years. It was through the Makowers that he was eventually introduced to the owners of a big textile factory in Lodz where he worked his way up to the position of a section manager. His girlfriend from Kolo joined him in Lodz. My parents went to the wedding.

Even so, my father did not approve of the marriage. In his opinion, as with his first son Szlamek, it was not for the young man to choose his wife. My father still thought that the head of the family was responsible for his sons and daughters. In such a case, my father would have consulted the rabbi from Gur; he would have looked into the family history of the bride or groom, checked that there were no hereditary illnesses in the family, and ascertained the intended's financial and intellectual endowments. The status of their family in the community would also have been taken into account – and only after all these conditions had been met and checked and found to be satisfactory, would he have given the son or daughter his blessing. But times in Poland, even in Chodecz, were changing. Even my father was changing; he no longer had a beard although inwardly he thought he was the same man.

Peccio would come once or twice a year and visit us, always without his wife and son. According to Peccio, she was unable to join him because she cooked for the managers and assistant managers who worked in the same factory in Lodz as Peccio, and besides, she naturally had to stay behind to look after their small son. So I never once saw his wife or the little boy. Whenever Father went to Lodz, he stayed with cousins and not with Peccio. When Peccio visited, on the surface things seemed fine but one had the feeling that the rift between my father and Peccio had never healed since the days of his apprenticeship to the calligraphy teacher, the son of the rabbi from Kolo.

During his stay with us, Peccio would read books and go for long walks. Often I would accompany him. He would put on his heavy lace-up boots and together we would set off at a brisk pace for a walk around the lake. His pace was fine for me for about half a mile. Soon after that, I would find myself out of breath and exhausted and plead with him to slow down and tell me the story about when he was a barber in Kolo or when he ran away to go to Africa, for the family always referred to his running away as 'Peccio's African Adventure' although he didn't manage to cross the borders of Poland. I liked the bit when at one station at night, he was chased by the ticket collector around the outside of the train with a spotlight on him. But being young, small and fast he had managed to get to the dark side of the train where he sat on the entrance step to a compartment and moved his legs in the air at the same time as pulling himself up into the interior of the train, but the shadow of his moving legs deceived the ticket collector, who thought that Peccio was disappearing into the distance and away from the train. I would question him about where he had slept and what he had eaten, for I too wanted one day to run away – to Paris. Why Paris? Someone from Chodecz had visited Paris and talked about it for years after and I heard some of the talk and thought that running away to Paris sounded like fun.

Then Peccio would tell me how he started his barber's apprenticeship by sweeping the floor and soaping the faces of customers for the first month; and how he had later progressed to waxing the moustaches of peasants and making them look like Marshal Pilsudski, who was a great Polish national hero and government leader.

In the second month Peccio had been assigned the task of shaving and cutting the hair that protruded from the nostrils and ears of customers. By the third month there was little for him to learn. For he knew that those who were fanatically religious never wanted their beards to be trimmed; their heads could be shaven up to the *payyot* but the beard had to remain untouched. The shop in which he worked was divided into two halves; one half was solely for non-Jews, and it was here that he put his inventive ideas into practice, and learned from his experiments so rapidly that before the three months were up, Peccio had had enough of being a barber.

On the first Shabbat after my three-month illness in bed, I walked slowly, hand in hand with my father to the synagogue. Grandfather had left earlier. Had I gone with Grandfather, he would have told me the story of the weekly Torah portion that would be read that Shabbat. Father walked in silence. As we walked, some people on their way to the *schul* would pass us, and others would join Father for a chat.

'*Gut Shabbas, Gut Shabbas!*' was the way everyone greeted one another and they would chat together in Yiddish about this and that. I would trail along holding Father's hand and trying to understand what the grown-ups were saying.

The women followed a bit later: we saw them filling up the gallery. By then, we were in our places; those who came to greet my father also greeted me.

'Don't pinch his cheeks,' Father would tell acquaintances who approached me with their fingers bent and open like the claws of a crab.

'The lad's pale, but I know how to make his cheeks rosy,' and they'd pretend to do it instead.

Some of the faces looked like the face on the bronze paper-weight of Karl Marx on my Uncle Ignac's desk. Grandfather had a beard but he looked quite different – he looked like Grandfather and no one else.

I sat next to Father. I would have loved to have sat with Misio, but Uncle Ignac, who was a far more fervent believer in Communism than Judaism, only brought his son to synagogue for the high holy days.

When the service started I would use my own prayer book which my grandmother had sent me from Jerusalem. She had sent an identical one to Misio, too. They both had olivewood covers. Father would show me on which page we were at certain stages of the prayers. I knew less than some of the Jewish boys of my age in Chodecz when it came to reading the Hebrew prayers, as some of them knew all the prayers off by heart. I was more interested in what was going on around me in the synagogue than in the prayers, and so I kept losing my place.

I could see the women in the gallery above from where I sat. I could see Mother. She wore a kind of mantilla, with a veil over her face; in synagogue most women wore these attractive veils so one shouldn't see their bare faces; yet I could still recognize a large number of them. I liked seeing them all dressed in their Shabbat best.

The *bimah*, the central raised platform, where the Torah readings took place, was generous in size. Before the readings, there would be a weekly ritual that was intoned in 'letters' auctioning the *haftarah* to the *maftir* – the person who would be reading it aloud. The money went towards payment for food for the elderly and the pious who spent entire days studying in the shtebel.

The *shamas,* the beadle, began intoning the *Alef* first letter as he collected nods, and then progressing to the next letter and the next. We children would be tempted to prompt him to say, '*Dalet… Dalet,*' but the grown-ups would keep us quiet. Later, it was the beadle who would chant the weekly portion of the Torah – with a beautiful, tuneful voice.

The cantor – the *hazan* – had two additional functions in Chodecz: he was also the Jewish ritual slaughterer and the *mohel*, who circumcised the male babies. He knew he was good at these three tasks and walked erect, full of his own self-importance. Mother had once sent me to him to find out whether I could join the children's choir, but he didn't waste much time with me. After I had sung my bit, he gave me a candy and said: 'Run along, little fellow. And if you love your family, don't sing to them!'

I had been so annoyed by his remark, that I tossed his candy away.

Now the hazan stood on the bimah next to the rabbi and the shamas. As he sang, everyone was quiet; even the ladies in the gallery who often chatted quietly through the prayers, leaned forward not to miss any of his quieter notes. The wooden synagogue had become filled with the music of his rich tenor. It seemed that the structure itself had been transformed into an instrument. I felt as if I were inside some marvellous giant violin.

It was almost impossible for me to reconcile the fact that this man, the hazan, who was singing so melodiously now, would cut the throats of all the fowl for the Jewish families in our town.

Every Thursday, Mrs Lewandowska would wheel her two-wheeled trolley to him, which contained a hen and a duck for kosher slaughtering for our Shabbat meal. One day, I decided to accompany Mrs Lewandowska as far as the slaughterhouse, and then go on to my aunt. We were about half-way there when Jadwiga, Mrs Lewandowska's daughter, who was about my age, came running up with the news that one of her brothers had been injured falling off a tree. Mrs Lewandowska acted fast. She said, 'Jadwiga, you help Romek. Here are the tickets; this one is for the duck and that one for the hen,' and having said that, she ran home to attend to her injured boy. Jadwiga and I went straight to the slaughterhouse and joined the queue.

Two women came in and stood behind us. One had a chicken inside a basket with a lid; the lid had an opening, and the chicken stared out at us. The other woman held her chicken upside down by the legs, which were tied together.

Jadwiga was fun, she was always saying things that made me laugh. Now she pointed at the upside-down fowl. 'You know what that chicken is trying to tell us? Please turn me round; you're giving me a dreadful headache.'

'Let's check if the duck and the chicken are from our home-bred brood…'

'Why, what will you do if they are?'

'I'll untie their legs and let them go. They'll find their way home.'

Our home ones were all ringed. We took them out, both the duck and the chicken, and examined them.

'No, they aren't ours,' I pronounced with relief.

The woman behind us with the chicken in the basket said, 'Don't put them in your bag because one of them may suffocate. Aren't you Lewandowska's daughter? I thought so! You hold the duck like this.' And she picked up the duck and we all moved a few steps forward, and when we stopped and turned, we saw her blowing the duck's bottom feathers apart.

'Oh, what lovely flesh, pure gold!' she said. 'Whoever bought it knows a thing or two about ducks.'

We moved forward again.

'Pass me your chicken and I'll show you how you have to hold it,' she said.

As I tried to gather up the chicken and pass it to her, she showed Jadwiga how to hold the duck and then took the chicken from me.

'What a chicken – it's the size of a turkey,' she said. The woman standing next to her said, 'After that duck, I'll believe anything.'

Then the woman with the basket put her forefinger into the hen's bottom. '*Oy, voy, voy* – what a layer!'

The other woman said, 'I don't believe it…' and she put her own forefinger into the chicken's bottom and exclaimed, 'It's a crime to have such a hen slaughtered, there's a treasure trove inside her… I can feel the eggs.'

Jadwiga opened her eyes wide and looked at me. I knew

something about treasure troves, both from Grandfather who told me stories about treasure and, of course, I had the clay cockerel with the slit on top into which I had put all the coins that were given to me during my illness. Jadwiga gave me the duck to hold.

'Really?' I said. 'What can you feel inside?' But they had lost interest in us and in our duck and chicken. They heard the voice of the hazan who was performing the function of the shochet, as he sang out a little ditty to amuse himself and the ladies – as he cut the throats of the fowl, and now they were keen to step inside the slaughterhouse to see the man and hear his song better.

The woman returned our hen to Jadwiga. The hazan sang during the short pause, when he was sharpening his knife. His song made the women laugh. He was still singing when Jadwiga, the duck, the hen, and myself with our trolley, squeezed inside the slaughterhouse. He looked around. 'Ticket?' he said, wiping the blade of his knife on a rag and then he ran the sharp edge of it along the nail of his thumb and began to work again.

I passed him the ticket, which he put in his apron pouch, and took the duck from me. He checked to see that her legs were securely tied.

'He always checks the legs,' said Jadwiga.

'The string is coming loose,' he told me. 'When I cut her throat, you'd better hold her by the legs, because if I handle her by the bindings, and they come undone, she'll drop down into the trough, and your mother won't be very pleased with me, or you – will she?!'

With his left hand, he held the duck under her wings, pulled her head back, plucked some feathers off her throat, said a prayer, took the knife which he'd been holding in his mouth into his right hand, and slit the duck's throat.

I stood rooted to the spot, looking at him.

'Here, take her,' he said. 'So – you want to be a shochet when you grow up?' He gave me a big grin before wiping his knife on the rag in front of him, and then placing it between his teeth and taking up the duck again. 'I tell you, little fellow, you've got a better chance of becoming a shochet than a hazan. Here, take her… take her and hold her over the trough,' and he thrust the bleeding duck at me.

The only way I could manage to hold the duck, which was struggling and beating its wings, was to hug her to my chest. Jadwiga was handing him the ticket for the hen and had left me to cope with the duck. I became covered with blood, and the duck's struggling legs had come untied. Jadwiga hung the hen by its tied legs in the trough, and came to help me. The duck gave an enormous convulsive beat with her wings and a forceful thrust with her legs, and I dropped her. She started running around.

'If you ask her nicely, she'll follow you all the way home,' said the hazan-shochet. Everyone laughed. A woman took a rag and began wiping my face with it.

'Now, just look at you – you've gone and spoiled a lovely

shirt… what a shame. Next time your mother sends you to the slaughterhouse, ask her to put some old things on you… it's safer that way. You never know what might happen. I once saw a cockerel flying about with his throat cut here in this very slaughterhouse. They do the most unexpected things before they settle down to die.'

On the way back, we went first to Aunt Sabina's shop with the slaughtered duck and hen inside the trolley's bag. Aunt washed me and changed me into some of Misio's clothes.

I couldn't sleep that night. The leaves of the tree outside cast shadows on the wall by my bed. They shifted, changing shapes. I vividly saw cockerels, ducks and hens flying about… moving their wings, dipping and soaring, and, as I looked, I thought I could hear them making those slaughterhouse, throaty, choking noises. I closed my eyes and thought that my grandfather would never be afraid of flying cockerels, ducks and hens. So I got up and quietly tiptoed to my grandfather's bed. I whispered to him that there were flying ducks and hens on my wall, and he said, 'Hush' and pulled me towards him and fell asleep again with his arms around me. In the morning, I found myself lying in my own bed again. I thought about the slaughterhouse a lot, but never told anyone about it. I was not going to be called a 'softie' by any member of my family.

When the service was drawing to a close, my mother, together with some of the ladies in the gallery, would begin to leave. The women would always hurry home to set the table for the most important and the biggest meal of the week, the Shabbat lunch. In winter, when the meal had to be hot, I would leave the synagogue before the service ended to help Mrs Lewandowska fetch the cholent stew from the bakery. My task was to hold the pot steady on the sledge while Mrs Lewandowska would do the pulling. All those who made the cholent for Shabbat would bring it to the bakery on Friday afternoon with instructions about where the pot should be placed inside the oven. It depended on how rich the contents of the pot were: if it contained a lot of meat and fat, it would be placed near the centre; but when some of the inhabitants of Chodecz could only make the cholent out of potatoes and barley and onions and carrots, then that pot would go to the cooler side of the oven.

Shabbat lunch would begin with *Kiddush*. In the winter, the grown-ups had an additional small, strong drink with an appetizer of chopped liver, salted herrings in olive oil with onions. On Friday nights we would have chicken soup from a large urn, and we all helped ourselves, starting with Father and Grandfather. Noodles would be added to the soup. In winter, the cholent of brisket meat, potatoes, barley, beans, onions and carrots, was a meal to look forward to. This would be eaten with pickled cucumbers or pickled beetroots, then came carrot and raisin *cymes*, and this would be followed by tea from the samovar, and then the Grace after the meal. It was a blow-out.

After the meal, we dispersed into the different parts of the house in a contented but semi-conscious state and only began coming back to a full and happy Saturday afternoon life by about 3.30 p.m. or so, when Aunt Sabina and Uncle Ignac with Misio, or other friends of my father and mother, began arriving.

When it was light and not too cold, we would all set off for a long walk around the woods or around the lake and then return home for tea. But the walks were mainly during the spring, summer and autumn. When the Shabbat finished, there would be music from Aunt and Uncle and Misio, and singing from their friends, who had lovely voices. Aunt would accompany the singers on the mandolin. Sometimes there were games in which we children were allowed to take part.

Even though our food was delicious and there was always plenty of it, I was sometimes tempted by non-kosher food, Podlawski's *zur*, for instance, which he ate every morning. Podlawski, my father's estate manager, worked full time. He looked after the horses, ploughed our fields, took the massive tree trunks to Wloclawek amongst many other things. He would arrive at 4.45 or 5 a.m. every morning, groom and feed the horses and get things set up for the day's work. At about 7 a.m., his wife, who was a sister of Mrs Lewandowska, would arrive, bringing his breakfast. This consisted of a soup of sour milk, called *zur,* which was garnished with *speck* – smoked bacon fat – and onion pieces. Podlawski would get this, and two chunks of brown home-baked bread covered in pork dripping, every morning. Mrs Podlawska brought the soup in a pint-sized milk can. She would place the can on our kitchen cooking range, stir it and heat it, and then serve it to her husband in an area of the washhouse, where there was a little table in the corner and the privacy for him to sit down and have a little rest and eat his breakfast.

The smell of this soup made me lose my senses. I would follow it the way a dog picks up a scent. I would go into the washhouse half-dressed, chat to Podlawski and his wife, and salivate. His wife would take off the lid from the milk can, put a potato and some liquid soup with the delicious fried *speck* in it, and hand the portion to me saying, 'Go on, Romek, this is for you. Have some, eat it.' And although I knew that this was completely not kosher, and that God might punish me, as we'd been taught in the *heder*, I was unable to resist Mrs Podlawska's *zur*.

Once, a boy said to me about my operation, 'My mother said that you must have been eating non-kosher food, and that's why they had to cut your stomach open.'

Surely, I thought, hearing the boy's comment, his mother must be wrong. To have had my stomach cut open, to have had to lie seriously ill in bed for three months – this all seemed just too severe a punishment for eating yogurt soup with pieces of *speck* in it.

One Sunday afternoon in the same year I started school, Emma came to see my sister Zosia. She came without her father. She said that momentous things were happening in Germany and that her father was listening at home to the new 'crystal set'. Not many people in Chodecz had radios and this was a way of telling us that the Hoffmanns had recently acquired one.

'With how many earphones?' I had seen one or two now to be able to ask expert questions. 'Is it brand new?'

Emma looked down her nose and ignored me and my questions and went on talking about it to the others. Then sometime later, she said: 'Of course it's new; Daddy wouldn't buy me a secondhand birthday present.'

'So it's really yours?' I said, greatly surprised. I had been given a pencil on my fifth birthday, the previous year. For her twelfth birthday, just recently, Zosia had received a tiny ring set with a blue stone from the whole family – which had been given to my mother when she was *Bat Mitzvah* age. But to be given a radio for one's birthday at the age of twelve… ! That seemed to me to be the most luxurious and fantastic gift imaginable. 'That's what I call a present!' I found myself uttering out loud. No one took any notice of me or what I was saying.

I was just about to ask Emma if I could come to her home and listen to it for a while, when Iccio announced that he was thinking of making a crystal set. He had read up all about it, and in fact would be getting the spare parts from a store in Wloclawek. That was great news for me; of course it would be a most scientific and revolutionary radio.

'When do we start on it, Iccio?'

Iccio looked at me coolly across the table without saying a word. I couldn't understand that look; I thought that after he had taught me to swim in the lake this amply qualified me as his right-hand man in making the radio, so I returned him a cool look and waited.

Iccio put me in my place pretty quickly.

'All the parts,' he announced, 'will be locked in my drawer and when I work on it, don't dare come into my room. Understand?'

Emma grinned, looked at Iccio's dark eyes and fluttered her eyelashes and said, 'You may come and have a listen on my new model, Iccio.'

'Thanks,' said Iccio.

A few days later, Iccio took me aside and said, 'Do you know what a secret is?'

'Of course I know,' I replied. 'Do you think that I'm a little baby?!'

'Now listen, if I tell you something which is a secret between us, you won't go blabbing it to Mother and Father?'

'Of course not,' I responded. 'Secret' – I thought. At last Iccio was taking me into his confidence and recognizing me as his pal.

'All right. I believe you,' said Iccio. 'Tomorrow, tomorrow at the crack of dawn, I'm setting off with Podlawski for Wloclawek.'

I knew that Podlawski was off there because three big tree trunks were already loaded on the wagon.

'I'm going to get spare parts to build a radio, and I think I may be short of a little cash. Can you lend me some of the money that you have inside that cockerel of yours?'

The money had been given to me by my relations over the

course of my three-month illness, when I had my appendix out, and I had been saving it for some time.

'But you can't get the money out. I tried it, and it doesn't come out. Only if you smash the cockerel, and you know what Mother would do to me if I did that...'

'I've thought about it,' said Iccio. 'I can get some of the money out without smashing the clay monster. Bring me the cockerel and I'll show you.'

I was impressed: Iccio was my hero – he could do anything! I went and got the cockerel. He put a knife blade into the slit, shook the cockerel so that some of the money inside landed on the blade, and slowly pulled out the knife, with the money still on it. There were silver coins of one and two *zloty* pieces on it.

'I think one more dip like that will be enough,' said Iccio.

'Can I come with you to Wloclawek tomorrow? I could help you choose the radio parts.'

'No, I will do all that and I will have lots of running around to do to get my books and see people... I tell you what: I'll get you a present.'

'Can you please get one for Misio, too, because he's not only my cousin but my best friend and I would...'

Iccio didn't let me finish, he just said, 'Yes, I'll get something for Misio, too; but don't ask me what it's going to be, because I don't know until I see it and buy it.'

'Don't get me a pocket knife, I'll have one. Peccio promised to get one for me when I turn seven.'

'No, I won't.' Iccio was now placing the second dip of money into his pocket, and he handed me the cockerel back, saying, 'Remember: not a word of this to anyone – Grandfather, Zosia, Misio… anyone. I will see Szlamek when I arrive at his sawmill. Shall I ask whether he has a day for you next week?'

The tree trunks which Podlawski had to take to Wloclawek were too large in diameter to be cut on our saws and they were to be taken to the sawmill managed by Szlamek.

During the springtime, summer and early autumn, almost every Monday, the horse-driven cart loaded with tree trunks would set off at 4.30 in the morning for the twenty-mile journey to Wloclawek. They would return with the cut planks very late on the Monday night or early on Tuesday morning.

Before Szlamek married Eva, Mother used to send him items of food and even dishes that she'd made, even though he had his own little place and a woman to clean and cook for him.

'Yes, please tell him to write a note to Mother that he'd like me to be with him for a day next week.'

'… that he needs your help,' Iccio interrupted me sarcastically. I was about to agree – I couldn't imagine anyone not wanting my help.

'All right, all right, run along now and put the cockerel back and don't fall and smash it… If you stay here any longer you'll be dictating the note that you'd like Szlamek to write to Mother and Father about *The Importance of Romek's Visit to Wloclawek.*'

I didn't like Iccio's tone now; he had become the condescending elder brother again. So I lifted the cockerel higher to my chest, drew myself up, and said coolly, unblinkingly into his eyes, 'Don't forget the two presents,' and walked away with my clay treasure trove.

Late the following day, Iccio returned from Wloclawek with books and boxes. He gave me a tiny, tiny, packet and said, 'Open it carefully; there's one for you and one for Misio.'

I was a bit taken aback by its size; I'd never expected anything so small.

Iccio was busily putting all his things in drawers and locking them up.

'Well,' he said, 'what's wrong?'

'Iccio, are you sure you haven't made a mistake by giving me the smallest parcel? You don't think it's perhaps one of the large ones which you've just put in the drawer that you ought to have given me?'

'I know what I'm doing. You run along to Misio and unwrap it very carefully in his house, and you'll see. You'll be thrilled with the present.'

Could it be two watches inside? I shook the little package and put it to my ear. No, no ticking from within.

'Did you speak to Szlamek? Did he give you a note?' I said.

'What about?' said Iccio, not even looking around.

'What about?! About me, of course, and about going to him next week.'

'Oh, I forgot all about it,' he said.

•

Deep in thought, I walked to Misio's house with the tiny present for both of us tucked into my pocket. Hmm, I mused to myself, you can't call such a puny thing a present. And what's more, he's forgotten to speak to Szlamek about me. What a useless journey – he's come back without so much as a note from Szlamek, which might at least have said, *'Dear parents, please send Romek to me next week with the load of tree trunks. I long to see him now that he is not dead. Your loving son, Szlamek.'* Something like that; short and to the point. I should have written a note to Szlamek, I thought. Grandfather would have helped me. Now, as I walked, I began to kick little stones and twigs out of my way, as Misio did when he was sad or angry.

But when I saw that Iccio's present was two fishing hooks, I was overjoyed. 'This is great; this is just what we need. I'm now going to make us fishing rods.'

Misio was less enthusiastic. He wouldn't be able to come because in the early mornings, after his father had scrubbed himself and they had had breakfast, he would give Misio lessons.

'See you tomorrow after the lessons; come as early as you can. By the time you arrive I'll have dug out a few worms and we'll be ready to set off.'

The next day, when Misio finally arrived, I had the worms in a tin. I had made a bag out of an old sock, put some earth in it, and put the tin of worms inside the bag. I handed Misio the sock and his fishing rod and we set off. I suddenly remembered that we needed money for the day's fishing permit and we went to get it out of my cockerel. I picked a knife from the kitchen on the way, and was just about to insert it into the slit when Mrs Lewandowska saw what I was doing.

'Ouuh, that's a naughty thing to do!'

I loved Mrs Lewandowska; who I thought was super. Zosia once said to me, 'You know why you love Lewandowska? It's when mother couldn't breastfeed you; Lewandowska gave you swigs from her big bosom. She's your milk mother.'

Lewandowska had about a child a year. She brought the little ones to our house and they slept and were kept very near the kitchen, in the area close to the washroom. From time to time she would pick up the smallest baby, unbutton her blouse, and feed it. I liked watching her; she would smile and wink at me. 'Would you like to have a little go yourself?' and I would turn all coy. When she finished with the smallest, the next in line would be brought in.

I told Mrs Lewandowska that I had made two fishing rods and now I needed money for the day's fishing permit.

'But if you go now, you won't be back in time for lunch,' she said. 'Wait here.'

She was gone for a few minutes, and returned with a coin and a sandwich for each of us. 'Look after one another, don't do anything silly, and don't come back too late. Go first to Mr Kaczewski and he'll tell you where to fish. And never let me catch you pinching your own money from your own little safe. Now, off you go.' And she gave me a kiss and a hug and a little tap on my bottom. I was just turning round to remind her to tell

Mother, but she'd read my thoughts: 'I'll tell your mother that you both went fishing to catch the biggest pike in the lake.'

I'd carved the floats on the string out of pine bark. Grandfather helped me to do it and showed me how to shape the float and make the hole in it for the string to pass through. As we walked together, I told Misio, 'We could make lots of these floats and sell them to other boys; I can get the bark from our timber yard for nothing.'

Misio gave me a wry smile; he didn't take my business ideas seriously. Instead, he pointed out that the string was on the thick side: it might frighten away the fish. I was proud of what I had made with Grandfather's help and didn't really like his adverse criticism.

'Oh no, they don't take much notice of the thickness of the string; they go for the worms and hook,' I told him with the authority of a seasoned fisherman.

'You see, the hooks are the best that Iccio could get; we aren't like the boys who fish with bent safety pins. We're well equipped; these are real hooks.'

Misio still looked a little dubious, so I went on to reassure him.

'And our rods are hazelnut twigs – the best.'

Misio looked at his crooked little twig, to which the string with the float was attached, the piece of lead and the new, proper hook at the end of it, and said, 'Actually, bamboo rods are the best.'

'Yes, but they don't grow in Chodecz. Where could we get bamboo rods from?'

Misio wasn't his usual self; I felt he needed cheering up.

'I'll tell you what… If we catch a very big fish, we will ask either your mother or my mother to pay for it, and then, with the money, we can buy a bamboo fishing rod from Wloclawek.'

'Yes…' said Misio hesitantly, still not fully convinced of my optimism. 'But I don't suppose we'll catch more than one big fish, and for one big fish, we won't get enough money to buy two fishing rods.'

'Well, we can share one between us.'

Now we walked on in silence, thinking.

'We might even be able to get one that can be taken apart – it's got these tiny tubes for slotting bits of bamboo into them, and that way one can extend the rod and make it long…'

'Or short,' said Misio, 'or even make it into two halves, two rods: one for you and one for me.'

'Let's fish on the forest side of the lake,' I said in a definite tone of voice. 'You see the town side is very noisy, and fish don't like that side.'

But no matter what I said, I wasn't able to make Misio enthusiastic; his mind was not on fishing. He would have been much happier, I felt, playing chess or his violin. Usually, when Misio and I went walking in the forest by the lake, we were equipped with pencils and paper and not with fishing rods. We would bring back drawings of birds which all had similar shapes, but some were drawn small and others large.

We arrived at Mr Kaczewski's hut. He was there, wearing high boots that came up to his knees, his trousers tucked into them, legs apart, his loose, thick shirt tied around his waist with a big belt. On his head he wore a triangular cap with a peak that was creased in the centre; and he had his rifle slung over his shoulder. He always carried his rifle. With the two fingers of his left hand he held the end of a leash, reining in his salivating bulldog. My mother knew my fascination for deformed limbs or cut-off fingers, and had told me that Mr Kaczewski had lost the other three fingers of his left hand in a straw-cutting machine. So the big landowner, who employed him and also owned the lake and the forest, had had him transferred from his work on the estate and appointed him lake guard. His title was 'Mr Keeper'.

Eyeing his drooling bulldog with some apprehension, we greeted him politely, calling him by his surname. Neither Misio nor I liked strange dogs because around Chodecz they were trained to bite, and so from experience we had learned to keep a respectable distance from them.

'Now, what do you want?' said Mr Kaczewski, barring our way and looking stern.

'We'd like two tickets for one day's fishing on the lake, please.'

'Not so fast, not so fast, young man. I need some answers first. Can you both swim?'

I decided to reply for both of us. 'I can, I swam in the middle of the lake, and Misio is my cousin and he is well over five.'

'We'll come to your age soon. Can he swim?'

'Well, not as well as I. You see... my brother Iccio...'

'So he can't!'

Misio was now squeezing the can with the worms in it, and shuffling from one foot to the other.

'Is that all, Mr Kaczewski? May I hand the money over to you?' I said, looking at the hand with the missing fingers.

'Not so fast... not so fast,' repeated Kaczewski. 'Now, how old are you?'

'I'm six.'

'So what have we got here? We've got one swimmer, aged six, and one non-swimmer, aged five... just a moment. Aren't you the son of the gentleman who conducts the fire brigade orchestra?' he said, fixing his stare on Misio. The dog suddenly became interested, too, and sat up.

'Yes, I am,' said Misio weakly.

'Damn fine musician, damn fine,' muttered Kaczewski.

It was hard to see where this was leading, but I offered, 'Misio plays the violin. Do you play an instrument?'

Mr Kaczewski opened up his belted-up shirt and produced a kind of short bugle, which he put to his mouth and blew. The forest resounded with the noise, and then came the echo of his blast. The dog began to bark.

'Were you always a bugle blower?' said Misio.

'I was in Marshal Pilsudski's brigade, liberating Poland and blowing the bugle.'

'Is that where you lost your fingers, Mr Kaczewski?' asked Misio. His mother, obviously, had not filled him in.

'Ah, that's a long story,' said Kaczewski, and told us to follow him. He led us to a place where there was a shallow stream and told us to fish there.

'Don't move from this place, and you hang on to that money of yours, little fellows. The fishing's on me today. Fine musician, damn fine musician, Mr Gora,' we heard him mumble as he walked away.

'I didn't know we had sandwiches – you never said anything about them,' said Misio.

I unwrapped the packet; they were a little squashed.

'Oh, eggs,' said Misio. 'I like eggs.' Now he'd cheered up, his mind on the food.

'But let's first drop our lines into the water and turn the worms around the hooks, so when the fish come to nibble the worms, we can jump up, pull in the line, and catch one or two with the hooks…'

'Let's not fish; let's just eat our sandwiches and throw stones into the water…'

'But why, Misio? We've come to *fish*.' I just didn't understand him.

'I really don't like this business of putting hooks into the mouths of fishes… Imagine if one of them swallows this sharp, nasty bit of metal… Anyway, would you like it if someone made a hole in your cheek?'

We stood in silence, looking at one another.

'Come on, Misio,' I said. 'We'll put our lines in the water, and if a fish is stupid enough to swallow a hook, then we'll pull it out and take it home. I'll carry it. Do you agree?'

Misio happily accepted my compromise. So we sat on the bank, ate our sandwiches and threw stones, pebbles, the earth and the worms which were in the tin into the water. I began to whistle what I thought was a tune – but Misio asked me to stop, he told me that it hurt his ears when I made that noise.

'I'll tell you how it goes,' and he sang it, and then repeated it with all the facial contortions of Emma Hoffmann when she sang.

We laughed, and then I tried to sing, and Misio started to laugh even more, until tears rolled down his cheeks. The sun shone and it was warm and sunny and for a time we forgot all about the fishing hooks that lay on the bottom of the shallow stream.

At the start of 1937, Iccio, who was nineteen, had been eight months in Bereza-Kartuska, the one and only internment camp where communists and other political dissenters were punished. The Polish secret police had come to our house the previous year in early 1936, and raided his room. They had forced open the drawer in which he kept all his writings and taken them away, together with all his books. Father told Iccio, who at that time was living away from home, about the police raid. Yet, despite this clear and obvious warning, he still chose to take part in the 1936 May Day parade in Wloclawek. Father and Grandfather, sceptical of all 'isms' (Communism, Pacifism, Zionism and Nazism), only regretted that Iccio, who displayed such promising writing skills and showed such imaginative powers, had, in their opinion, wasted them by becoming a communist.

In Bereza-Kartuska, the situation for any Polish Jews who were communists was pretty terrible, worse than for Roman Catholic communist Poles. In 1937, anti-Semitism was virulent. After the death of Marshal Pilsudski in 1935, an anti-Semitic government had taken over. Marshal Pilsudski had been pro-Jewish ever since his life had been saved by a Jewish family. As a young soldier, escaping from the Cossacks, whom he was trying to drive out of Poland, he ran into a Jewish house, and asked to be hidden. The man praying had the presence of mind to throw his prayer shawl over them both, and when the Cossacks burst in, they didn't see him, and went on.

This new government admired Hitler's screeching about 'the

Jewish conspiracy', and bought into his allegations that all the current evils and wrongs were due to 'the exploitation' by European Jews. This attitude towards Jews existed even in Bereza-Kartuska.

The letters which Iccio was allowed to send were heavily censored. Yet, intelligently, he managed to convey a lot. He told us that the camp was set in a swamp area and they had to work in the swamps to clear them. That the guards were as gentle and kind as those much-admired couple of families on the way to Przedecz, on top of the hill. (We of course understood, for he referred to two families whose members were infamous as butchers and thugs.) He wrote in a way that Mother and Father knew how to read into and decode the meaning from his words, which was often the opposite of what was written. Iccio told us that they were allowed only one blanket at night. To get as much warmth out of it as possible, they would make a cone and squeeze into it. My mother made him quilted trousers and a jacket in the form of an overall. When he received this, he had to surrender his other and only garment to the authorities in Bereza-Kartuska.

In the meantime, my father collected statements from people like teachers, the chief of police, wealthy landowners and others saying that our Iccio had been misled by others, that he was young and innocent and impressionable and had been put up to it by the leaders of the Wloclawek Communist Party into carrying the Red Flag on 1 May 1936. For some of these statements my father had to pay, others he obtained freely. He travelled to Wloclawek, Ciechocinek, Klodawa, Konin, Kolo, Izbica Kujawska and as far as Lodz to get these statements. They all began 'X, Y, Z knows Iccio Halter personally.'

My parents were terribly worried about Iccio, and then, in the midst of this, there was the calamity of Ruzia's death.

My half-sister Ruzia was eighteen in 1937. One Sunday in June, she went rowing on the lake with two of her Jewish girlfriends, who were the same age as her. Roman Catholics didn't swim in the lake till after St John the Baptist's Day on 24 June, no matter how hot the summer was and how warm the water was. We Jewish people had the lake to ourselves till then.

Ruzia and her friends had rowed here many times before. Perhaps one of them had leaned out to pick a water lily from its stalk, who knows? but certainly this time their boat capsized and the three of them began to drown. Ruzia was the only one who could swim but her other two friends clung to her resolutely and pulled her under with them. They struggled and from time to time came to the surface. Each time they did so they screamed for help. Village people who passed by did nothing because it was before 24 June and they believed that anyone who ventured into the lake before that date and got into trouble was rightly being punished by the saint and were not to be helped in any way.

The man who eventually came to their rescue was the fisherman who had the sole fishing rights for the year. He should have been on his way home, like the other peasants who passed by from church, but this Sunday he had decided to do a bit of surreptitious fishing, and then he heard screams.

'Just another rape...' he told himself and carried on casting his nets. Then he saw splashing and more screams close to the bend by the reeds. He rowed over and waited. When Ruzia's head came out of the water, he grabbed her and pulled. But she went under the water again, leaving him with a fistful of hair. It was a little while before she came up again. She didn't scream this time, but now he was ready with rope and oar and began to pull her into his boat. The other two, he recounted, 'clung to her like leeches.' It wasn't easy to get the three of them into the boat.

'It was the biggest catch of my life,' he would say later.

He rowed them to the shore and pulled them out onto the grass. Ruzia was still just alive and vomited. 'The other two were as dead as rocks,' he said.

My sister recovered consciousness and was terribly ill for the next two weeks. She had a terrible cough and temperature and kept bringing up phlegm. Eating made her sick. My father asked her to drink hot milk with butter in it and honey, but this made her even sicker. The doctor said that the fisherman ought to have pumped all the water out of her lungs immediately; but he was a simple man, who knew a lot about fishing but nothing about First Aid, or what to do in such an emergency.

Ruzia died.

The entire family was shattered by her death. My father, who in 1937 was sixty years old, aged by a number of years.

Everyone arrived back home for her funeral. Most stayed in our house for seven days, during the *shiva*, the period of mourning after death. My half-sister Sala, who lived in Brzesc Kujawski, came with her husband, Gershon, and their two children. Gershon designed and made shoe-uppers, mainly for ladies. He was a Zionist Youth leader, and a follower of Zeev Jabotinsky. Szlamek and Eva came from Wloclawek, and so did Zosia who was now sixteen and was apprenticed in Wloclawek with two sisters, friends of mother's, who were corset makers. She lived in lodgings with a family who were distant relations of the Makowers. She could have lived with Szlamek and Eva, but Zosia preferred to be independent, and so my father had to pay for her lodgings.

Peccio came from Lodz without his wife or child. He didn't stay for the whole period of the *shiva*; he said that he would have let down his section had he taken the entire mourning period off. But I knew that the real reason was that Father did not get on with his daughter-in-law.

At the end of the seven days, the family gathered and discussed the deteriorating situation for the Jews and the idea of leaving Poland. They considered all the pros and cons for a further two days. The general situation for the Jews in Poland was terrible by then: the anti-Semitism which had always been bad was now rife, there was a general lack of trade and now Poles were refraining from buying from Jews. Daily, the news that was coming out of Germany was awful, and all of this produced tremendous sadness and caused great worry to my grandfather, father and mother that even I – an optimistic and boisterous ten-year old – couldn't help noticing.

I was considered too young to sit and listen to what was being discussed. Moreover, the family hardly considered me trustworthy enough to keep my mouth shut about the family's confidential plans. Yet, in my very youthful, cocky state, I felt I had an important contribution to make. I told all the family that my school holidays had begun and that they should bring their problems to me and I would provide them with answers and solutions; that my advice might prove of great value to the family! After all, didn't Grandfather keep telling me that I had an original way of looking at things and coming up with answers to questions.

Once at the luncheon table, when I was told to keep quiet when politics were discussed, with the logic and sense of justice of a ten-year-old, I objected roundly:

'Why should I keep quiet when I have something to add to this general discussion?'

'Because you chatter away stupidly and say much too much,' said Zosia, six years my senior. Whenever there was an opportunity, she would try to put me down.

'So at what age did *you* acquire so much wisdom?' I shot back.

Then, at the end of July 1937, less than two months after Ruzia's death, we were burgled. All our silver was stolen, along with many other valuable things. One thing after another.

Naturally we thought at the time that things could hardly get worse – but this was well before the onset of the Holocaust.

In the autumn of 1937– I don't remember the month – a Polish government official arrived to see my father. He said that if a certain sum of money would be guaranteed to be paid by Christmas, Iccio could be released within a week. He explained that all my father had to do was to sign before witnesses that this sum would be paid. As most fathers would, my father signed, and a week later, to the great joy of us all, Iccio came back. He looked thin, but was well and fit. He promised my father that he would have nothing further to do with the Communist party or indeed with any other party. He kept his promise.

As a big timber merchant, Father had bought up chunks of forests where the trees were cut down and then transported to our sawmill. Now Iccio was sent to these remote areas to supervise the cutting, sorting, storing and transporting of the tree trunks and logs. He lived in a little wooden cabin, just as Father himself had done before he had been conscripted into the Czar's army in 1898. It was Mother who made sure that Iccio was sent food and books to keep him going. He, in turn, would send us lyrical short stories, mainly about nature, which Father read aloud – and he read them so well – every Friday night after the Shabbat meal. I was allowed to stay up and listen; a special treat for me.

Mother, meanwhile, took it upon herself to try to obtain visas for us to leave Poland. She wrote letters to her sister Jadzia in Haifa, to my father's sister, Aunt Sarah Weiner in Lausanne and to a cousin in Bolivia. Nothing came of it. In 1937, Mother had turned forty. She sensed that a tragedy of unprecedented proportions was about to befall all the Jewish people in Poland. She wanted to save us all. Very often I would find her crying. When I asked her why she was weeping, she would pull me towards her and give me a hug and kiss.

'Things may work themselves out… even big clouds disperse!' she would say with a sigh.

Before the end of the school year in June 1939, our teacher, Mrs Wisniewska, had explained to the class that Herr Adolf Hitler wanted to take the Danzig corridor away from Poland in order to link his Germany with Prussia. 'Such a corridor,' she said, 'will cut Poland off from our Baltic Sea which is of the utmost importance to us. Poland must never consent to Hitler's demands or give Herr Adolf Hitler anything, not even a button. We cannot allow ourselves to be strangled by our neck, Danzig, and deprived of our "head" – the Baltic. We have no quarrel with the Germans, and they should leave us in peace.'

She went on to say that Poland had signed a treaty with Great Britain, so that a declaration of war against Poland meant declaring war against Great Britain as well. Who in his right mind would pick a fight with the mighty British Empire when it was allied with lion-hearted Poland, a country, as we all knew, with the finest cavalry in the world. Most of us cheered. The

Volksdeutsche boys and girls sat impassively through this lesson. 'Not even a button,' the rest of us chanted on our way home.

One Sunday, sitting around my own family table with everyone enjoying my mother's cake and tea, I hoped that Emma, who was also tucking into her cake, would take her left hand out of her muff. But she ate expertly with her right hand, and kept her muff on the table with her left hand in it.

'Please, Emma, could I borrow your muff for a moment? I would like to have a close look at the flowers on it.'

Mother shot me an icy look, and Zosia followed it up by saying: 'You aren't blind, are you? You can see the flowers across the table. Don't give it to him, Emma; he would only make it grubby.' As if Emma had any intention of parting with it for a moment.

Father was now engrossed in the newspaper. Grandfather was writing to his wife in Jerusalem, and he sat there at the end of the table in his own world, a glass of tea in front of him, with his left hand supporting his forehead and writing with an indelible pencil, which he would dip into his mouth from time to time. Iccio read his thick book, with its covers wrapped in brown paper.

Zosia brought Emma's birthday present and gave it to her. It was a handkerchief, with the letters E.H., which she had embroidered in the corner.

'It's much nicer, Zosia dear, than the one I gave you,' said Emma. 'Look, Mrs Halter, how prettily the E.H. is entwined, and the colours are so nice, too. Thank you. Look, Mr Halter...'

And then a strange thing happened. My father, as if he hadn't surfaced from reading the paper – it was a Yiddish paper – looked at us all and his eyes filled with tears. None of us had seen him that way before. Even Iccio stopped reading and looked at Father. Only Grandfather was busy writing and licking the tip of his pencil. Slowly, Father transferred his gaze and was staring at Emma. This lasted for quite a time. We all sat quietly and tried not to look at him. Then Emma said, 'Is something wrong, Mr Halter?'

Father still kept looking at Emma and then shook himself as if from a nightmare, and he said, 'Would you sing for us, Emma? Would you sing "*Ich weiss nicht was soll es bedeuten, Dass ich so traurig bin*"?' ('I don't know what it can mean, that I feel so sad.')

Emma stood up, adjusted her muff, cleared her throat, and sang, sweetly and beautifully.

Chodecz – the Descent

In 1939, there were close to eight hundred Jews living in the town of Chodecz. Just before the outbreak of the Second World War, there were some 1200 German Poles – *Volksdeutsche* – and around 2200 Poles in Chodecz's very mixed population.

Between September 1939 and September 1940, half the Jewish population of the town had either been sent to forced labour camps on the Berlin-Poznan highway or was being systematically murdered. Chodecz was in that part of north-west Poland which Germany had designated as integral to the Reich, so with virtually no delay, the SS set about making this area *Judenrein*, free of Jews.

A few days after war broke out in September 1939, a brigade of uniformed Polish soldiers came to town and rounded up most of its German-Polish citizens for fear that they might form a

Fifth Column. The *Volksdeutsche* were marched away from Chodecz and two days later, they were marched back again. The long column came to a halt on our street, Ulica Pilsudzka.

It was a warm and sunny September day. The people in the line looked tired and dusty from the dirt roads around Chodecz. We knew most of these *Volksdeutsche* extremely well. My mother handed me a bucket of drinking water, a ladle and a cup and sent me out to offer it to the thirsty people standing in line. I saw Mr and Mrs Hoffmann with Emma, and I saw our neighbours, the Eszners and their family, including Karol, my great friend. I ladled out as much water as I could until a soldier with a rifle slung over his shoulder came up and kicked me from behind. I fell flat on my face, spilling the rest of the water, more indignant than hurt by this act of brutality. Then I approached the top-ranking officer and asked him if I might offer water to the people in the line.

'Water, yes, but no food,' was his reply.

Soon others came out of their homes to offer water to the 'Fifth Column'. When I returned home, my mother wept.

Around mid-September, Hitler's armies entered Chodecz. All those of German descent who lived in the town and the surrounding villages turned out to welcome and cheer their 'liberators'. They lined the main streets through which the troops passed and they shouted *Sieg Heil*, giving the Nazi salute, and the young girls hugged and kissed the soldiers. Some even made swastika flags, which they waved with great enthusiasm. My family and I watched through netted curtains.

Only three months previously, Karol Eszner had finished his studies at Szkola Powszechna. He was now ready to enter the high school in Wloclawek. Both my parents and his attended the prize-giving ceremony. I had come top in my class at drawing and painting and he was awarded first prize in his class for the best essay and also received a prize for drawing. His parents and mine walked home proudly together after the prize-giving. Karol and I followed them and we all chatted together happily.

After the regular German forces came and went, the SS troopers settled into the towns and villages. The first thing they did, with the help of the *Volksdeutsche*, was to draw up a list of potential leaders and troublemakers among the Poles and the Jews.

It appears that my brother Szlamek was on that list, because one night he was taken away. Mr Hoffmann, who had always been a key figure in the German community of Chodecz, must have arranged for his release, however, because early next morning, Szlamek returned home. He would say nothing about what had happened to the others, but the news quickly spread that they had all been shot, like the Polish and Jewish leaders in the adjacent towns. Amongst those killed were our Jewish physician, Dr Baron, the 'new' doctor, and the old Polish doctor as well, the man whose standard method of treatment had been to dispense castor oil.

•

For their billets, the SS requisitioned any house they liked the look of. The family of the local blacksmith, Mietek, who lived only a few doors away from our home was one of the first to be evicted. Their house was a rather elegant one and it had a few distinctive architectural features: a rounded balcony and steps leading up to the front door. The Germans decided that they wanted their officers to be put up in this home, and they just evicted the blacksmith's family, who were Roman Catholic, took them to the forest and shot them. The Germans behaved with brutality not just towards the Jews in the town, but also towards the local population who were Polish and not *Volksdeutsche*.

Within two months of the SS establishing themselves in Chodecz, my family had been evicted from our house and put into three small rooms on the outskirts of the town. We were forced to leave most of our belongings behind. Everything had been taken from us – land, house, horses, timber yard. Every day there was a new proclamation on the noticeboard of the SS police station, which we Jewish people were ordered to read. First there was the notice that every Jewish person had to wear a yellow star on the front and back of one's coat or outer garment. Those who failed to do so would be 'suitably pun-ished'. Any Jew seen outside the perimeter of Chodecz without a permit would be shot. Jews were not allowed to walk on pave-ments, but had to walk on the roads or close to the kerb and in single file. There must be no gathering in people's houses. And so on and so on. Every day, new, humiliating and dreadful things were demanded of us. The local school where everyone had gone, the Szkola Powszechna, had now become a school only for German Poles. Then one day, our lovely wooden synagogue, the precious parchment Torah scrolls and the prayer books (which we kept in the lockers of our seats) were all torched. Everything burned to the ground. My grandfather was held up in the street by young local 'Germans' who cut off his beard with a knife. When Karol passed me, he walked along the pavement, while I had to walk along the road. He looked away.

One day I was rounded up, together with three of my Jewish friends and taken to the lake. It transpired that we had been brought in to help with a duck shoot, in the capacity of dog-retrievers. The man who had ordered us to be rounded up was the Oberst, Herr Oberst as the Germans called him, or Major.

By now, this man was practically running the town, and was also the chief training officer of the SS in our area. He, his wife and three children lived in the largest Jewish house in Chodecz which had been confiscated from a family who were related to us, the Czyzewskis. The house, office headquarters, sheds, stores and stables had all belonged to one of my father's cousins, a corn and grain merchant.

We went to the lake. The Oberst had two guests with him, and his dog, Fritz. In among the reeds there were ducks. It had been a successful shoot. Instead of sending the dog each time to retrieve the catch, the Oberst shouted out that we should retrieve the prize. Apart from the dog, I was the only one who could swim and I kept on volunteering to get it. So I swam out, got into the reeds, got hold of the duck by the wing with my teeth and somehow made my way back, stopping now and then to do a little backstroke with one hand and holding the duck on my chest with the other. That was a little easier for me and allowed me to breathe. Then, when I got to the bank I would put the duck on the grass and Fritz would run back with it and place it by the Oberst's feet.

This worked out for a while. I swam naked as I was afraid to catch a cold by jumping into the October water with my clothes on and then walking around in wet trousers, shirt and sweater. So I stripped very quickly and performed my task. By the time I got back to the shooting party, I was practically dry and would quickly dress again. But on the third occasion one of the guests insisted that one of my three friends go to catch it. They chose Szlamek, who had been hit in the eye on the *heder* playground with an arrow when he was seven and had only partial sight in that eye. He came up to the Oberst and said in Yiddish that he might not be able to find the duck because he was blind in one eye. The Oberst and his guests didn't quite understand the Yiddish and so my two other friends tried to explain what Szlamek said. When they heard, the Germans roared with laughter. I knew that neither Szlamek nor the others could swim but it was too late. The Oberst said something to his guests and one guest got hold of Szlamek and told him to get the duck quickly. We could see that it lay partly on the reeds and partly on a clump of water lilies. But to get the duck meant swimming across clear water for some fifty yards. Szlamek began crying and pleading. Then the Oberst shouted, 'Halt.'

Szlamek stopped crying and stood rigid and to attention. By the end of September 1939, we Jewish people in Chodecz had learned that if we dared to move when a German shouted 'Halt' we could expect to be shot.

'One of you get it!' he shouted.

I knew that none of my friends could swim, so I quickly started to strip but the Oberst made me stand there naked. Szlamek stood rigid to one side. I stood naked next to the other two. They were still fully dressed and clinging to one another and pleading in Yiddish, 'We can't swim, we can't swim!'

The Oberst went up to his guests and spoke with them and they began to laugh together. Then he turned to me and motioned with his hand and pointed in the direction of the duck on the water lilies. Fritz followed me to the edge barking excitedly. I dived in, swam across a corner of the lake and then had to search amongst the water reeds and the lilies till I found the duck. Then I heard shots. I caught the duck, held it by my teeth and began swimming back. It was heavy, and the way I held it prevented me from breathing. I kept on adjusting it to make certain not to lose it; I was afraid that it would sink to the bottom of the lake. When I came to the edge, I saw Szlamek still fully dressed, drowning. He kept on going under and coming up making horrible coughing noises.

The Oberst and his guests stood by the edge and shouted to

me to swim towards them with the duck. I did as I was ordered, placed the duck on the shore. Then I asked if I might now help Szlamek to the edge. This part of the lake had no shallow end. I was told to get out and get dressed.

'You are almost as good as Fritz and we may need you again next week for another shoot,' said one of the guests.

They all laughed, Szlamek had no chance. He not only couldn't swim but he wore trousers tied just below the knee. They must have pulled him under when they filled with water.

I carried the ducks back. On the way we passed my other two friends who lay on the ground groaning and bleeding. The Oberst and his guests went past them. Fritz barked. I managed to whisper in Yiddish, 'I will come back to you.'

I returned as soon as I could with members of their families. The Oberst and guests had told them that since they couldn't swim they might as well run back home. As they ran, they were shot, mainly in the bottom, back and legs. Their bodies were peppered with tiny plugs of lead. Szlamek drowned.

Towards the end of October 1939 I was summoned to report to the police station. Although we Jewish people referred to the place as the 'German police station' or the 'Komendatura' – all the men working there were SS men.

My parents and my grandfather were terribly concerned, afraid that something appalling would happen to me. They kept on asking me whether I had done anything that might deserve punishment. My mother wanted to come with me. She spoke and read German very well and she told me that she might be needed to translate things for me… But I insisted on going alone.

When I got there, an SS man led me to a large room, where a man in uniform sat behind an imposing desk, and beside him was Mr Hoffmann. Seeing Mr Hoffmann there, I now felt that nothing bad would happen to me. The man in the uniform was Herr Oberst. I recognized him, but for some unknown reason, had no fear of him. I bowed and then stood to attention the way our teacher Mrs Wisniewska had taught us to do in school before the war.

This Oberst, this man in uniform slouching in the big chair, looked me up and down and then for a time he stared into my eyes without saying a word. I had been taught by our teacher that when a person does that, one should not look away or down, but straight back. Then the Oberst said: 'The duck Jew' and gave a nod to Mr Hoffmann.

Mr Hoffmann said to me in German that from the next day I would be working for the Oberst's family. He instructed me to report to the back of their house at 8 a.m. And then he told me to go. So I bowed, turned and went home to my family. I was then just over twelve years old. This was when I began my working life.

My duties for the Oberst started at 6 a.m. My first task in the early morning was to carry two large buckets of pig-swill on a yoke. This was a kind of buttermilk that had to be taken from the dairy to what was now the Oberst's home. The distance I had to walk was roughly a mile. It took me about half an hour. Every day of the week and twice on Saturday – there was no Sunday collection – I struggled with the two full buckets of buttermilk. The kitchen maid who spoke both German and Polish would open the side gates and let me in.

Having brought the swill, I would mix the liquid with a prepared roughage, which was delivered in sacks, and feed it to the pigs. Then I would go to the porch and see whether there were boots and shoes, which had been put outside for me to polish. Later, I would clean the sty, sweep the yard, sort out potatoes (the tiny ones were to be boiled for pig food), work in the vegetable garden, run errands, and carrying my yoke and two large buckets, I would draw soft drinking water from the spring well, and generally do anything that the Oberst, his wife, children or maid ordered me to do.

The Oberst had two boys, one was my age, twelve, and one was three and a half years old. There was also a little girl, Ingrid, who was eight years old. Neither the Oberst nor his wife nor any of the children would communicate with me. Jorgen, the youngest, sometimes came out and followed me about and chatted until the children's maid (this maid spoke only German) would spot him and quickly lead him away.

In November 1939, around the time that we were evicted from our home, the Oberst began training the young local *Volksdeutsche*. I knew most of them. They had been pupils at our school. Some used to come with their parents to buy timber or building materials from my father. Now they were no longer the polite and quiet Polish-German clientele of ours but fervent supporters of Hitler who proudly considered themselves German through and through. They took their military training and keep-fit very seriously. At daybreak they would gather by the fire station and the Oberst would drill them with press-ups, arm swings, jumps and squats. On my way to work I would see them doing exercises, and by the time I got back with the pig-swill, the Oberst would be home from his run. Every morning at 5.30 a.m. he would take the *Volksdeutsche* SS volunteers (and there were plenty of such volunteers) jogging. The run also included toughening-up exercises and marches. Those volunteers who lived some distance from Chodecz – now renamed Godetz – were billeted in the block where, before the war, the Polish teachers of our local school had lodgings.

Sometimes on my way to the dairy in the morning mist I would see the recruits led by the Oberst jogging towards the lake. By the time I was on my way back they would also be returning, marching and singing. The kitchen maid had instructed me that when I passed the recruits I should stop, put the buckets on the ground close to the kerb, place the yoke in front of me, and if I was wearing a cap, I should take it off and stand neatly to attention, cap in hand.

Karol Eszner also took part in these early morning runs and toughening-up exercises and marches, although he was only just past fourteen years old. He was not the only German fourteen-year-old in the group to do so. One morning, as I stood to attention by the kerb, my cap in hand, the buckets carefully placed next to me, the yoke on the ground in front of me, waiting for the singing recruits to march past, the Oberst halted the column. He motioned to me to come closer to him. He then asked these SS volunteers if one of them knew this young Jew.

I knew almost all of them: the younger ones from school, others used to come to buy wood or building materials or even coal from my father... A few of the SS volunteers in this group were the sons of those German smallholders who carted our coal from the railway station to our place in Chodecz and knew me well. So when the Oberst asked whether any of them knew this young Jew, Karol Eszner stepped forward and said in good German (I had never heard him talk German before that) that their house was next to where we used to live and that he knew me very well.

'Come over here,' ordered the Oberst to Karol, 'and knock this Jew to the ground.'

Karol came up close to me, and with absolutely no hesitation, he hit me hard with his fist on the side of my face. It hurt. I swayed, tripped, and fell backwards to the ground. And as I lay there on my back, the Oberst ordered Karol to drag me to the kerb and to tell me to look down at the ground the next time. As I lay there dazed by the experience, the group started singing again '*Gagmen England*' – 'We're off to England soon!' as they marched off.

•

The kitchen maid was quite indifferent towards me and the other hired hands, two Polish lads in their twenties who looked after the pigs and horses and did the heavy labour. They lived in Przedecz a few miles away and used to ride their bicycles to work.

Before going home each day we were to knock on the back door and report. My job was supposed to be done by midday but often the maid would ask me to stay a little longer or to come back after the Oberst's siesta (he didn't want anyone in the yard while he slept) for extra chores.

Normally when I had to report back in the afternoon it was to force-feed the geese and to clean the Oberst's muddy boots again according to the maid's instructions: first, gently scrape the mud off the leather with a cloth wrapped around a stick. Then clean the boots with milk (milk didn't stretch the leather) and let them dry a while, or, if they were not needed for the rest of the day, leave them overnight and shine them the next morning with polish, a soft brush and a shoe rag.

One afternoon, as I sat on the porch working on the Oberst's boots, the two Polish lads reported to the Polish- and German-speaking maid that they were setting off for home. This maid normally spoke German to me except when I couldn't understand something and she would have to translate it for me. To the Polish lads she spoke in Polish. The two of them were getting ready to cycle home. Their trouser cuffs were tucked into their socks, their satchels were slung diagonally over their shoulders and they stood at the door ready to say goodbye, their caps in their hands. 'What do you have in your bags?' asked the maid. They looked at each other and at her and made no reply. 'Empty your bags here,' she ordered. There was another silence. Then one of them glared at her, his eyes blazing with hatred, and said something like 'Go to hell!' And they both turned on their heels and mounted their bikes. The gates were open and they cycled away.

The two men did not report back the following day, or the day after that, or ever again. Two Jewish men were hired in their stead to look after the horses and to do the heavy labour. The maid showed me how to look after the pigs and clean the sty, to mix the mash with the small cooked potatoes and the swill and to set out straw for their bedding… From that day onwards this too was my job.

I told my grandfather about the two Polish men who never returned to work for the Oberst and he told me that I must always be polite, truthful and hardworking and never ever take anything that was not my own.

Around that same time, November 1939, Szlamek was taken away, together with the other fit young Jewish men in the area, to work on the Hermann Goering highway somewhere beyond Poznan. From time to time, our steward Podlawski, who had been with my father now for a full fourteen years, would receive letters that Szlamek had somehow managed to post. The letters were written to his wife Eva and to his little son

Danus and were composed in such a way that Podlawski would not get into trouble if they were opened by the Germans. By that time, Jews were not allowed to send or receive mail. (As far as I recall, a few months earlier, we had managed to send food and clothing parcels to Zosia, who was now in Warsaw, and her letters still reached us. Zosia had been sent to Warsaw to take Iccio various things when he ended up there under German occupation after having been conscripted to fight for Poland. Father had written to Iccio saying that since he was both a communist and a Jew, he would be shot immediately were he to return to Chodecz. Iccio had then left for Russia, and although Zosia wanted to return to Chodecz, she was not allowed to leave. A Jewish ghetto had been set up by the Germans, and Jews were sealed off from the rest of Poland.)

Then we heard no more from Szlamek. Eva wrote to the address that Szlamek had provided in his last letter and her opened letters were returned to Podlawski.

Soon afterwards another Jewish family managed to get a letter from their son who had been taken away the same day as Szlamek and sent to work at the same place. They informed us that Szlamek had been hanged. David 'Dudek' Czyzewski, his best friend (whose parents' house had been commandeered by the Oberst), had been forced to string him up, but because Szlamek was so tall that his feet touched the ground, Dudek had to bind Szlamek's hands and gag his mouth and hang him again and watch as he swung from the rope. Other letters arrived with reasons for the hanging: some said Szlamek had been caught smuggling arms into the camp. Others wrote that he had been caught trying to bring more food into the camp and when the guard tried to take it from him, Szlamek had hit the guard… All this was little comfort to poor Eva or to us. Our beloved Szlamek was dead.

It was now almost four months since Aunt Sabina, Uncle Ignac and Misio left for Kiev. We – Grandfather, Father, Mother, Eva, Danus and I – were all crammed into three rooms on the outskirts of Chodecz.

Early in 1940, we had a letter from Peccio. He sent the letter to us via Mr and Mrs Podlawski. He wrote that he, his wife and child were now in the Lodz ghetto, but had plans to get out and go south. We didn't hear anything more from him. Father took all this very badly. He would sit for hours now, just staring into space or weeping. We didn't know what to do or how to help him. When I came from work I would shave him and Grandfather with a cut-throat razor which I sharpened on a leather belt. Mother asked me to massage his face gently after the shave and to speak to him about happy things.

But it was hard to find happy things to talk about.

Each day brought new sorrows. Then I thought of asking him how to do certain things at the Oberst's and that worked wonders. So after the shave, Mother would boil some water, tear a towel into squares and dip them in the water. I would ring the squares out and spread them over Father's face while he leaned back with his eyes shut, enjoying the hot towels and my gentle face massage. I did this for Grandfather too. As I worked on my father's face, I would ask him how best to hold the goose I had to stuff-feed with thumb-sized noodles made of a grated potato and flour mixture ladled with a spoon into boiling hot water. 'Bring me my walking stick and I will demonstrate it to you... well... here is the goose...' and momentarily he would come back to life.

One day in the springtime of 1940, I finished my work at the Oberst's and went up to the back door to find out whether there was anything else that they needed me to do before setting off for where we now lived. I stood there with a strange feeling inside me. I remember it was partly fear and partly apprehension. I knocked gently on the door and waited as I had so many times before.

The Oberst's wife came to the door and said that I must listen carefully and that I must note every word that she would tell me. It was the first time she had spoken to me – before that the maid had always communicated their orders. She said that today, within the hour, I had to set off with an envelope that she handed to me.

'It's a farm near Izbica Kujawska.'

She said that if I didn't know where the place was my father might be able to help me. But that he is not to go there, and only I should carry out this task.

'Do you know Izbica Kujawska?'

'Yes,' I replied, 'my auntie and cousins live there.'

She told me that I must not go to them or to anyone else but directly to the address on this envelope, which was about two miles away from Izbica. She said that if I was stopped by a German soldier, I should show the envelope and say that the Oberst's wife had sent me.

'They will let you go on if they see the envelope. Now, don't waste time and you can get there before dark. You may come back tomorrow after lunch and bring with you the things which they will give you.'

As I came out of the house, Mr Hoffmann was coming out from the front. He saw me holding the envelope in my hand and called me over. 'Put the letter in your pocket and get going. Don't waste time.'

I ran home. My mother rolled a blanket over my shoulder. She gave me some food for the journey. Father explained to me where the place was. Now I knew exactly; I could get there with my eyes shut. They kissed me, including little Danus and I was off. Outside, my instincts told me to turn round. Grandfather and Father stood by the window. Father looked serious and motionless, Grandfather smiled and I gave a little wave and began to run.

For most of the eight miles, I ran and walked fast. Dogs came out from small farmyards and barked at me. I passed some Polish people walking from the opposite direction. Sometimes a cart would pass me. Occasionally I overtook people walking in the same direction.

'*Hej Zydek*, where are you running to?'

'If they catch you they will shoot you.'

I didn't reply, but just ran on. When I got tired running, I walked and ate the food Mother gave me. From time to time I checked whether the letter was still safely in my pocket. As long as I have this letter with me I am safe, I thought. I ran on, I knew exactly where I was. I was over twelve years old, fit and confident. But to give myself that extra courage I recited the prayer that one says after reading the Torah.

'Blessed are You, O Lord of the Universe, who has given us the true Torah and has implanted everlasting life in us; Blessed are You, who has given us the Torah.'

My grandfather who was coaching me for my Bar Mitzvah, preferred this blessing to the one recited before reading from the Torah, explaining how beautiful this one was, with its reference to giving us the Torah and implanting eternal life into us, and that was good enough for me. Now it made me feel good.

When I reached the farm, it was dark. A maid opened the door and I gave her the letter and stood outside. After a while she asked me in Polish to wait inside the porch. I must have waited for about half an hour. Then a servant came out and said in Polish that I ought to follow him. He called me *Zydek* – little Jew. Although I didn't look particularly Jewish, each Pole in our area knew as if by some sixth sense who was and who was not a Jew.

The man carried a paraffin lamp and led me to the stables. There he kicked together some straw into a corner and said: 'You can sleep here. Mind you don't snore because I wouldn't like you to frighten the horses.' He gave a kind of horsy laugh, snorting at his own funny remark. Then looking at me as if I was another animal in his temporary care he said, 'I will peg the door from the outside, so if you want to shit go now. The bog is to your right when you come outside and right again. Do you want me to show you? I wouldn't like to start fishing you out of the hole this time of night.'

'No thanks, I'm all right,' I replied. 'Could I please get some water, I am very thirsty.' He dipped the bucket into a barrel which stood in the corner and handed me the bucket. 'Don't finish the barrel, leave some for the horse.' And he began to laugh again. He didn't give me any food or ask me whether I was hungry. Paraffin lamp in hand, he shut the stable door and pegged it from the outside. The blanket came in very useful.

Next morning two Polish stable boys came at dawn to groom the horses; they wanted to know what I came here for. 'I brought a letter,' I told them. They went about their work. One of them said, 'Did you sleep well?'

'Yes, all right.'

'You weren't bitten in the night?'

'No,' I said.

'Sometimes the rats go for the nose or the soft ear bits or your hands.'

I didn't reply but I thought that I must remember to ask my grandfather or my father about it.

'When you sleep in a stable, it's a good idea to have a piece of wood with a nail on the end of it and when you feel them trying to bite you, you biff them with the nail and the shriek of the one that has been biffed sends them all scurrying away. They don't come back to you again that night…'

'Or go to sleep with a big Tom cat, for the rats would kill a small one,' said the other stable boy and they both laughed.

When they had finished grooming the horses they gave me a piece of their bread and one of them went outside and brought me an egg. He showed me how to pierce a small hole at one end and then plunge in a straw into the other end and suck the raw egg.

Later I saw the Polish maid who told me to wait in the porch last night and I asked her if she could find out from the master or his wife whether I could go back to Chodecz now. 'You came to collect something and you had better wait in the stable until we have it ready for you.'

It must have been past ten when I was given a sack, which the maid helped me to strap like a rucksack on my back. It wasn't too heavy. I was also given the original envelope with the Oberst's stamp on it and the German writing and another one to hand to the Oberst's wife. 'You've got some plucked fowls in there, so get going and deliver them safely.'

She gave me a couple of pieces of black, homemade bread spread with pork dripping. I stuck the bread inside my blanket, which I wore diagonally across my shoulder. I left without having set my eyes upon the German owner or his wife. My father had known the previous Polish owners who, as rumour had it, had all been sent to work in Germany.

Polish fields and forests in spring are beautiful. I was happy to be on my way home. It was a sunny day, and though the weight on my back was too heavy for running, I walked at a pretty brisk pace. Soon, I settled into my stride and I took out the bread with the pork dripping and began eating it. Knowing that I was eating *treife* food somewhat marred my enjoyment of it, yet I thought it tasted good. 'Can it really be so bad for me if it tastes so good?' I mused.

I thought I should stick to the road; it would be safer and someone might give me a lift. Some two miles on, I was overtaken by a Polish peasant driving a horse and cart. He stopped and asked my name.

'Which Halter from Izbica?'

'No, I'm the youngest Halter from Chodecz.'

'Jump on.' I climbed onto the cart. 'What's in your sack?' I decided not to answer.

'What's inside it, little Jew?'

'My name is Romek.'

'Don't you know that if the Germans catch you half a mile out of your town they will...' and he passed his right hand along his throat, indicating that I would be a dead pig, for pigs were slaughtered like that.

'So let's see what's in your sack and I will see whether I can help you. Do you understand me?'

I understood him well. There wasn't a living soul within sight. In his eyes I saw a blue coldness. I knew that I had seconds to react.

'You see, sir, I work for the German chief of police, the

Oberst. He is a powerful and important man. He trains all the young German recruits who have skulls on their caps and collars. My German chief sent me to collect pigeons, chickens and ducks for the party tonight.'

I made this up about the party. 'Here is the letter which I have to deliver with the sack.'

I waved the letter close to his nose. It was upside down. He was either not interested or he could not read; suddenly he had lost all interest in me and the sack. He mumbled something, which to my ears sounded like 'Chicken-carrying little Jew...' and turned to his horse, smacked his lips and shouted 'Gee up! Vio!' The horse began to trot and we jerked and rolled from side to side inside the cart. The peasant was sitting in front holding the reins. I sat behind him, somewhat sideways against the hay, still with the sack on my back. The sun was pleasantly warm and with the warmth and together with the jerky rhythm of the cart I felt sleepy.

For a while I slept like a bird dozing, opening one eye or both and watching what the peasant driver was doing. Suddenly, at a point when I must have been asleep, I heard him call me. 'Hey, young Halter, why don't you ask your father if he wants a basket of potatoes in exchange for a watch? If he does, let him send you here to this spot, the same time next week and I will have the potatoes in my cart. But don't come empty-handed...'

'I'll ask him,' I replied.

'Now out you get and start walking because I go to the right and Chodecz is to the left.'

I thanked him for the lift and began walking. Soon I recognized where I was – some three miles from Chodecz. I took a cut across the fields towards the forest. From time to time I heard sounds of shots from the sandy ravine which dipped down from my side. A few years ago, when I was about eight, we children would go there with metal trays or old washing tubs to slide down the slopes of fine sand. This was one of our happiest playgrounds.

Now, as I approached it, some inner prompting told me I should creep up without being seen. I hid under a bush and looked down. I saw all the SS recruits wearing helmets, belts and diagonal straps. They were all armed. The Oberst wore the boots and the belt which I polished and cleaned. He was in his full 'funny-shaped' cut-off-on-top helmet. The whole of the SS police force were in their uniforms and wearing these 'funny' helmets too and holding rifles with bayonets fixed to them. Then immediately opposite, men without uniforms were dragging bodies along the sand. Further on, surrounded by uniformed men with rifles, I recognized familiar figures, eight in all – they were my Jewish friends with whom I grew up and went first to *heder* and then to school together.

When the dead bodies were out of the way, the Oberst gave the order and two SS police went inside the huddled group of boys and girls and began pulling some of them out. Henryk and Hanka, brother and sister, two close friends of mine, were pulled out. Henryk embraced his sister and the SS policeman tried to tear them apart. The Oberst shouted something and one of the new SS recruits stepped out. By his walk I thought it was 'Piggy' who had been in Zosia's class, six years ahead of me. Now in his boots, helmet, belt, SS uniform and rifle, he looked quite lethal, transformed. Piggy turned his rifle upside down and with the butt end, like with an axe, hit Henryk on the head. Both Henryk and Hanka fell to the ground. Two men ran up and dragged brother and sister to the bank of sand where they propped up Henryk in a sitting position. His head, face and body were covered with blood. Hanka was also propped up and now she stirred, as if waking up. She screamed and threw herself onto Henryk. The other six, groaning, were led and prodded by the SS police with bayonets. From the rest of the ravine at the far end came a sound like the roaring of the lake on a windy day: it was a sound of moans blended with prayers and sobs. I knew the other six very well and I looked at them from within the bush quite forgetting who I was and where I was… I don't even remember feeling afraid. I was not in this world.

Things below were happening quickly. Someone gave an order. It was not the Oberst's voice. The eight recruits stepped out. Each one positioned himself about twenty paces from each of my friends and directly in line with their bodies. Henryk slid further to the ground together with Hanka. She was still clinging to him. I thought I saw Karol among the recruits. The Oberst said something and the two SS recruits who covered Henryk and Hanka went up to them, put bayonets into their rifles and standing astride over the bodies plunged the bayonets again and again into Hanka and Henryk. No sound came from either of them that I could hear. The Oberst shouted and the two SS men kicked over Hanka and Henryk, bent down over them and went back to their former positions. My other six friends who stood with their faces to the sand cried and wept. An order was given to the remaining six SS men, who raised their rifles and aimed. Then came the short bark of an order, and they fired. Shouts rang out and my friends sank slowly, but so very slowly and almost gently first onto their knees and them some fell on their backs and some sideways in a heap.

I found myself saying the *Shema*. The six SS came and inspected the bodies, and some kicked them so they would lie face up. The men in civilian clothes came nearer and when the Oberst waved his hand, they began pulling the bodies away.

I suddenly realized that if I were to be caught in this place, I would also be killed. Inch by inch, on all fours, I began to edge my way backwards out of the bush. Then I crawled for a time. When I thought that I could no longer be seen, I made for the fields where I threw up, then shook with sobs. After that I walked until I came to the proper road to Chodecz, which brought me very close to the school house. Suddenly something touched my hand. It was Fritz, the Oberst's dog.

Fritz followed me; he had come to know me well since he saw me every day at the Oberst's place. I was stopped by two SS policemen who were not from Chodecz station but were guarding the school. One of them escorted me to the Oberst's home to make certain I was telling the truth. I asked the SS policeman whether we could go by way of the river and past the place where we now lived. I'd hoped I might catch a glimpse of my family and be able to wave as we went by, but he took me the short way round past our old house instead.

At the next junction we met other SS police who laughed and said, 'Put a bullet in him now and spare yourself a walk.' They all laughed at the remark.

At the Oberst's house the maid said, 'He's right, Mrs Oberst sent him,' but the SS policeman insisted on seeing the Oberst's wife himself, and only then did he leave me and go back to his post at the school. I was sent to clean out the pigsty and ordered not to come out till the maid told me to do so. The piggery was one pig short.

Later the maid brought me something to eat and said the Oberst's wife had ordered me to stay in the piggery overnight. I was not to step out till the morning until they told me to fetch the pig-swill.

It was a noisy, festive evening at the Oberst's house. I was sound asleep in the corner when there was a knock on the door that sounded more like a kick. As the door creaked open I saw the maid holding a bowl of bones with some meat on them for me. She was a little drunk.

In the morning I heard a great clamour of comings and goings. Then everything was still and I was told to fetch the buttermilk-swill. I took a chance and went the round-about way, past the house where my parents, Grandfather, Eva and Danus lived. I knocked on the window and when Mother saw me she fainted. Father opened the door and said 'Are you all right?'

'Yes, I'm fine. Here's some cooked meat, I'll be back later.' And I walked off briskly to get the pig-swill.

When I came home that night I said nothing about what I had witnessed. Mother said some children my age had been sent away on a 'transport'. Again I said nothing. The meat I had brought that morning was eaten by Eva and Danus. Father told me gently that unless we were starving, we would not eat *treife* so long as we remained in Chodecz. He wanted to hear about my trip; whether I found the place and all about it. I told him and my grandfather everything except the murder of my friends. I also left out about the bread and pork dripping which the maid gave me. I went to bed that night, like the night in the pigsty, with pictures of Hanka and Henryk and my other friends before my eyes, and said the *Shema* over and over again.

When later my grandfather told me in the Lodz ghetto just before he died that it was the German plan to kill off all the Jews, what he was trying to pass on to me was something I already knew. After I had witnessed my friends being murdered in the ravine, I had felt certain that this would be the fate of all of us Jews. Up till that time, I had been protected by my family from all forms of horridness. 'Bad' things were not discussed in front of me. I thought this a mistake and told my parents so.

Later on in the war, there were encounters that I found strange, new and very shocking, yet they did not produce in me the convulsions of shaking and quivering. These encounters appalled and frightened me. I felt sickened by them, but I managed to get through them without shakes or quivers. But witnessing the murder of my Jewish friends, this particular experience penetrated not only my consciousness but embedded itself so deep, that to this day I still get nightmares about it.

It's hard to understand how, at the time when it happened, I did not tell my parents or my grandfather anything about it. Did I instinctively want to shelter and protect them from this knowledge of such a terrible deed? I simply kept this all within me and quietly wept at night.

A few days after I had witnessed the murders in the ravine, two carts arrived in town, each drawn by a pair of horses. They halted in the marketplace where all the Jews of Chodecz, young and old, were rounded up and loaded on with a rifle-bearing SS policeman for an escort. I was the only member of my family to be shoved onto cart number two. The Polish cart drivers told us that we were being taken out to pick potatoes. And so we were. We arrived at a field about three miles from Chodecz and were given digging tools and baskets in which to carry the potatoes to the collection wagon. I had often watched Mrs Lewandowska and the other women digging for potatoes in our fields before the war, so I knew how it was done, and when the Polish overseer asked, 'Who knows how to pick potatoes?' I stepped out with half a dozen others.

The overseer gave us each a quick test and asked us to wait on the side. Then he began to try out the rest, and if they did well they joined us on the edge of the field. There was a lot of mirth and banter, for no one really took the overseer seriously. The SS police stood some distance away, smoking and chatting with each other. Eventually we began to work, but it was not going very well for us, unskilled as we were at potato-picking. The Polish overseer muttered curses at us and eventually went back to the estate. Soon afterwards the new German owner of the estate (the previous owner, a Pole, a man called Werner, had left when the Germans arrived), galloped up on his horse and began thrashing everyone in sight. He was a friend of the Oberst, one of the guests who had accompanied him on the duck shoot. Straight away the joking stopped and everyone started digging frantically for potatoes. Then, still mounted on his horse, he inspected the baskets. When he saw that some of the potatoes were cut or damaged, he called the pickers out and thrashed them again with his whip. Suddenly his face turned red, and as the overseer held down one woman after another, he whipped their faces and their breasts, shouting something like '*Halte sie bei die Haare!*' The Polish overseer could not understand him so an SS policeman demonstrated how to use one hand to pin the woman's arms behind her back and the other to grab her hair. If the woman screamed, the German whipped her even more violently and ripped her clothes off with his riding crop.

Mrs M. had been one of the women who was thus beaten by him, and a few days later she sat with my mother and told her she'd had no word from her two sons, her only children, who were a few years older than me. Her husband had been sent away on the same transport as Szlamek. 'Have you heard anything, Romek?' she asked. I didn't want to lie but I didn't know what to answer, so I just sat there, staring at the faded lines of her scarred face. Mother said, 'He comes home so tired, you know, getting up before dawn the way he does for work. I would just leave him alone.'

Then one day later in the year, in September 1940, an SS policeman and a chief SS officer arrived in Chodecz, something that boded ill for the Jews, as we knew from experience. I had finished my work at the Oberst's and knocked on the back door as usual to ask whether there was anything else to do before I went home. The maid announced that the Oberst's wife wished to see me, and that I should wait outside. I waited and waited. Then the maid came out again with the Oberst's daughter, Ingrid, and gave me some food in a bag. There was nothing very unusual about the occurrence, since they had given me food before in the past, but this time, when the maid said that the Oberst's wife was still busy and could not come out to me, Ingrid said, '*Morgen fa'hrst du weg, Romek.*' ('Tomorrow you're going on a journey.') The maid pulled her inside and shut the door. I wanted to ask whether, in view of what little Ingrid had said, I was expected to come the following morning.

When I reached home, Father, Mother and Eva were packing hurriedly. Grandfather was praying. Father had been informed by Mr Hoffmann that very early the next morning the

Jews of Chodecz were going to be transported. I was convinced that we would all be shot the way my friends in the ravine had been. 'Let's go now and leave everything here, and when night falls, we'll hide in the woods or travel to another town... only, please, let's leave...' My parents didn't understand what had come over me. I wept, I pleaded...

That night I couldn't sleep. I conceived a plan: when they stood me before the firing squad I would turn around at the last minute and shout, 'You murderers... may God never forgive you!'

It was still dark outside when we heard a knock at the door. Two SS police and a German civilian told Father that we were all expected to assemble at the marketplace in half an hour, bringing with us the barest essentials. Horse carts began to arrive. Mr Hoffmann said to Father, 'Take more belongings with you; you can always throw them away later. I will see to it that you get everything into the cart.' Mother sent me back to fetch another eiderdown. 'What's the point?' I thought to myself. 'This is only a blind. Soon enough they'll shoot us all. There are no new SS men here. They're all waiting for us at the ravine with their guns and their brutal faces...'

I got the eiderdown and was putting it into a sack as Mother had told me to, when I saw a big glass jar of cherries. I opened it and poured myself a glass of juice and drank it down. It was delicious, and I had some more. Then I saw a bag full of kidney beans. I thought I will put this around my heart and that way the bullets won't penetrate. I staggered out with the eiderdown in a sack and a big bag of beans and found my parents in the marketplace.

We were loaded onto a train. I remember waking up on the floor of the wagon next to Father, Mother, Grandfather, Eva and Danus and some fellow Jews from Chodecz.

'Did they shoot us?' I asked.

'No one has been shot, sssh, go back to sleep,' said Grandfather.

Lodz, Auschwitz, Stutthof, Dresden – Living in Hell

The Jews of Chodecz were sent to the Lodz ghetto and we were amongst them.

On arrival in Lodz we were taken to a school building in Marysin on the outskirts and held there for three days and nights. The ghetto area was sealed off from the rest of Lodz by a high barbed-wire fence, with SS guards in sentry boxes every fifty yards or so. There was one gate for entry and exit, controlled by the SS. About 360 Jews had been sent to Lodz on our transport, but only 120 got into the ghetto; one third were taken in, and homes (crowded rooms) found for them, and the remainder were put on a train and taken to another place. I was certain that the 200 or so who were taken to 'another place' were taken to be murdered.

We were given a room on 3, Storchen Street.

Later that autumn, we were told that about eighty more

people would be coming to Lodz from Brzesc Kujawski where my half-sister Sala and her two children lived. Like we had been, the new arrivals were held in the Marysin school building until other accommodation became available for them inside the ghetto.

Sala and her husband Gershon had two children, Danusia and Henryk. They were younger than me, but I was very attached to them. They would all come to visit during the high holy days, and in the summer of 1937, I had spent some time with them during my summer holidays.

Sala painted prettily in watercolours, and for my birthday, she would always paint me a card with strawberries on it, and Gershon would make me a leather pouch or small purse, and these two presents would arrive without fail the day before my birthday, on 6 July, and I would open them happily on 7 July.

Now I wanted to go to the school to find out whether Sala and her children had arrived there with the group. I planned to go on my own because although we had only been in the Lodz ghetto for a few months, we were all starving, I thought Sala might have some food with her. The scant food we had brought with us from Chodecz, a little flour and a small bag of beans, were gone within a week. Rations in the ghetto were meagre and unfairly distributed. Those relatively strong and well connected received a bigger share. Newcomers were cheated and had no way of fighting for their starvation ration. Mother would send me to the soup kitchen to wait for a tiny ration of potato peelings from which she managed to concoct a kind of bread loaf. Every imaginable and unimaginable sort of thing went into it. We had grown so weak we began to look as though we were starving – it was the first stage of starvation, as we later learned. A more advanced stage, the *klapsedra* (this was a ghetto word meaning 'a walking skeleton') with swollen legs and swelling under the eyes, lay in store.

After a month in the ghetto, Father discovered an acquaintance who was an important person there and knew Chaim Rumkowski and other Jewish leaders of the Lodz ghetto. Eventually this acquaintance helped get Father into the home for the aged, though he was only sixty-three years old at the time. The aged received a little extra soup along with their starvation rations. There were many heart-to-heart discussions between Mother and Father, and eventually they decided that the extra soup would make all the difference and Father could save a little liquid or half a potato a day for us when we came to visit him.

We went to see him every other day. The highlight of our visit was the bit of potato he had fished out of his soup to share with us. Mother, Father and I would share the little fragments that amounted to a half a potato which Father served on a board, divided into three equal portions.

'No, no, you have more,' Mother would say. 'I am not hungry and Romek needs less food than you do.' But Father insisted. 'We will all get the same portion and we will eat and enjoy it.' With a liberal sprinkling of salt, we nibbled on our minuscule shares, savouring them, trying to eke out as much nourishment as we could, eating in perfect silence, so as not to disturb the illusion of eating a meal.

Grandfather was not living with us either. He was in hospital. He had caught a cold, which had developed into a cough and now he was dying of pneumonia. It all happened so quickly. I would visit him every day, and he would try to be cheerful and tell me it was all the will of God, that he'd had a good and happy life, and that I must never give up the will to live. He said I would survive these times and live to tell the world in the clearest and best way all about our present sufferings. He told me to be fearless and strong in spirit and mind. Hope, like the light of day, would always surround me if I didn't lose courage.

As I stood before him, unable to say anything of comfort, he asked me to remember how he and I used to walk to synagogue together. He told me to keep him always in my heart, with joy, not with sadness.

He spoke to me, though his lungs were filled with water, and I listened, my eyes brimming with tears. I tried to remember the precious days we spent together in Chodecz not so long ago. I told him that Sala and the children had possibly arrived in the ghetto, and that next morning I would go to the school in Marysin and try to find them. If they had managed to bring some food with them I said I would 'race right back' to him.

Eva still lived with us, but she seemed to have lost all concern or warmth of feeling for Mother and Father, though she was still kind to me. Little Danus was in the children's ward of the same hospital as Grandfather on Lagiewnicka Street. I was unable to find out what was wrong with him or see him. Eva had found other friends in the ghetto, and she seldom came home now that Szlamek was dead and Danus was so ill.

Under her bed she kept a wooden strong-box that was screwed to the floor and padlocked. From time to time she would show up at our room either to take something out of the box or put something into it. Mother and Father did not like her very much, but I did, remembering how she had been good to me before the war when I was sent to stay with her and Szlamek for a few days. Danus had been a small baby then. How I loved Danus. Now I pleaded with her to let me see him in the hospital but she only stroked my face and said firmly: 'Out of the question.'

'What's wrong with Danus?'

'He's very ill and I am the only one in the family allowed to see him.'

The next morning I set off for Marysin. Sala was there with Danusia and Henryk. We embraced and kissed each other. Sala wept. 'You look so thin, Romek.' She told me that Gershon was 'no more'. I knew from the letter we had received from her in Chodecz that Gershon had been shot along with other Polish and Jewish leaders in October 1939.

Sala wept and Danusia and Henryk clung to her and reached out to touch me, frightened by my gaunt and haggard look. I told Sala we were all starving, that Father was in the old people's home and Grandfather was dying and that Eva shared our room, that Szlamek had been hanged and that Danus was in the hospital, gravely ill. Sala listened and then said, 'Romek, my dearest, my thin little boy, this is what you must do,' and she wrote a note to Eva. 'Find her immediately and give this to her,' she said, handing me the note.

The Jews of the Brzesc Kujawski transport were not allowed to leave the school in which they were shut up, guarded by the ghetto police. I didn't know how to find Eva so I stopped in at the hospital where I saw Grandfather and told him of my meeting with Sala.

'Go wait outside the ward where Danus is,' he advised. 'Eva is bound to visit him.'

I waited there for some time and sure enough, Eva came out of the ward, crying. 'Danus has passed away,' she said, embracing me. We both wept.

I handed her the note from Sala. She read it and wept, then turned, leaned against the wall and sobbed. My heart was with her. I too loved Danus, the darling child who came running out to greet me every day when I returned from the Oberst's house. Eva was shattered. First her husband had been hanged, and now her son, her light, her lovely Danus, had been extinguished. She, so small in stature, looked even tinier now. Shrunken. Her face contorted with sobs.

Through tears she said, 'Go to your mother, Romek. Tell her that Sala is here with the children, but not a word about Danus's death to her or your father. I will tell them soon enough.'

'What will you do about Sala? Sala needs help.'

'Leave that to me. Go back now and tell your father that we'll need a couple of rings and a gold watch… We must help Sala and the children so they'll stay in the ghetto instead of being sent off on a "transport". Bring me whatever Father gives you to this address,' she said, jotting it down on a piece of paper. 'You are weak, I know, and have done more than enough walking today, to Marysin and back… but I will have something for you to eat when you come with the watch and the rings… and we will help Sala and her children…'

I went straight to Father and told him Eva was going to help Sala and the children but that she needed a couple of rings and the gold watch. Father asked: Did Sala look well? How are lovely little Danusia and Henryk? Did they bring food with them? I was not surprised by his last question. We all had food on our minds most of the time, if not a hundred per cent of the time… Anyone who is starving thinks first, last and always about food.

My father had many precious items left, sewn into the lining of his coat. He handed me the watch and the rings and I went straight to the address Eva had given me.

She wasn't there so I curled up in the narrow hallway and waited. I was awakened by a kick. 'What are you doing, dozing here, *Klapsedra*?' said the voice. I showed him the piece of paper with the address on it. 'What's your name?' I told him. 'So Szlamek was your brother!' Yes, I said, but corrected myself, 'He was my half-brother.'

He told me to follow him and to wait there. The room was three or four times the size of the one in which we now lived in Storchen Street. It was furnished with chairs and a table and looked like no other place I had seen in the Lodz ghetto, almost, in fact, like the pre-war home of a well-to-do family in Chodecz.

My thigh was sore from the kick. The skin was bruised of course, but since I had very little flesh or muscle there, I felt the pain in my bone. The man looked long at me again and said, 'Eva has gone to see Szlamek's sister. She will be back soon... Would you like a lump of sugar?'

What a question!

Occasionally, very occasionally, we would receive a minuscule amount of brown sugar in our starvation rations which we would stash away and lick in times of emergency. When this well-fed man with the thick neck – in the Lodz ghetto in 1940, the starving were distinguished by their necks – asked me if I would like a lump of sugar, I could not believe my ears. I thought he must be joking. 'Sir,' I said, 'might I ask you for four lumps please, one for me, one for my father, one for my mother and one for my grandfather?'

He didn't laugh. He went to the wooden chest across the room, and without a word, unlocked it and took out two lumps of sugar. 'Eat them yourself,' he said, 'or swap them for some bread with someone else.' I forgot all about the pain in my thigh; I could hardly believe my good fortune. Carefully I bit off a tiny smidgen and felt the sweetness spread through every cell of my body.

'Sit down in the corner here,' he said, pointing at the floor. 'You don't have lice, do you?'

'I don't think so,' I answered, settling myself on the floor with a lump and three-quarters of sugar safely in my pocket. The morsel in my mouth tasted so delicious... for a moment, all was bliss. Then there was a knock on the door. Eva, I thought. But it wasn't Eva. The man with the thick neck put on the chain and unbolted two bolts; then he let a man in. They exchanged a few words in Yiddish and then the man with the thick neck turned to me and said, 'You had better go home now. I will tell Eva that you came to see her. Do you want to leave something here for her?'

'No, not really,' I said, and walked out the door which they bolted behind me right away.

Mother was in bed when I came in. I gave her half a lump of sugar. It seemed like a miracle to her and she sucked on it for a long time. Next morning, Eva came and said that Sala was inside the ghetto now and that she and her friend, the man I had met, had helped obtain the corner of a large room for Sala and her two children, and that I should return the rings and the watch to Father, as they were no longer necessary. She told me where to look for Sala, but if we couldn't find her there, she would probably get a space of her own the following day.

The man with the thick neck had friends in the Jewish police force that patrolled the ghetto on the lookout for 'space' vacated by the dead to allot as 'rooms' for newcomers. Later on, the system of space allocation became more efficient but

knowing the right people and having 'Protekcja' in the Lodz
ghetto was always of cardinal importance.

Mother said we should have brought Sala and the children to
our place, since we had two beds, one in which she and I slept
and Eva's bed. Our room was a kind of narrow corridor
between two living areas occupied by other families. Mother
must have thought Eva would give up her bed for Sala and the
children.

One day when Eva was paying us her weekly visit, she told me
I should come see her in the soup kitchen where she now
worked. When I arrived I was surprised to find the man with
the thick neck running the place. Eva gave me a can of soup. I
ate a little and took the rest to Father first and then to Grandfather. I meant to save some for Mother and Sala's children too,
but when I came to Grandfather and heated the can up, he
thought it was all for him and gulped it down with such relish I
couldn't bring myself to say or do anything to stop him. Then he
asked me to bring him some water in a cup and he rinsed his
hands in a bowl, and muttered *berkat ha'mazon*, the grace after
meals. His eyes were shut. Only his lips moved in prayer from
time to time. I stood and watched him.

'Romek,' he whispered, beckoning me closer. He put his
hand on my head and for some minutes, between coughs, he
uttered more prayers, and then, very slowly, pulled something
from under his pillow and gave it to me. It was the silver watch
I knew so well. He said something but I could not hear him.

'What is it, Grandfather?' I asked again and again. 'Shall I come again tomorrow?' He nodded and smiled.

'I will, I will come tomorrow morning.'

He gave me another smile and waved his hand.

When I came the next day Grandfather was dead. I told Mother that he had passed away. She merely gazed into space and nodded. She had no strength left to weep.

'When?' she said after a while, and I told her. There was another silence.

'What day and month is it in the Jewish calendar?'

'I don't know, Mother.'

'Find out, find out.'

We sat in silence. 'My father was a *tzaddik,*' said Mother and I nodded. A holy man.

It was a long journey to the Marysin cemetery. We walked very slowly on that cold December day, Father, Mother, and I, and Sala with her children. We all embraced and wept. It was the first time my parents had seen Sala in the ghetto.

The two men wheeling Grandfather's corpse on their push-cart wanted a 'reward', otherwise they said they wouldn't have enough strength to fill in the grave… Father gave them a ring. They haggled. I said I would help.

'Will you say a few words, Father?'

'I have neither words left nor the strength to say them, my son.'

'But Grandfather was such a good man,' I pleaded.

'Yes he was, he was, we know it and the Almighty, blessed be his name, knows it too, but I can't – my heart is so heavy.'

One of the two men interrupted 'Who's going to throw the first spade of earth over the grave? Come on, we haven't got all day here.'

'Let me say something first,' I replied. 'We loved you, Grandfather and we will not forget you...' I promised before the grave and burst into tears.

Father added, 'We will remember your teachings and your wisdom and your pious ways, may Almighty God...' He, too, broke down, and we all wept. Father scattered the first handful of earth over the grave and murmured the prayers.

Two months later, it looked as if we might have another death in the family.

Sala had taken on a strenuous job at the washhouse in order to be able to bring the soup that was served there home to the children. But she had become ill, and was now lying in hospital. Neither of my parents could tell me what was wrong with her.

With Eva's help, Sala and the children had been moved into the smaller area of a room that had been divided by a partition for two families. The toilets were outside. Meals were cooked on a gas ring in a common room. Whilst Sala was in hospital, I went to stay with the children. The weather was bitterly cold. At night before going to bed we had to get dressed and cover our heads well, because people used to freeze to death in their sleep. We all slept together and put everything we could find on top of the blankets and huddled together to keep warm. I would tell them happy stories before we all fell asleep.

We would visit Sala regularly. One day on the way back from the hospital with Henryk and Danusia, we saw a cart with two Jewish policemen and a pile of Swedish turnips. Children would sometimes put stones on the road to jolt the cart as it drove by in the hope that a swede would fall over the side, which is just what happened now. I picked up the fallen swede and gave it to Henryk who was still capable of running fast, and by the time the policeman jumped down Henryk was out of sight. What a feast the three of us had that evening, with some left over for Mother, Father, and Sala.

Just before the spring of 1941, factories were set up in the ghetto to make all kinds of things for the German forces. I was accepted to work in a metal factory. Those who worked there received an extra ration of soup. I was assigned to work in the sheet metal cutting section.

Father was in a bad way now because the home for the elderly had stopped serving an extra bowl of soup, and the Jewish Council of the ghetto, headed by Chaim Rumkowski, had decided to cut down the rations of anyone not working in the factories. Our survival depended on getting a job in one of these factories.

Every day, before or after work I would look in on Father. He felt tired and was getting weaker by the day. I would find him

either sitting or lying on his bed. People of his age were reject-
ed when they applied for a job. The other residents in the home
for the elderly used to play cards or chess with him. Now they
were all starving to death, and were lying or sitting around and
waiting for death to come.

When I walked in, Father would glance at my hands, to see
whether I had brought him any food, and most of the time I
had none to give him, so I would sit at his bedside and hold his
fingers. Although spring was on its way, we still wore our fin-
gerless gloves against the cold.

Father and I sat in silence for a while. I told him that Mother
had found work in one of the factories. I brought him news of
Sala and her children and the latest ghetto gossip about the
world outside. Unfortunately, Hitler's armies were doing well
everywhere.

By this time, Father had exchanged all the valuables that
were sewn into the lining of his coat for bread or potatoes. The
only 'treasures' he had left were his good books, his coat and
one of the two feather eiderdowns we had brought with us –
Mother and I had the other. Although he saw that I was empty-
handed, he asked, just to make certain, whether I had brought
him any food. I could only shake my head in the negative,
feeling too ashamed to say 'no' out loud.

I changed the subject. 'Sala is getting better. They may let
her out in a couple of days' time.' This was true, I didn't invent
it.

'That's good, that's good. How is Mother?'

'Still too weak to come, she sends you her love.'

I invited him for a stroll outside in the fresh air and helped him up. He put on the boots he had brought from Chodecz and the *onuckas*, the way he had taught me some time before. *Onuckas* were pieces of cloth which were folded around the foot inside our wooden clogs to keep the feet warm. Our socks had worn out and it was impossible to replace them. I could not do it as well as Father because my clogs were now too small as my feet had grown and the big toes felt cramped. Father put on his coat and we went outside.

'You ought to go see Eva more often,' said Father. 'Tell her I'm starving. She works in the kitchen. Maybe she can help us.' I promised I would.

That winter of 1941 was extremely harsh and we had little means of keeping ourselves warm. Children went to Marysin, where before the war there had been a coal bin. Now there was only coal dust left in the bin which the children, working in gangs, collected into sacks and loaded onto prams or home-made carts and then pushed and pulled them all the way home. Coal 'cannons' or *kneidels*, as they were called, were made out of this dust to use as fuel, but the children would not tell outsiders how they made them. It was their secret.

I asked Father about it, figuring he would know since he had been a coal merchant, but he had no idea what to mix with the dust to give it shape and make it burn.

That winter we had used all our furniture including chairs as firewood to keep ourselves warm and to boil water for drinking. We were getting desperate, and so one morning before I went to work at the metal factory, Henryk, Danusia and I set off for Marysin, full of hope, carrying some empty sacks and a sieve. Since we didn't know how to make the coal cannons, I had constructed a sieve to let the coal dust through and trap the hard bits. We had hoped to keep some of this residue for fuel, and trade what was left for bread, potatoes or flour.

But it was too late in the year. The ground was frozen solid, and all I could do was scrape it with the end of a sharply-pointed stone. Others there were doing the same. It was no use. Even a pickaxe could not break up this ground. Danusia and Henryk stood by, shivering and watching me in silence.

When we returned to the ghetto with our empty sacks I discovered that my big toe was frozen. The tip was white. Mother tried to revive it, but two days later I hobbled to the hospital and waited in the casualty ward.

A nurse took me aside and told me that she would give me a wink when Dr Kleszczelski came out and that I should go up and tell him in my fine Polish what was wrong. It worked. Dr Kleszczelski gave me something to hold in my hand and something else to bite on 'if it hurts' and then he quickly cut off the white skin around my toe and pulled it off like a sock. He had to do this, he said, to prevent gangrene. Then he put an ointment on the toe and the nurse bandaged it up. He told me that he knew where Chodecz was because he and his wife sometimes passed it on their way to Ciechocinek.

With the doctor's help I obtained a pair of wooden clogs and made some metal tips for them at the factory, to keep them from wearing down. With the *onuckas* around my feet, allowing the air to circulate in the clogs, there was a little more comfort in my life. Little things make such a difference!

When Sala was released from the hospital, I went back to Mother. Sala was transferred to somewhat lighter work; cleaning and mending German uniforms. These uniforms, soiled and bloody, some of them full of bullet holes, were brought back to our ghetto for repair.

Eva, who continued to work in the soup kitchen, did not keep in touch with Sala or with us. When I worked on an early shift in the metal factory, after work I would go and see Eva in the soup kitchen with my aluminium can, which I had made at work. Whether she couldn't or wouldn't hand any spare soup to me, I couldn't tell, but instead she would give me a can full of potato peelings. She said that I could come to her for the peelings once a week. Mother and I would share the peelings with Sala and her children.

Winter turned into spring, nettles were growing, and Sala, Danusia, Henryk and I would go to the cemetery in Marysin and pick the ones growing there. Mother was too weak to make the journey there and back. Her hunger swelling was beyond her ankles now.

The potato peelings from Eva would be thoroughly cleaned, and then chopped up with the nettles into a fine pulp. Before this the nettles were put into boiling water for a minute or two. Had we had any oil, my mother would have been able to fry the pulp like cutlets. Sala used to steam her mixture. We were all so starved and so hungry that we ate it with gusto, and we could not have had enough of it. We felt ourselves grow stronger after eating it... Then, the soup kitchens decided that they would stop peeling their potatoes, and only wash them instead, and so the extra provisions came to an end.

The metal factory had its own soup kitchen which was located on the side of the building and isolated from the rest of the ghetto. Each person working in the factory would receive a ladle of soup on their shift. You handed over a coupon and your container with it to one hatch, and received the soup from another hatch. Then you would move aside and begin checking with a spoon whether the soup was thick or thin, and also how many potato pieces it contained. It was a tragedy if the soup was weak and there were no pieces of potato there... but there was nothing one could do about it. The weekly starvation ration was just too small to enable one to survive – you needed the soup at work. This soup made the difference between a slow death, or life.

One day Mother came to me. She had found bread somewhere and I took a piece to Father and to Sala. Next day she gave me half a lump of sugar.

'Where did you get this from?' I asked.

'Never mind,' said Mother. 'Call it a miracle. Manna from heaven.'

During that week we regained our strength. This on top of

our starvation ration made all of us, Father, Sala and the children, Mother and I felt that we had a new lease on life. In addition, I was given an extra soup ration at the metal factory. Father grew more cheerful, Mother could walk more easily now. She came home from work and said that the only hard part was crossing the bridge.

One day I came home to find Eva, the man with the thick neck and a Jewish policeman who was a friend of Eva's shouting at Mother. They were accusing Mother of stealing sugar cubes from the box Eva kept under the bed. Then the man with the thick neck started hurting Mother who lay prostrate on the bed. I screamed at him. He lifted me by the collar and shouted at Mother, 'You have two seconds to tell us where you hid the sugar,' and then he shook me till I thought my head would fall off and said, 'I'll count to ten.'

They had ransacked the place before I walked in and had found nothing.

Mother got up and unscrewed the top of the metal bed post. From the tube she pulled a stocking and inside it were the sugar cubes. The man with the thick neck dropped me and slapped Mother's face and then the three of them walked away. I stood there, swaying. My head felt disconnected from my body. I thought of Szlamek. Mother sobbed without tears, and suddenly shouted, 'This is not the end; this is not the end!'

There were more rumours about the war. Father kept asking me what I knew, what I had heard. We were all waiting for some sort of miracle, something that would end the war and the torture, the starvation and the murder of Jews – something that would set us free.

I was not well informed. Most of us in the Lodz ghetto didn't really know what was going on in the outside world. From the 'vibrations' of the Germans who came in and out of the ghetto we sensed that Hitler's armies were winning everywhere. This was not what Father wanted to hear. He wanted news that would keep his hopes alive.

It was a clear and a fairly warm day in April 1942 when Father suddenly came to see us. We knew that something was up, since normally we would visit him in the old people's home. For him to come to us in his weakened state, all that way, was most unusual.

He sat on our bed and told me to memorize his sister's address in Lausanne: Auntie Sarah Wiener, 8 Chemin des Cèdres. Then he said, 'Outside our house in Chodecz, on the right, after the sheds, twenty paces from the last shed and twenty paces from the fence, buried about three feet down, there is an oak chest with soap and clothing in it and some other things.'

Mother sat next to him on the bed, the only place left to sit. Tenderly she stroked his face as if she sensed the inner voice that made Father speak this way. He didn't seem particularly sad. He talked about Chodecz and even about his youth, and then he said, 'Have you any food left?'

We had no food. The next ration started the following day and Mother and I were going to collect it.

'Never mind,' he said, 'let's lick some salt.'

And we sat together and licked salt. Mother and I walked Father to the home, but Mother left us half-way there. As we continued walking together, Father said to me, 'You remember the man who came to see us when we arrived at the school in Marysin?'

I remembered.

'He was very friendly with Peccio and was his tailor. When I die, take this coat of mine to him, Mother will tell you where he lives, and he will remake it into a coat for you.'

'But you're not going to die. Father, you'll live, you have to live!' Father made no reply. He smiled at me and gently stroked my face with his hand.

He died the following day on the 7 April 1942. I came to see him after work and was told that he was asleep. When I went in and touched his cheek, it was stone cold.

The people in charge of burying the dead gave priority to those with '*Protekcja*' or food. We had neither, so they said, 'We'll put him in the ground tomorrow or maybe the day after tomorrow… or…' Eventually they showed me where the grave was to be.

I began to dig there myself. Sala and Mother came with me.

Sala thought it would be too upsetting for Danusia and Henryk to attend the funeral. 'There is nothing but death, starvation and misery… Let them remember Father the way he used to be when we would come for the holidays and he would smile and lift them both up on Felek.' (Felek was our tamest horse.) 'I'll tell them about his death when they're stronger.'

Sala told Eva and she came too.

'Why are you digging the grave, Romek?' she asked.

'Because we have nothing to give the gravediggers,' I answered.

She greeted Mother but Mother didn't reply. At the morgue, Sala told me later, Eva lifted the sheet and looked at father to identify him, and then she left. Eva had told Sala that I should drop by to see her in the soup kitchen. Sala said she was sorry she could do nothing to help me because she felt so unwell. She, too, left. Mother stood by, watching and weeping.

I had to return the next morning to finish the job, as the ground was hard and I was weak. First I went to the metal factory to tell Leon Chimowicz, my section manager, that I needed the day off to finish digging the grave. He made certain that I would be given my portion of soup even though I didn't work that day.

Mother went with me to the cemetery. One of the gravediggers said, 'Did you bring us any bread?' I replied that we had no bread so he lent me his spade and said something like 'Good luck' and 'Bring it back to me when you're finished.'

The same gravedigger helped me set Father face down, on something that looked like a metal bedframe. 'Don't worry,' he said. 'When you tip him into the grave like this, he'll fall the right way round.'

Mother was in no state to help me carry Father, so I kept turning the metal frame round and round in an arc as I advanced. This proved hard work and I had to take many rests before I managed to bring Father close to the grave which was now only a short distance away. But the frame had to be lifted over the other graves and I was unable to do it.

'Maybe they could lend you the two-wheeled cart with the horizontal platform?' Mother suggested, but they obviously couldn't or didn't want to perhaps, and I don't know whether I could have even coped with the cart all on my own.

We were stuck. Neither of us knew what to do. Mother uncovered Father (he was covered in a sackcloth which I had been asked to return to the home for the elderly) and wanted to turn his face and look at him.

'Max, Max is this the end of the world?' Father's name was Mordechai, but Mother called him Max.

I went back to the morgue and began pleading with the men to come and help me. 'One day if I have a potato or a piece of bread to spare I will bring it to you,' I said to the man who lent me the spade and he agreed to help.

'You're not from Lodz?' he asked.

'No, I'm from Chodecz.'

'Where's that?'

'Near Wloclawek.'

'Aha,' he said. 'It's always hardest for the provincials in our Lodz ghetto. They're like lost sheep!'

He helped me tip Father in and I covered him with earth. I found that I didn't remember the Yizkor prayer by heart. Mother did. So I repeated it after her.

'Say another prayer you know, I'm sure God will understand,' said Mother.

I said the *Shema* and then we stood in silence for quite some time, just looking at the ground, each thinking our own thoughts. I put a few stones on the grave so that when I was able to return later with a metal marker which I was going to make in the factory, I would be able to recognize where Father was buried.

Mother carried the spade and I dragged the bedframe and the sackcloth. We rested and slowly made our way back to our room.

I made an embossed metal plate engraved with the number 642 (the number given to me by the people who ran the cemetery), the date, 07. 04. 1942, and the name Mordechai Halter on it. The hardest part was finding the wood, but eventually I found some and fixed the plate to it and took it to the cemetery where I stuck it on the grave. On Grandfather's grave there was only a number. Danus was buried in a common grave, so Eva told me. I don't know why.

My section manager's brother, Alfred Chimowicz, was appointed manager of the metal factory. Leon and Alfred's third brother, Hermann, had joined the Jewish police and was in charge of a prison.

Leon and his wife had two small boys. He took an interest in me. We usually had a short break at midday (depending on the shift) and because talking used up so much energy, I would use the time to read or write. 'Write,' Mother had said to me. 'Write about everyday things, in a sort of diary. Mrs Wisniewska said you write so well. Keep it up, it will take your mind off food.' And so I read or wrote.

One day while I was scribbling away, Leon Chimowicz passed by. He was thin and tall with dark hair and dark penetrating eyes and a large nose. To me, he looked like a noble eagle – if an eagle can be noble.

'Come to my office and bring your writing with you,' he said. I did as I was ordered. 'Read me a page, here, this one.' He sat down and put his feet up and I began to read. Suddenly his brother Alfred walked in. I stopped reading and stood up to greet Mr Alfred. He was also dark-haired and dark-eyed and fairly tall, with an interesting face. Neither Alfred nor Leon looked starved. Alfred was the most important person in our factory.

'What's going on?' he said. When Leon explained that he had asked me to come in during the break and read him a page from my notebook, Alfred replied, 'Leave your writing here and go back to your work.' I did exactly that.

The following day someone delivered my notebook without any comment. About a week later, Mr Alfred's secretary came to see me. 'Being a country boy,' she said, 'you probably know something about growing vegetables and gardening. A friend of Mr Alfred's could use your help. Go see him and if he engages you, you can do your factory work during the 2 to 10 p.m. shift and your gardening in the morning.'

●

Life now improved for me and Mother. We had a little more food. What I received in payment from the man with the vegetable garden made all the difference. On top of that, Mother got a portion of soup a day at her place of work and I got one at mine. The weather turned warmer and we both felt stronger. I was transferred from the sheet metal cutting department at the factory to Mr Glazer's engraving department. Sala was growing stronger and occasionally I was able to bring a little something for her and the children from the vegetable garden. Eva was now living with the Jewish policeman who had come to take the sugar away from Mother.

The summer of 1942 was not a good summer for us. We grieved over Father's death and Mother was feeling so very weak and her legs continued to swell. When she came home from her factory, she would sit on the bed and press her thumb into the swelling. Whenever I could, I would meet her by the wooden bridge and help her across it.

'They say that if I drink less the swelling will go down,' said Mother. 'Anyway, there's no point worrying. It's only swollen around the ankles. If it was up to my knees, then it would be dangerous...' Meanwhile, I was as thin as a skeleton but my ankles were not swollen.

Days passed and we clung to one another and to life.

Sala and the children had Father's eiderdown. I now had his coat, remade for me by Peccio's tailor friend. Someone had stolen Father's boots, the good leather ones he had had made especially for himself before the war.

During the winter the pump outside had frozen. Now it worked again. Mother said we were lucky that our pump was not infected; in some pumps the water was spreading illness and people were dying everywhere.

Mother spoke to me quietly and slowly. Starvation had slowed even her speech, and she didn't want to waste any energy. The tenderness in her voice was still the same but her looks were so altered. In my mind's eye I tried to imagine us as we had looked in Chodecz. But the person I saw in the mirror had a strange starved face that wasn't mine. I showed Mother what I had written in my notebook and she said, 'Record, don't judge,' and then she added, 'Mrs Wisniewska taught you well.'

At the factory I made a metal soup container for someone and he gave me a piece of bread for it. His father worked at the bakery. Mother decided we should share it with Sala and her children. We went to see them, walking slowly all the way, and found the three of them sitting together and crying. Henryk, now six, had unlocked their ration box and eaten all the food and there were three days to go before the new ration would be given out. We left them with the bread and the next day I told Leon Chimowicz what had happened and asked if he could please help.

'I am a section manager here, not...' He couldn't find words to finish his sentence. He had two small boys of his own and well understood this tragic situation.

'Go away, go back to work and don't bring me such stories.'

But before I left my shift, he sent a portion of soup to take to them. And he did it again the following day.

I was very religious at the time, that is, I prayed a lot. But I didn't like people to see me pray. I didn't wear a *tzitzit* and didn't put on *tefillin*. I had a small prayer book that had belonged to Grandfather which I carried around with me. Whenever I had a chance, I would go off where no one would see me and say a prayer. I felt that praising God was a way of communing with my father and my grandfather. They would have been happy that I was praying. Also, it made me feel stronger when I prayed, and I was convinced that my sincerity and faith, even though I didn't understand most of the words I was uttering, would lessen Mother's pain from the swelling in her legs and from hunger. After each prayer I would ask God to help Sala and her children and reunite us all in Chodecz one day – Sala, her children, Mother and I, Zosia and the others who must surely still be alive somewhere.

In the autumn of 1942, the SS sealed off one area after another inside the Lodz ghetto, and began taking away the very young, or old, or the weak and starving and all who, in their opinion, were not fit for work.

Everyone from our side of the ghetto had to gather in a central area where the SS performed the selection. Mother and I were bundled onto a horse-drawn cart with those unfit to remain. There were many horse-drawn carts around, full of people bound for transport. The carts took them to trucks parked on the other side of the ghetto, as some of the streets were too narrow for the large trucks to get through.

Mother drew me close to her and said: 'I'm too weak to save myself, you can still run. When I tell you to jump, you must not hesitate. Do it! Take your clogs off and run. Your life depends on it. This is the end.' I understood her fully.

Eva, who had been registered in our living area was there, too, with her friend the policeman, on hand with other members of the Jewish police to assist the SS in the selection. She had come to say goodbye to us. Mother pleaded with her, 'Help Romek, for God's sake, help Romek.' Her friend spoke to the policeman guarding our cart. We turned a corner. There was an opening ahead that led to a field used as a shortcut to another part of the ghetto, and about forty yards further on, an outhouse with a latrine, one of many in the ghetto that were emptied from time to time by the 'shit brigade'. Nearby was a high fence that screened off the Lodz ghetto fire station.

Mother gripped me with an unexpected strength and said, 'Take your clogs off, carry them in your hands and don't lose them. Run zigzag. Throw your clogs over the fire brigade wall and climb up on the roof of the outhouse, then onto the fence and over it. Lie close to the fence on the other side with your clogs beside you and don't move. Go, don't stop, when they shout or shoot, just run. Look after yourself my son, my light – may God be with you. Now jump! Run!'

I did as she had said. I heard shouts but did not stop. I lay behind the fence when the SS came and fired shots. They must have thought I had jumped into the latrine. They left and I lay there for a very long time.

Much later, I went to the fire brigade office and said that I had been selected for transport and had escaped from the cart. I told the firemen where I lived. They replied that the SS had finished with our section and moved to another part of the ghetto, and that I could return to our room.

After the escape I went back to the tiny space in which my mother and I lived. I entered it and looked around. Suddenly the hollowness of this miserable little space brought to mind the fact that I was now all alone. That my mother whom I loved and who cared for and loved me was gone. That I would never see her again and that Sala and Danusia and Henryk were also gone. I had grown so close to those children. When Sala was in hospital, I had looked after them, told them stories and felt a deep love for them. Now they were gone for ever.

As I stood there by the door, rooted to the spot thinking about them, my body began to shake and quiver uncontrollably. I went to the bed and sat down on it. The duvet, which we brought from Chodecz, was still there. Surprisingly no one had taken it yet. This duvet, filled with down, had saved our lives during the winters of 1940–41, and 1941–42, when others froze to death in their beds. I sat on the bed shaking uncontrollably. It was the second such attack in my life. My mind was clear. I felt a great mental pain at the loss of Mother, Sala and her children. I could not cry. After some moments, still shaking, I went to the pump outside, washed my hands and face. Then I returned, covered my head and said part of the *Shema* prayer. My grandfather once told me that 'it is not the quantity of the prayers that matter, but the sincerity with which they are uttered and how this affirms belief in God.'

Then I made up a prayer to my father, mother and grandfather. I told them that they would always live in my mind and that they should guide me in all my actions and I would need their help to protect me throughout life.

My body still quivered and I felt tired, so very tired. I took off my wooden clogs and lay down on the bed and covered myself over with the duvet. It was still light outside.

I must have slept for twelve hours or more, for when I woke feeling refreshed and optimistic, it was daylight again. I sat on the bed feeling very hungry – but this I felt all the time in my state of starvation – yet an inner calm also invaded my being. The shaking and quivering stopped and now I started thinking about the future. I thought that when I survived I would go back to Chodecz. (Chodecz, and the joyous life there until I was twelve was frequently on my mind, joy and Chodecz together representing happiness.) Iccio, who had gone to Russia, would surely come back, I thought; and Zosia might also return and so would Peccio with his wife and child, and surely some of the relations from Izbica Kujawska would have survived… Our Aunt Sarah from Lausanne would be bound to help us financially to get back on our feet, because she lived in

Switzerland and all Swiss are well-off – so I thought. The Polish people of Chodecz who knew me from birth and whom I held in affection will welcome all the Halters back with open arms; they would be so pleased to see us!

'I must be strong and live,' I told myself. This is what my mother would have wanted for me. I remembered the time when my grandfather blessed me before he died and told me that 'When I survive' and not 'If I survive', I must hold on to life. When I survive I will tell the world the truth of what I saw and experienced. Everyone in the world will want to know, so I thought.

I will go now to the metal factory and tell my section manager what happened to me during the Selection and ask him if I could get my old job back.

I locked up the duvet in the wooden box screwed to the floor under the bed. Other things of Mother's and mine were in it. I hid the key to the box and left for Lagiewnicka 63, for the metal factory.

Some days later Leon Chimowicz called me into his office. He told me he was going to adopt me. As an adopted son I would be entitled to a *birat* ration (this was the bigger ration that managers and big shots received), part of which I would give back to him. 'Do you agree?' he asked. 'Yes, of course,' I answered. His wife was pregnant with their third child and found it difficult to do housework, he said, so every morning before work, I would help her out. Did I agree to this? My reply was the same, 'Yes, of course.'

The Chimowicz family occupied a big room with a small kitchen, in the corner of which I was to live for the next two years.

Mrs Leon Chimowicz was kind to me. She told me from the outset what my duties were and she never changed or increased them. In the morning when I finished the domestic chores, I would go to the factory and do my work there. I was still very thin, and some still called me *Klapsedra*, but being adopted by one of the Chimowicz brothers gave me considerable protection and a degree of security.

Mrs Leon Chimowicz gave birth to another son in the spring of 1943. To the circumcision celebration, the *brit*, Leon invited six foremen from the metal factory and his brother Alfred. Leon had managed to procure some potatoes, which were grated, mixed with flour and fried as pancakes. Everyone made a speech, either in Yiddish or Polish, praising our leader, Alfred C.

I was hovering somewhere in the background when suddenly Leon announced that I would now read them something from my notebook which was not in praise of anything or anybody. He ordered me to bring it from the kitchen, and chose a chapter for me to read out loud.

I was so taken aback by this that I did not read very well. I glanced at Alfred and he said, 'Read it again, Romek, and slowly.' Again I read the words aloud, about being abandoned, forgotten by a world where no one cares or gives a thought to our suffering and our fate. Although Mother had told me to record, not judge, from time to time I had to let other expressions surface.

'How do you know that no one cares?' asked Alfred.

'That's how it seems to me,' I replied. Everyone but Alfred and Leon started laughing. Alfred waited a while and then said quietly, 'I think he's right. We can't remain scattered amongst the other nations, united only by our determination to survive.'

Alfred, I later learned, had been the driver of the Zionist leader Zeev Jabotinsky before the war.

Months passed, and one day in 1943, a new group was brought into the ghetto. On the list of arrivals was the name Szlamek Halter. My heart missed a beat when I saw this. I thought it was my half-brother.

But how could that be, I wondered, when Szlamek had been hanged in 1939? No, this Szlamek was the eldest son of my Uncle David from Izbica Kujawska, my first cousin. I was astonished to see how well and normal he looked. Like my half-brother of the same name, he too was tall and strong. He on the other hand was distressed by the news I told him and couldn't get over seeing me so thin and starved.

Within a very short time Szlamek became the head of a soup kitchen. This was a dream of a position. I would go and see him and receive extra soup. What a joy it would have been for Mother and Father, Grandfather and Sala and the children to get a container of thick soup like this every day. What a difference it would have made. I began to feel stronger and more energetic.

Szlamek invited me home with him one day. 'Romek,' he said, 'in case you survive and I don't, I want you to remember an address and a name.' Like our Szlamek, he told me, he and others from Izbica had been sent to work on the Berlin-Poznan highway and the railway nearby. There he had made friends with a Pole, whose wife picked up his little daughter in Izbica and adopted her for the duration of the war.

Szlamek's daughter, like Sala's, was called Danusia. She was nearly five now. When he had worked on the railway under the SS guards, the kind Polish woman who adopted her used to bring her with her other children and show her to him from afar. 'A glance at my child was a very great joy.' Now, he said, it was his wish that whoever survived from the Halter family would collect Danusia after the war. Every time I saw him after that he would quiz me to make sure I remembered the name and address of Danusia's adopted mother.

'But Szlamek,' I said to him, 'you are a man, you're strong and fit; but I'm just a skinny starving youngster...' Szlamek looked at me and did not answer. A few weeks later he was picked up by the Gestapo and sent away from the Lodz ghetto on a 'transport'.

I had stopped praying for a time after Mother and Sala and the children were transported. Now that Cousin Szlamek was gone, I began to open Grandfather's little prayer book again and read the 'magical' Hebrew words, 'magical' because I didn't know what they meant, and the little prayer book had no Polish translation. Compared to some of the other factory boys who were well versed in the Five Books of Moses and Rashi's Commentary, I was quite uneducated.

I would still say a prayer in privacy from the little book, and then address God, 'Please, unite my Cousin Szlamek with his daughter Danusia in health and joy after this war is over.' Bereft of everyone I loved, I felt spiritually and religiously naked. Yet this lapse of faith did not last long. The will to live brought back my faith in the values that supported me and kept me from losing my human sensibility, the capacity to distinguish between the human and inhuman, the sane and insane.

Often, in those dark days when I searched the starving faces of others my age for signs of sanity and humanity, I would find a certain character and resolve, a life force shining with hope and a strange form of optimism. They did not question or analyze or compare the past with the miseries and sufferings of the present, but were determined to survive, and after every 'knock-out' sprang back to life. And so did I.

To adapt in this way was quite difficult for adults like Mr and Mrs B., who had been sent to the Lodz ghetto from Düsseldorf. Mr B. was a professional engineer and knew a lot about metal. Alfred Chimowicz found a job for him and his wife at the factory, but within a few months he began to look thin and starved.

I was fascinated by them and their dignified behaviour.

When the soup was served we had to queue up, but most of us would try to get in later to get the thicker bits from the bottom. Mrs B. would ignore these terrible tactics and march up erect to collect the two soups for herself and her husband, put the lids on the cans, and walk back to her office. There she would set the little table as for a feast with knives and forks, spoons, serviettes, plates and a salt cellar. They would first eat the thin liquid, placing the bits of potato on a little wooden board to eat, sprinkled with salt, while they made polite conversation about matters unrelated to Lodz ghetto or our suffering.

'Why do you eat like that Mrs B.?' I asked. 'This is a ghetto and all we get is watery soup.'

Mrs B. would give me one of her smiles. Her hair, parted in the middle was neatly gathered into a bun at the back. Her neck was thin and long and her eyes were beginning to bulge from starvation.

'You see, *mein lieber Junge*,' she explained, 'part of their plan is to rob us of our dignity, our civilized manners, and if we submit to that, if we let ourselves go, we'll be well on the way to our own self-destruction. That is why little things are so important.'

One day towards the end of 1943, an inspection team of army officers and SS commanders showed up at the factory. Bibov, the German head of the Lodz ghetto, and Czarnulla, another big-shot, were there with them.

Czarnulla had been coming to the Lodz ghetto from 1940 or

1941 onwards. His job was to take out all the gold, diamonds, foreign money, etc, from the Jews. Whether he was actually a friend of Eichmann or Goering, or even Himmler, I cannot say, but he must have had great Nazi connections. When he came to the ghetto, he would come to the metal factory and deal directly with Alfred Chimowicz, load up and leave. Later, he must have somehow become affiliated to Albert Speer's department of armaments, because he began to take an interest in what the metal factory was producing.

Alfred Chimowicz lined up his foremen and the engineers who were experts in different fields of metalwork. Mr B. stood amongst them, proudly wearing the medal he had won fighting for Germany in the First World War. The army officers were impressed both by Mr B.'s knowledge of metals and by his decoration. They spoke to him at length and passed on, but the last of them, a high-ranking SS officer and his sidekick said something to Mr B., grabbed his medal and tried to rip it off. When it wouldn't come off, his sidekick, a more junior SS officer, tried to pull it so fiercely that Mr B. landed on the ground. Bibov, Czarnulla and Alfred C. stood watching in silence. No one dared to say 'stop it' to the high-ranking SS officer or his sidekick. At this point the junior SS officer put his boot on Mr B.'s chest and yanked at the medal till it flew off, tearing part of the jacket. The action must have torn out Mr B.'s heart as well, for he died a few days later, and a week after him, Mrs B. died too.

•

In the summer of 1944 the Lodz ghetto was liquidated. Everyone who was left was sent on transport. There were rumours that the transports were going south or southwest, but no one really knew for certain.

We workers were sealed off from the rest of the ghetto and awaited transport to somewhere unknown. Others, those with '*Protekcja*', joined our compound, among them Dr Kleszczelski who had removed the frostbitten skin around my toe a couple of years before. We had to pack up all the machines which were to be collected by lorries.

A few weeks later, at the end of August 1944, Bibov and the SS arrived at the factory compound to thin down our group of 1200 metalworkers to 500. Only when they began to take away people with the wrong skills – in the opinion of Alfred Chimowicz and his foremen – did Mr Alfred plead with Bibov to start the whole selection process over again.

We had to line up outside the factory in single rows, and Alfred Chimowicz and his foremen chose the 500 people themselves, including of course the wives and children of their nearest and dearest friends. Those who were not selected were in despair. They were convinced that this meant certain death. Some tried to run across and join the 500 and were shot.

Bibov strode about with his pistol in one hand and a whip in the other. The SS were taking orders from him now. People were weeping. Families were being separated. Being the adopted son of Leon Chimowicz and by now a skilful metalworker, I was among the 500, as were Leon's wife and children, the youngest of them barely one year old. The other people were led away, and the remaining 500 of us remained within the factory compound for another few days.

Then one morning we were marched off to Radagoszcz railway station.

The march was not easy. The SS men made us walk 'on the double'. Those who carried too much weight shed bags and bundles along the way. We were starved and weak, clinging to our most precious possessions, a duvet, a water jar, a photo album, a blanket, a prayer book. I accidentally dropped my photo album and as I stooped down to pick it up, an SS man kicked it into a ditch.

At Radagoszcz stood a long train. I counted 35 cattle trucks. We were made to walk fast to the front, past these covered cattle trucks with people locked inside who must have been there for days. We could hear them groaning and calling out in Yiddish, Polish and German, 'Water! Water!' and 'Air! Air!' The only vents on the trucks were two small horizontal openings criss-crossed with barbed wire.

Bibov and Czarnulla arrived and Alfred Chimowicz spoke with them. Our wagons each received a container of water and two large buckets with lids for excretions – in the metal factory that was one of many items that was produced. Now people were being packed aboard – into the 35 cattle trucks, 80 to a car – some 2,800 persons in all.

Suddenly we heard shouts, whistles and dogs barking. A few of our men had slipped away, intending perhaps to free a friend or relative whose familiar voice they heard issuing from one of the wagons or perhaps they were trying to escape themselves – in any case, they were all caught and brought back. Those of us not on the train yet were ordered to stand to attention and watch while the SS, instead of shooting the captured men, made them kneel and smashed their skulls in with the butts of their rifles. We were made to watch this. It had the most terrifying, paralyzing effect on most of us.

I had no idea where the train was going. It was a puzzle. If we were being sent to work at a factory in or near Germany, why was the train carrying so many people who were *not* metalworkers? Where are they being taken? Things were not making sense. Then we too were locked into the cattle wagons and the train moved out. A few hours later it stopped, began shunting, then stopped again. The train halted there until no more daylight came through between the boards, the knot-holes and the two vents criss-crossed with barbed wire.

There wasn't enough air, crammed together as we were, and people were pleading with each other for a 'drop' of water. The buckets, one in each corner, for bodily functions were rapidly filling up. Those who couldn't reach the buckets urinated where they stood. There was no room to lie down. Slowly, very slowly, people slumped down and fainted on their neighbour's feet. The place began to stink. Over and over we heard the pleas of 'Air, Air' and 'Water, Water'. And all the time the train stood still.

Daylight was long in coming. It entered through the gaps in

the boards, the rust holes and the vents. The train was still not moving. By now most of us were groaning for air and water, but mostly for water. Those who were pressed against the walls were able to peek out through the chinks. Others stood on their neighbour's shoulders for a wider view through the slats and tell the rest of us what they could see. We seemed to be at some railway station. I was trying to suck air in through a knot-hole, and peering out from time to time.

Hours passed and the train remained in the station. The buckets were all full. The floor under our feet was wet. The stench hung about us like a cloud. Those who had slumped down were now mired and sat upon. It was very difficult to remain upright, decent and strong.

When darkness fell, the train began to move again. We travelled for hours. Groans and the rhythmic sounds of the wheels became intermixed. I slept on and off, pressed upright against the side of the wall. The knot-hole was my life-giver, letting in sweet, fresh air with every gasp. We rolled on till daybreak when once again the train halted, reversed, shunted and stopped. At first we could see only the mist outside, and then we began to make out the tall barbed-wire fences, and beyond them, long sheds set out in a grid formation with guard towers at intervals above the fence like so many nests with little roofs on top. I continued to peer through the knot-hole. As the description of our surroundings was passed on, a great fear entered our souls. Some started praying, others groaned or cried. I began to sweat. I could no longer pray. I had prayed so fervently a few years back, begging God to save my father, my mother, my grandfather, my sisters and brothers.

Now, amid this sea of sounds, the prayers, the groaning, the suppressed sobs, the moaning for water, and the foul air, I stood by the knot-hole, my throat parched, remembering the faces of all the members of my family who were still a part of me, although most of them, I knew, were dead. Perhaps Zosia in the Warsaw ghetto, and Iccio in Russia, were still alive? They were vividly present in my mind's eye when the wagon doors slid open.

Men in striped pyjama-like garments stood before us. No one moved. We remained where we were, riveted together in a tangled mass of weak, confused, starved and thirsty bodies. Then the SS approached with their dogs shouting 'Out! Get out! Faster – faster…'

Together with this great sense of fear, something had entered our being, the realization that we had perhaps arrived at the last stop on the journey of life… the end of our existence.

'Where are we? What is this place?' we kept asking the men in the striped pyjamas. They only answered the first of our questions.

'This is Auschwitz-Birkenau,' they said in Yiddish and added, 'Get out, quickly, leave your things behind.'

We began to spill out, literally dropping to the ground on top of each other, but this was too slow for the SS who sent in the men in pyjamas first to drag out the dead and the very weak and to speed us on.

When they learned that we were metalworkers from the

Lodz ghetto, they said quietly in Yiddish, 'Get out, stand tall and look strong.' One of them said to me, 'Pinch your cheeks to give yourself colour and if they ask your age say that you're eighteen.' I was seventeen then and I couldn't understand what difference one year would make to the SS.

Compared to others on the train, the metalworkers were in fairly good shape. However, having seen what a weak and confused state most of the people were in, the SS selection team on that infamous ramp decided to take the entire train to the gas chambers.

Alfred Chimowicz realized this. He began to shout in German that he had a document on behalf of all our group that he must personally deliver to the officer in charge of the selection. One SS officer came and knocked him down to the ground. He stood up again and he shouted that he had to see the officer in charge. He was badly bleeding and he was being hit again and again. Then Mengele motioned that he be brought over to him.

He stood tall and presented the document to Mengele which Bibov and Czarnulla had given him. Then a strange thing happened: the column of people being led to the gas chambers was halted (although we didn't actually know where we were being led at that moment, it was our instinct that told us that this was probably the end), and Chimowicz was directed to gather his group of 500 into groups – women and children in one and men and youths in the other – and wait at the ramp while the Auschwitz office verified the document. An SS man on a bike was sent by Mengele to check this out.

I was with other young men, making our way to the group of our men from the 500, (with cheeks reddened by pinching and trying to look taller), when an SS officer shouted out something, and in response to that, some of my friends turned and walked back to help the weak and very old people from the train, over 2,000 of them, who were lined up to be marched in the opposite direction.

Some of my friends went. I didn't quite hear what the officer had said, but a hand pulled me back, and I went in the other direction with the group of 500.

'What did the SS man say?' I asked someone.

'That we're heartless, walking away from those poor weak people who were going the other way. He said: Why don't you go and support and help them, and then come back?'

Those who had gone to help never came back.

We all waited. The 500 of us, men, women and youths, were counted and re-counted and set to the side on the ramp. (By now our group of 500 were a few short.) Then we were re-counted and checked again. The Nazis were fanatical about numbers, records and lists. They also counted the dead, who were piled on carts pulled by the inmates.

Hours later, still standing there without water or food, we began to smell the terrible stench of burning flesh.

Now we understood – we knew with great clarity what had just befallen the others who had shared our train, all the Jewish children, and their mothers and fathers.

Near us was an electrified barbed-wire fence, with the

women's camp beyond it. A shrill woman's voice shouted something in Polish and then we understood: 'You'll be dessert,' she screamed. 'You're the *kompôt*,' and she added in German that the main course was over, and it was our turn next – words that made us freeze where we stood. The SS guard laughed. A wave of fear passed through us. We stared at one another. The 'Canada Commando', who had taken away all our possessions, were now scrubbing the wagons. These men were so called because they took all the rich pickings from the Jews and gave them to the Germans. The Germans regarded Canada as a wealthy country, and the nickname seemed appropriate.

Then, in the late afternoon, they began marching us in the same direction they had led the people from our train that morning. Those who hung back were kicked or hit by SS guards with heavy clubs. Other SS stood some distance away, holding rifles or dogs on leashes. A group of inmates waited for us around the bend. They began shouting and hitting us to make us walk faster. The women with babies were taken around the side of a building. Mrs Leon Chimowicz was not amongst them.

We were told to undress in front of this building. Screams from the women's side could be heard and we thought they were being murdered. Naked now, we were ordered to enter this structure and shower. The word went around that there were no showers inside, that this was the place where we would all be gassed. We refused to go in. The SS laughed and so did some of the men in striped pyjamas who made us stand against the wall and began to beat us. Anyone who disobeyed was dragged to an SS man to be shot.

More men in striped pyjamas arrived. These were criminals who had been sent to Auschwitz from the Lodz ghetto in 1943. They spoke to the SS, then began to search for familiar faces amongst our group of 500. The chief of the Jewish police was amongst us. He was dragged out, knocked to the ground and choked to death by two guards pressing a wooden club down on his throat and rocking on it. Others were dealt with in a similar way.

Then we were ordered into the building again, and once more everyone hesitated. A high-pressure water hose was turned on us and the force of the water peeled us into the opening. While the SS laughed, we were toppling over each other, so weak we couldn't withstand the pressure of the water jet.

Inside were men with razors waiting to shave us and chop off our hair. They worked quickly and expertly, although sometimes they cut people just for fun.

Then we had to step into a trough full of thick brown liquid. Four *kapos* stood on top of the trough, one in each corner to make sure we submerged ourselves fully in the disinfectant. They would either step on us or hold us under with a crook-like pole. I had a cut somewhere and the brown ooze stung terribly. I took a deep breath, shut my eyes and held my nose. A heavy pole held me under, and when I no longer felt the pressure on my head I surfaced from the dip. Others were held under for a longer time than necessary and came up coughing and choking. The *kapos* laughed sadistically and joked with each other. After that, we passed through to another area where water poured down on us from the shower heads. It was a strange relief. Some of us wept and others laughed but it all sounded the same.

The *kapos* were criminals of any nationality. They enjoyed brutalising and murdering people and did all the SS asked them to do.

We hung about naked for a long while after the showers. They had intended to tattoo us and eventually decided against it. A young man who sat waiting to tattoo us, one of many, called me over and pricked the side of my left thumb. 'One day when you get out of this hell,' he said in Polish, 'look at this and remember you were here!' We waited for our striped pyjamas. Eventually they came. Everything I tried on was too big. Other men had the opposite problem.

Shortly before we arrived in Auschwitz, the SS had gassed all the gypsies. Now they took us to the gypsy blocks: the women in one block and the men in the other.

That night the *kapos*, their assistants and those in charge of the main blocks of Auschwitz-Birkenau came to rape our women. Married men wept when they heard the shrieking of their wives and daughters. I understood their pain but after a few minutes, not being a father or husband, I fell asleep on the boards of the small space allocated to each of us on the bunks.

•

The head of our block was a murderer. On his striped jacket, next to the number, there was a green triangle – signifying that he was a murderer. The other triangles were: black for repeat murderer, red for political prisoners and pink for homosexuals.

When we were brought in he lined us up and gave a pep talk that began like this: 'I don't like shouting or saying things twice, so listen well. Anyone who breaks the rules in my block will be dispatched to heaven on the express route.' This, according to one of the assistants, was his standard introduction to new arrivals. He was a homicidal maniac, they said.

When we entered the block we had seen a well-fed man standing in the corner, quaking with fear. Later we found out that he had been brought there to be punished. Next morning at roll call – our first roll call – his corpse was carried out to be counted: the dead and the sick were laid on the ground. I had slept through his torture during the night, but others had heard him groaning and pleading as the life was squeezed out of him.

We were kept inside the block for days. We were forbidden to communicate with the adjoining block where the wives, sisters, mothers with children and other women from the 500 group were interned. The only task we were given was to polish the long chimney, a horizontal painted structure, and to keep the block immaculately clean. We were beaten and kicked by the guards and drilled on smartly removing our round caps and putting them on again. This was done just outside our block.

'*Mitzen auf Mitzen...*'

•

Towards evening on the second day, Mengele arrived at our block with an entourage of SS men. Our head of block felt that he was specially honoured.

We were all asked to stand smartly to attention along one side of the block. A waist-high rope had been stretched the length of the building and Mengele asked us to approach it, stretch our arms out, palms up, and remain standing like that. The fittest, the strongest and biggest managed to get to the front position. We younger people were in the second or third row behind them.

'Anyone who moves will be dealt with.' We knew what this meant. Mengele then began inspecting our hands. We in the third row spat on our hands and rubbed them on the floor trying to pick up as much dirt and grime as possible without being seen. One by one, he questioned people about the metal work they had done at the factory in Lodz. 'What, with these soft hands?' and then he would say in Yiddish: 'Who are you kidding?' His Yiddish was good – some said he could speak it quite fluently.

Then he signalled to a *kapo* who approached with two assistants holding a bucket of indelible liquid, and painted N/N (*Nacht und Nieblung* – 'night and fog') on one hand, which we later learned meant 'mark for disappearance' – and on the other hand, the number 3, 4, 5 etc. Many of our men were marked thus. The head of the block appointed one of his assistants to check the men daily and make sure no one dared to remove the marking. When the marks became faint the men were marked again. Those whose hands were marked died a thousand deaths a day. They didn't know when they would be led off to the gas chambers.

About five or six days later, the head of the block announced, 'You haven't been tattooed and you are not being sent to work in Auschwitz because you may all be dispatched to heaven any minute, which is why the men with marked hands have not been taken yet. You may all be taken together.'

Leon Chimowicz began to act strange and unbalanced. He was worried by this announcement, by the lack of news from his wife and children, and by the death of his good friend, who although not marked N/N and numbered, had run towards the electrified barbed wire and thrown himself on it. Now Leon barely talked, and seemed not to recognize people. His brother Alfred kept saying, 'Ignore all this, any day now we're going to be sent to work in the metal factory where we sent the machines from the Lodz ghetto.' Alfred went around trying to give everyone strength and heart.

I ate my piece of bread after roll call. I looked around at the suffering faces and saw my reflection in them. I went on dodging kicks and punches. I said the prayers I knew by heart.

'Are you praying?' asked a man from the 500 group.

'Yes,' I replied. 'Why do you ask?'

'You're praying, here, in Auschwitz-Birkenau?'

I couldn't make out what he meant.

Whenever Alfred C. spoke to anyone, I would try to listen. I thought he was a great man.

'Will you remember all this?' he once asked me.

'Will we live to remember it?' I replied.

'Don't talk nonsense, just store it up in your mind.' I was flattered that he had spoken to me like this.

After ten days at Auschwitz-Birkenau we were led off again, whether to the gas chamber or the train, we did not know. It turned out to be to a waiting train. There was a cart full of bread there and each of us received about three daily rations. People were hugging one another as if the war had come to an end. We saw the women and children being marched towards us, and the joy in people's eyes was something to behold.

The women and the children were put in separate wagons and we were counted and loaded on the wagons too. 'You, in here,' someone would say and we obeyed. Auschwitz inmates were added to make our group exactly 500 in number.

Dr Kleszczelski was in my wagon. He took charge immediately. Since there was not enough room for us to lie down we would have to sit zip-fashion. Each person would sit with his legs spread and the next person between them, and so on down the line. In that position we would all be able to sleep. This worked out very well. The wagon doors were not locked from the outside but each wagon had two SS men and quite a large area was occupied by these two armed guards. However, we had as much water to drink as we needed and there was air in the wagon because the SS left the sliding door fairly open most of the time.

We were going north. Most of us were convinced that we were heading for the factory near Poznan where our machines had been sent. But we passed Poznan and headed further north. Once again we arrived just before dawn, this time at the Stutthof concentration camp, near Danzig. The munitions plant we had been supposed to work at was located somewhere between Danzig and Poznan, but Russian troops were advancing westward, and an order had been given to transfer the machines to Dresden.

It was October.

Leon C. found out that his youngest son, the one-year-old, had been taken from his wife at the showers in Auschwitz.

'We take the little ones to our Auschwitz nursery,' said the *kapo* as he took the babies from their mothers' hands, screaming and weeping.

Mrs Leon Chimowicz had arrived in Stutthof with two of her boys and was put in the 'special' block together with the other women from our transport. The men's blocks were on the other side, separated by a barbed-wire fence. At first the camp looked small and cosy, and we found out that it only had one crematorium. Anywhere was better than Auschwitz, we thought, and this place seemed tolerable at first, especially since Alfred told us that we would probably be there no more than a few days.

Stutthof was not like Auschwitz, it is true, but it was hell nonetheless. We had to sleep two to a narrow bunk. Bugs from the bunk above kept dropping on our faces as we slept and we were covered in bites from the lice and fleas. The morning roll call was at 7.15 a.m., but the block leaders would switch on the lights at 5.30 a.m. and literally within seconds we had to be out. Anyone who lingered was beaten with a stick. In our frail and starving condition it was hard to recover from such beatings.

We were made to wait outside for one hour and a half in the freezing Baltic winds with nothing on but our striped pyjamas. The only way to bear the cold was to form a human oven by clustering together in groups, depending on each other, rotating rhythmically left and then right and then left again, stamping our clogs to keep our feet warm. Sometimes the *kapos* would charge at us with sticks to break us up, so we would wait for them to go and then start over again. Anyone excluded from the 'human oven' was doomed, and even with it people were getting sick and dying off.

We always had to be on the look-out for food, any food. Once on such a search for food, I came upon a block within the camp that was fenced off from all the other blocks. As I drew closer I heard a man inside say in German, 'Here you are, boy, take that,' and he threw a small paper bag out the window and over the wire fence. 'Ask other boys to come here, but no adults.'

The paper bag was full of lovely bread crusts.

'*Danke*,' I said, and disappeared with the bag under my striped jacket. I ate some crusts and gave a few to Leon Chimowicz, and because I admired Alfred so much, I offered him a couple.

'Where did you get them?' he asked, and when I told him, he replied, 'That's the block where they keep the Danish resistance fighters. They get parcels from home through the Red Cross. Don't go there again, because if you're caught by a *kapo* you'll be killed.'

Alfred C. took only one crust and I swapped the other for a couple of carrots. There was a lot of swapping going on behind one of the blocks. A bite of bread could be traded for one drag on a cigarette stub. Those who worked outside the camp sometimes managed to hide vegetables on them and bring them back. I traded three carrots for one Danish crust and gave Alfred two of them, keeping one for myself to eat with the rest of the crusts the following day and the day after. I should have shared them with Leon C. but I didn't, I ate them myself. I told a few other boys that we might be able to get a bag of crusts from the Danish prisoners. This time the prisoners gave us something even better to eat, and we were not caught by the *kapos*.

Before the morning and evening roll calls, the men from our blocks would sometimes sneak up to the barbed-wire fence and communicate with their womenfolk on the other side. Leon C. did so whenever he thought it was safe enough. It cheered him no end, as much or more than a double portion of bread.

One morning after the roll call, all the women and children from our 500 group were led away. We all knew what that meant. The women wept and waved to their husbands; the men, Leon C. among them, started crying and ran towards the barbed-wire fence. The *kapos* beat them mercilessly with their sticks but they ignored this and called their beloved children and wives… I watched and prayed. I knew Mrs Chimowicz and the two boys so well. The SS led them away as if they were taking them for a stroll around the Garden of Eden. They turned and waved and wept. Leon C. never really recovered. He was a different person, and we all noticed it.

We, meanwhile, were taken out every morning for a course of 'toughening-up exercises'. After roll call, a drink and a piece of bread, the weaker ones were led by the *kapos* and the SS guards to an area about a quarter of the size of a football pitch where they each had to lift a boulder and carry it from one heap to another and back again. Those who collapsed were beaten and kicked, or set upon by the dogs before the *kapos* dragged them away, never to be seen again. The weaker-looking men were simply selected and 'dispatched' – another cruel euphemism.

One morning I was asked by two Poles to come to their block where they said that they would give me some food. I was starving so I went. They were eating when I came in and they said to me, 'Get up on that bunk there and warm it up, we'll join you in a few minutes.' I realized suddenly what they had in mind and for a split second I froze and then said that I must go to the toilet first. They agreed. Instead of going to the toilet I ran back to my block.

After this incident we, the 500 metalworkers, were only in

Stutthof concentration camp a few more days. But during those few days I lived in fear of my life. Had the two Poles looked for me and found me they would have murdered me. I discovered that they had an important position in their block and to murder a person was quite common. They would not have been punished for it.

It was our second week in Stutthof and one day, while we were out moving boulders as entertainment for our sadistic guards, an SS man appeared and ordered us back to camp. Czarnulla was there, wearing a long black leather coat, assisted by some Germans in civilian clothes, together with army men and a few SS. They began a selection. Alfred Chimowicz stood behind Czarnulla.

They were taking some thirty or so men out to dismantle the machines that were now somewhere near Poznan. We had to march past in single file. Alfred C. had a definite say in who would be chosen but I felt that I had to speak up, because if I wasn't chosen, I knew I wouldn't stand a chance of survival. So I gathered all my courage and took the chance and spoke up, saying, in my best German, '*Ich bin fingerfertig*' ('my fingers are dextrous') and showed him my hands. An SS guard was just raising his rifle, when Czarnulla said: 'No, don't club him.' He gave me a wry smile and glanced at Alfred C. My eyes must have pleaded with him: 'For pity's sake, say yes.' Alfred Chimowicz nodded. I was chosen as one of the thirty-two men, who were sent to clean, oil and crate the machines for transport to Dresden.

We arrived by train at a small plant near Poznan and were housed in a long wooden hut between the SS guards escorting us and the German civilian engineer who spoke both Polish and German. Our work on the machines was done in a tool shed near the railway station. Living with the engineer in an adjoining room was Panna Olga, a big red-faced woman in her late twenties who looked after him.

Leon C. said I was good at cleaning so the group chose me to sweep and clean our section of the wooden hut. Panna Olga asked me to sweep her section too. She was not permitted to give me food so she would put some in a can and call me to 'throw out the rubbish'. Of course I never threw it out but ate and grew stronger by the day. Sometimes there was sardine oil in the 'rubbish can' and I would drink it. It tasted marvellous, just what my body needed. When the engineer left, the younger SS men would come to Panna Olga's room and jump into bed with her, one after another. When she had finished with them, or they with her, she would sit on a low stool in the kitchen, make herself a drink and smoke a cigarette. Her eyes when she grinned squinted pleasantly.

When Czarnulla came to inspect our work with the same German civilians who had been with him at Stutthof, they were pleased with what they saw. Czarnulla recognized me. He watched me oiling the machinery and said something to the SS officer and to Alfred Chimowicz.

That afternoon I walked about ten paces behind Czarnulla

and his party, without an SS escort, carrying two buckets of coal to a flat where I was told to make a fire in the tile stove that looked very much like the one we had at home in Chodecz. There were three women in the flat setting the table for afternoon coffee, all of them chatting and laughing while I cleaned out the stove. When the table was set they decided to go out for a walk. Czarnulla told me to make the fire and then sit down in the corner and wait for their return. Did I understand his order? 'Yes,' I replied.

The fire was burning nicely but suddenly I thought, what if some SS friends of theirs came in and mistook me for a burglar, or if I told them that I'm a Jew, seeing me there without an SS escort, they could have taken me out and shot me. No matter which way I looked at the situation, it made no sense. The truth was too fantastic. I pressed myself into a small gap between the oven and the wall, and in a few moments, fell sound asleep.

I awoke to the sound of voices. They had all returned, and seeing my face, blackened with soot, they burst out laughing. The SS officer lifted me by the collar of my striped jacket. Where had I been hiding, he asked shaking me roughly, and when I showed him, he laughed.

On the way back to the shed, the German and Polish passersby who saw me with an escort of two SS men, one of them an officer, must have thought I was a very dangerous criminal on the way to be shot somewhere. I also half expected to be punished for ignoring Czarnulla's orders and hiding behind the oven with (no doubt) some sinister purpose.

•

It took us six weeks to finish our job on the machines, working carefully but not quickly. The SS guards didn't seem to mind. Far better and safer to guard us Jews than to fight the Russian troops. We also found conditions here better than in the Lodz ghetto, Auschwitz or Stutthof.

Days of cleaning and loading machinery, of not being outside in the cold, and the rations we received there did us good. When we arrived back in Stutthof towards the middle of November 1944, we looked and felt much fitter. There, we learned that in our absence so many of our original group had died from beatings, starvation, infection from vermin and the terrible Baltic winds. Because numbers had gone down and since the original order had been for a transport of 500 slave labourers, 500 it had to be, not one more and not one less. The SS, punctilious as always about such things, requisitioned more men and women, all strong and fit, from Auschwitz. They were all seasoned, tough-looking '*Katzetniks*' who had been in Auschwitz for one or two years. Now that the group again numbered 500, Alfred Chimowicz told us we would be on our way – though where to, no one knew. If he himself had any information, he never disclosed it, not even to his brother Leon. But we who cleaned and crated the machines guessed that it was Dresden.

This time we travelled in relative comfort – only 50 prisoners to a cattle car, with two SS guards who kept the doors open at all times. Again we sat on the floor in 'zipper formation'. While we grieved for those we had lost, it was a great relief to be out of that hell of a place called Stutthof. We were transported to Dresden, to work in an ammunition factory. The factory was at 68 Schandauer Street and there we made bullet tips out of wire. The machines making the bullet tips were operated around the clock. Our group worked in three eight-hour shifts, guarded by SS men. The machines were in the basement. I worked on the steel-hardening dies: the actual moulds into which the wire was thrust at great pressure, shaping it before it was cut off into a bullet tip.

The building was a section of a huge cigarette factory. Our sleeping accommodation was in two big halls, one for men, one for women, in bunk beds. The SS had the best quarters. Although we weren't in a camp, there was no relaxation of rules. We were the slaves of the SS. We never went outside, except once, before Christmas 1944, when we were marched round and round in a nearby yard for thirty minutes. We thought that to be able to breathe fresh air was bliss.

On the first floor and part of the ground floor there was a civilian administrative office. After some weeks, I was chosen as a 'runner' between the office, which was under Albert Speer's department, and the machine floor. I don't really know why I was chosen to be the runner. Maybe it was because of the soot incident, when I was told to sweep and prepare the stove in the hut for the little party for Czarnulla and some SS officers. Perhaps Czarnulla had been amused, and remembered me.

My new job brought me into contact with the civilian

Germans in the office, such as the director, Mr Braun, who turned out to be a kindly man. As runner, I was allowed to go anywhere in the factory area to deliver drawings and collect worksheets with information about those who worked on the machines – we were referred to by our numbers, not our names. The worksheets had to state the quantity of bullets each machine produced and how many coils of wire it used.

Czarnulla would sometimes come to the factory and stay for a few days. He was obviously of a high rank, and he and Mr Braun looked after Alfred Chimowicz. On the top floor was the kitchen where our daily soup was cooked (all we were given to eat apart from a kind of ersatz coffee and bread). Mrs Alfred Chimowicz was in charge of the kitchen.

Towards evening either Czarnulla or Mr Braun would give me a small milk can full of soup and ask me to take it to our kitchen to have it warmed up. Once when I opened the lid on my way up the stairs, I saw some pieces of sausage floating on top and ate a piece. It was delicious. On the way down, after it had been warmed up, I wanted to take another piece. When I handed it to Mr Braun, I felt myself going red and mumbled something like, *'Ich bin unschuldig'* ('I'm not to blame'). Mr Braun only laughed and patted me on the head.

Time went slowly but we didn't mind as long as we weren't being beaten, terrorized, threatened or shot.

It was Christmas 1944, and a new head SS officer allowed us to put on a kind of pantomime. They gave us extra soup and bread. The entire pantomime, or most of it at any rate, had been written by Mr Nussbaum, a very cultured man in our group who could play Mozart on a comb, and recite poetry in perfect German. The Auschwitz toughies used to make fun of him and Mrs Nussbaum, or 'Peezia', as she was nicknamed, for someone who is absent-minded, slightly confused. Mr Braun asked the deputy SS officer (the one left in charge of us for Christmas) if he and the German office workers could watch our pantomime too.

Mr Nussbaum performed a number of sketches, and had made up hilarious ditties set to well-known German songs about our work at the factory. He was dressed as a woman and another performer with a fine voice played the man.

We knew that it happened to be *Chanukah* that Christmas Eve, and in our hearts, that was what we were celebrating.

Around midnight on 13 February 1945, we heard an air-raid siren, but we were not very concerned. Having heard so many false alarms in the past, we were convinced no harm would befall this beautiful city, especially now that the war was drawing to an end. We didn't know, of course, no one told us. Instinctively, we felt that the end was near. We thought that the planes would simply fly over Dresden and continue to other cities nearby. But as the menacing hum of the planes grew louder, the higher-ranking SS officers ordered us down to the basement where they left us in the charge of the junior SS men, while they hurried off to a nearby air-raid shelter.

At around 12.30 a.m., bombs began to fall in torrents, with

such force that the whole earth seemed to tremble. The sick people from our group had been left up on the roof in the First Aid hut. The SS guards, normally so brash and cocky, now were looking pale and frightened as they scurried this way and that, and then huddled together under the support columns of the factory. We were glad to see our torturers in this state, and though the raid couldn't have lasted more than thirty minutes, to us it seemed much longer. Our factory wasn't hit. The 'all-clear' sounded and we had climbed the stairs to our dormitories, when all at once the loudspeakers boomed: '*Achtung, Achtung, Luftwaffe meldung...*' Another RAF sortie was heading towards Dresden.

We were ordered back to the basement, and more bombs began to fall. Looking out through the bars of the basement window grille, we could see flares parachuting through the air. This time the ground did not shake. Someone said, 'Those are incendiary bombs.' That second raid, coming straight after the first one, intensified the fires, so much so that buildings that were not bombed began to burn from the extreme heat of the adjacent fires.

The great fire of Dresden had begun.

When our factory was hit, the SS sent two men up to the roof to see whether the building had caught fire. The First Aid hut was ablaze, and everyone sick who was in it was burned alive. 'Dresden is a huge inferno!' they reported.

As soon as this raid was over, the junior SS guards decided to wait for the higher-ranking officers to return. We waited inside as the factory filled up with smoke. It was then that Alfred Chimowicz showed his leadership skills, wisely suggesting that the SS guards lead us out through the fire to the River Elbe before it was too late. He told us all to take a wet blanket, cut two small holes in it for our eyes, and wait for marching orders. The junior SS officers did everything that Alfred Chimowicz told them; the senior SS officers had again disappeared to their shelter.

Soon we were on the road, throwing ourselves down as huge cartwheels of fire, some several feet high, came repeatedly towards us. We would cover ourselves with the wet blankets, and throw ourselves down onto the road and let the cartwheels of fire go over us. Screaming humans were jumping from burning buildings which were collapsing all around us, walls crashing to the ground, and materials inside what must have been factories, exploding. The heat was enormous and we found it hard to breathe. There was just no air. We heard the screams, the creaking of wood snapping, the thud of masonry falling – and all the time, the thick, acrid smoke that made it almost impossible to breathe. We kept to the middle of the road, though the asphalt surface had become unbearably hot, and eventually we reached the River Elbe.

We remained by the river throughout the following day. Late in the morning, American planes dropped bombs over the fields surrounding Dresden, then turned around and flew away.

Towards late afternoon, new high-ranking SS officers showed up to take charge of us. They marched us to the tank factory in

Pirna, quartered us in the timber-curing sheds there, which were pleasantly warm, and in the morning, gave us some good soup. Then they decided to 'thin us out' – another euphemism for murder. This time those who felt themselves too sick to go on were given the opportunity of volunteering – they were sent to the sick ward, given a bed, more soup and a lethal injection.

The fittest among us were selected to collect the dead in Dresden. This was a time of great confusion, and among the people who disappeared at this time, were two men I had got to know quite well, Avraham Sztajer and Adam Szwajcer. We assumed they had been put in charge of the two collection groups and that they had managed to escape and were hiding in the ruins of the city.

Then twenty-four of us, together with five SS men, went back to Dresden to clean up the factory and the machines, to pump the water out, and arrange a dormitory for the corpse bearers who came back to sleep there at night. I was sorry to have been selected because life in the tank factory had been comparatively promising and cosy.

Dresden was still smouldering in places; everywhere we marched had been damaged by the bombs. Compared with the destruction of other parts of the building, our section of the factory had only been burned on the top. But there was now water in the basement where the machines were.

We first had to clean out a space for the five SS men to live in. Then we began pumping out the water and mopping up the basement floor. On top of the roof, where the water tanks were, there was also a long room. This was where our sick bay had been – which the fires had set alight on the night of the bombing. We had to remove the three bodies that had been caught in the blaze.

Czarnulla appeared one morning, and he and Alfred Chimowicz and one of the SS men went to get more people to help us clean up and to repair things. Fifteen more arrived, among them ten women, accompanied, of course, by women SS. Alfred Chimowicz told us that we had been appointed a new chief SS officer who would be in charge of both the men and the women.

We worked hard and we almost had the place ready when one morning the new SS chief, together with a woman SS officer, arrived in a lorry. The lorry was packed with SS men whom we knew and who had guarded us before the bombing, together with completely new men. They lined us up outside the factory, as if for a roll call. Absolutely everyone, including Alfred Chimowicz. The new officer handled us very roughly. Then the woman SS and the SS chief went to the office to see Czarnulla and Mr Braun. We stood to attention and had to wait. When they returned, they began selecting people.

They chose both Leon and Alfred Chimowicz, and I was kicked by the woman officer and made to go first. As soon as I stepped out, this woman officer got hold of my arm, pulled me towards her, and hit me with a hard object which she held in her hand on the left side of my head. (The others told me later that what she had been holding in her hand was a metal

T-shaped window-opening key.) My head started to bleed pro-
fusely; then she shouted something and an SS man advanced
towards me. I saw him turn his rifle round and lift it like an axe
by the barrel.

I knew that he wanted to crack my skull, for I had seen
it done to Hanka and Henryk in Chodecz in the ravine, in
the springtime of 1940, and many times since – and I knew
his murderous intention. It was normal for the SS to act this
way, particularly before an execution or murder, they would
smash the skulls of one or two people. They must have been
given instructions from their higher echelons about what to
do in certain situations in order to cow and terrify people
into paralysis.

Quickly and instinctively I covered my head with my arms
and the blow slid down my back and caught me on the left hip.
I yelled and staggered forward, fell to the ground and picked
myself up, sobbing. Another SS man stood me face to the wall
with my hands up. About a few feet away from me, also with his
hands up, stood Leon C., then Alfred and the rest, all twelve of
us, with rifles pointed at our backs. Then the SS officer ordered
the soldiers behind us to stand at ease. We could rest our raised
arms against the wall now.

My head was still bleeding but it did not hurt as much as my
hip. I sobbed quietly, afraid that if I made too much noise I
might be beaten again or shot. 'Shut up,' Leon Chimowicz kept
whispering to me. Passers-by gathered in the street to watch us;
the SS seemed indifferent to their gazes. After what seemed

like a long time, we were led back into the factory and put to work as before.

Later we learned that the SS officer in charge had asked Czarnulla and Braun for cigarettes. Had they not managed to produce any, we would all have been shot. Luckily for us, Czarnulla and Braun did find some cigarettes for the SS in the Reinsmar cigarette factory and so our lives were spared.

Dr Kleszczelski, who was in our cleaning crew, examined me. He didn't think my hip was broken, and as for my head, he pronounced lightheartedly, 'The brains still seem to be on the inside.'

By the beginning of March we had got the machines working again and the factory was back in action.

Among the new SS, there was one sadistic woman officer who liked to choose her victims from among the younger and smaller men. She would make them stand to attention and then kick them in the groin with her pointed boot. Being a runner, it was hard to avoid her, so I made myself a protective shield out of metal. Dr Kleszczelski told me how to put it in so it wouldn't clank when she kicked me. I was to throw myself on the floor and writhe as if in agony. While he and the others rehearsed me in this, I had them in stitches – but whenever I saw the female sadist I was terrified. I felt that she truly hated me.

The new officer in charge had the eyes of a killer. We all feared him, and rightly so. Rumour had it that the last SS officer in charge had died in the bomb shelter the night of the

Dresden bombings and his deputy had been promoted for his courage in taking us down to the river – Alfred's idea actually – and because he meted out harsh punishments for the smallest things. With the new officer in charge, we saw a definite change in the behaviour of the ordinary SS. Life became more unpleasant than ever. The German civilian office knew that the SS were just ruthless killers but there was little they could do about it. There was little cooperation between them and the SS now.

The Escape

In late March, 1945, the order came to move us out along the River Elbe. We were allowed to take a blanket and were given a loaf of bread each. When I said 'goodbye' to the office staff, Mr Braun took me aside and told me that if I managed to 'get away' from the transport and get back to the factory, he would be sure to find some clothes for me (we were all still dressed in the striped garb of convicts, which made escape nigh impossible) and he would also try to find me a hiding place.

The transport was to trudge some twelve miles a day, or at least this was the target set for us by the SS, but during our last few days at the factory, most of the group had been suffering from severe diarrhoea. We plodded along very slowly. The stronger ones took turns supporting the weaker.

Outside Dresden, in a more isolated spot where we rested for a while, the SS officer appeared with a couple of spades. Then the SS officer in charge shot two of our men. We left them at the edge of the field with earth heaped over them. 'That ought to make you march,' he said. 'Anyone who falls behind will suffer the same fate.'

We began to walk faster but only for about half a mile, and then we reverted to our usual pace. The women, many of them also suffering from diarrhoea, marched behind. We were not allowed to stop and relieve ourselves. Some of the women were shot and buried along the way.

We covered eight miles or so that first day. We were led to a field and told we were going to sleep there overnight. The SS arrived with a bucket of whitewash and a long brush. As a precaution against escape, they assigned two men from our group to paint the large letters K.L. (*Konzentration Lager*) on our striped jackets and to shave a two-inch strip from the front to the back of our heads.

We huddled together on the ground, trying to keep warm, under the watchful eyes of the SS men and women. Next day we trudged on even more slowly. There were more stops along the way and more shootings – murders, to be more precise. That second day, we covered six miles at the most. The men from Auschwitz – the seasoned *katzetniks* – and the fittest amongst us, were convinced that the next day we would all be shot.

There was a man in the Auschwitz group called Franz who spoke only German. The story had it (his story) that he had been in the German Luftwaffe and taken part in the bombing of London among other places. But then, while home on leave in

Vienna, he had helped his father slaughter an unaccounted-for pig. For this crime they were arrested. Then, during their interrogation, it came to light that Franz's grandmother was Jewish and he was promptly sent to Auschwitz. He never saw his family again. This was Franz's story and he stuck to it, feeling vastly superior to the rest of us and giving himself airs. He had some friends among the Auschwitz lot, including a girlfriend, but none amongst us from the Lodz ghetto. We didn't care for him.

The natural leader of the Auschwitz contingent was Moniek the Boxer, who had been sent to the camp at the end of 1942, and bore the tattoo of the startlingly early number of 55 on his arm. This meant that he had survived some twenty-three months at Auschwitz. This, combined with his physical strength and the strength of his will and character, commanded everyone's respect. He was a natural leader: what Moniek told people to do, they did. At Auschwitz, one of the punishments devised by Mengele for disciplining SS men was to send them singly into a darkened cell where Moniek would be waiting for them wearing a mask and boxing gloves. He would then punch the SS offenders until a bell rang. No one ever learned the boxer's identity. For these services Mengele allowed Moniek a special ration of food.

In Dresden, during our Christmas party, Moniek had fallen in love with another man's wife. Each time we halted on our march, he would ask for news of his beloved. He and Franz talked about escaping as they walked. I was all ears.

The news spread that we were nearing Pirna, the site of the

tank factory where some of us had been taken after the Dresden bombing. 'If they take us there today or tomorrow,' said Moniek the Boxer, 'it means they still need us for metal work of some sort, but if they march us on, then it'll only be a matter of hours before they murder us all.'

I understood his reasoning. 'Moniek,' I said, pulling at his striped jacket, 'I know how we all can get civilian clothes in Dresden.'

'What do you mean, all of us?' said Moniek.

'I can get shirts or dresses for at least five men and women.'

Moniek looked at me suspiciously. 'Stay close by and I'll talk to you later.'

We made a stop in a sloping meadow with a few trees at the top. We were half-way up the slope when the usual roll call was taken. The number of the living was tallied in with the number of those who had died or had been shot. The sum total was correct. No one had escaped. The SS men and women brought us a meal consisting of bread cut in strips, a carrot, a beet and a piece of cabbage, all raw, and a drink of water. Those who were still recovering from diarrhoea were advised by Dr Kleszczelski to save their food and only drink water for the time being.

The SS pegged and roped off the area where we were to sleep and a latrine area, a shallow V-shaped pit. Some began to make their bedrolls, blankets for three, one spread on the ground with the remaining two blankets used as covers to huddle under. There were different ways to arrange a bedroll, depending on how wet the ground was, but the slope was relatively dry.

Within the roped-off area we were free to walk about, but the women were kept in a separate area nearby. There was a stench of diarrhoea in the air. I decided to stick with the Auschwitz contingent because they were healthy and fit and planning an escape I wanted to join. They still had the strength and the will to take risks, risks that could well determine their survival and my own. I wanted to survive. With them, beside them I could still smell life!

I went to talk to Leon C. His stomach was all right and so was Alfred's. They were lying on the bare ground, wrapped in their individual blankets. One side of Alfred's face was badly bruised. Earlier in the day he had approached the SS officer in charge and asked for two sticks so that we might take turns carrying Mr Nussbaum on his blanket. The SS officer called for a stick and with it he smashed Alfred on the face and said, 'Here's your stick. That will teach you to come bothering me with requests.'

I felt sorry for Alfred C. He was a great man. 'Is there anything that I can do for you?' I asked him.

'Yes,' he said, sitting up, 'tell as many people as you can that tomorrow we may be taken to the Pirna factory.'

I passed the word around.

Moniek the Boxer, Franz and the others lying nearby wanted to know how I planned to get the shirts and dresses. I told a lie. I said that Mr Braun and the others at the Dresden office had promised me that if I escaped with them the office people would help us find civilian clothes.

Moniek sat up and beckoned me closer. He put his enormous

hands around my neck and squeezed it. 'You wouldn't lie to me, would you?' he snarled through his teeth.

'No, of course not,' I replied.

'Then keep your mouth shut. Not a word,' he said, and added, 'If you let out anything about the escape to anyone here or if you're lying about the civilian clothes I will personally snuff the life out of you with these hands,' and then he squeezed my neck again.

I was more afraid of being shot by the SS any time now than by Moniek's threats. I knew I was gambling with my life by lying to him but I had a hunch that I could pull it off when we got to the factory in Dresden.

The following morning we were awakened early. At roll call those who were fit had to stand while the weak and the sick lay on the ground. The chief SS officer announced that we were close to a town and he wanted volunteers to help carry the infirm to the station where they would be loaded on a train. Volunteers who stepped forward would also be allowed to take the train. Only a few came forward. The rest were chosen at random from the roll call sheet. Someone from the Auschwitz contingent who was close to Moniek the Boxer was also selected. Mr Nussbaum was taken away, and his wife could be seen pleading with the chief SS female officer to let her accompany him. Mrs Nussbaum was allowed to go. I felt sorry for all those who were leaving, but especially for that lovely person, the engineer and musician, the cultured, gifted and wise Mr Nussbaum and his wife, the tiny Mrs Nussbaum whom the Auschwitz lot had called Peezia. In my mind's eye I saw the massacre of my friends in Chodecz, and imagined their fate...

Some time later we heard shots in the distance. The SS men and women returned to us laughing. Word got around that they had been just in time to catch the train carrying Jewish people from other parts of Germany... but where, no one could say. Who had passed the word around? One of the SS men, supposedly.

We were not taken to Pirna. Instead we were led south through a small town with a railway station. When we reached the middle of the town an air-raid warning sounded and we were told to sit down on the stones in the middle of the market-place. Aeroplanes were flying overhead, dropping bombs that fell some distance away, closer to the railway station. Only a few SS men remained on guard, the rest took shelter.

When the all-clear sounded, the townspeople crowded around and stared at us. The SS counted us again and then ordered us to sit down in a tighter group. Some of the townspeople started kicking us. I figured they were angry about the bombs and wanted to take it out on us. They pelted us with bits of food. Although most of us were starving only a few pounced on these scraps. The onlookers laughed. '*Untermenschen!*' they shouted. Those of us who sat quietly on the cobblestones and did not fight over the food were kicked by the SS men or called out and beaten. I remembered the words Mr B. had said to me in the Lodz ghetto about dignity and refused to scramble for a few crusts of bread. One's stomach said, 'Yes, yes, go on, get the bread,' but self-respect won out: 'I will not do it.'

Obviously we weren't providing enough 'action' to satisfy our SS guards. The female SS officer who hated me singled me out, and made me stand to attention. I stood there before her, clumsily with my legs partly crossed. I tried to protect my lower body. Instead of kicking me, she punched me on the chin. Relieved not to be kicked I made myself stagger back and stumbled on top of the others who were still sitting on the ground. The onlookers laughed. They all hated us, I knew.

The SS counted us again and ordered us to march. I heard Moniek the Boxer tell a friend from the Auschwitz contingent: 'Tonight's the night.' This other man's name was also Moniek, but he was called Moniek the Testicle because Mengele had removed one of his testicles at Auschwitz as part of an experiment to see if this would reduce aggression in violent males. Some people spread the rumour that Mengele had selected the most virile Jewish men for this in order to collect testicles to graft onto German soldiers who had lost theirs on the Russian front, but Alfred Chimowicz said this was complete nonsense because no German would sew a Jewish ball on a German soldier!

With or without his full complement, Moniek the Testicle was one of the most lethal fighters among us, as all who knew him were quick to affirm. There was plenty of aggression left in Moniek's remaining testicle. Neither in Stutthof, Dresden or on this march did anyone ever pick a quarrel with Moniek the Testicle, for we believed the stories about him.

When we stopped for water later in the day, I clung to the Boxer. 'I will not fail you; I will do anything you tell me to do.' He just nodded. He was preoccupied: he had just heard that his beloved had diarrhoea but she was young and would soon feel better. She had not been taken away that morning with Mr and Mrs Nussbaum and the others.

Now the SS seemed more relaxed. They must have thought we were too far from Dresden and too exhausted to attempt an escape. And where would we go? We had all seen how the population felt about us. So the next time we stopped to rest and drink water, the men were allowed to talk to the women and sit with them. Also, only a few SS stayed to guard us while the rest got onto the lorry which followed the column at some distance. They drove off, returned in a jolly mood, counted us and marched us on. No one was missing.

I kept looking out for a ravine or a newly-dug pit in some field ahead because I felt certain that was where we were being led now, to our end.

But the SS kept us on the road. We walked and walked till we came within sight of the Elbe again. Then further on, the road was flanked with pine trees. A few miles later we turned left and walked a further half-mile or so until we came to a junction. From this point and as far as the river there were fields. To the right, about a hundred yards away, I saw two huge roofs, like bandstands in a park, and under these roofs, open on all sides, stood agricultural machines.

'This is where we'll stop for tonight,' said the SS officer in charge. The machines were taken out and a couple of men driving a horsedrawn wagon brought us new straw from the nearby estate. We couldn't understand what was going on, could this straw really be for us? For the past two nights they had made us lie on the damp ground and today, machines were being taken out to make room for us under a roof and on fresh straw too!

The whole thing was very unsettling, and then they didn't separate the men from the women. This made us even more suspicious. The Auschwitz men said that frequently before the SS murdered inmates in the camps they would amuse themselves by devising extraordinary tactics to confuse the victims and create the impression that from now on all would be well.

The Boxer gripped my arm. 'Were you lying about being able to get civilian clothes for men and women?' he said, shaking me.

'No, of course not... I wouldn't lie to you, Moniek.'

'Then listen carefully because I will not repeat what I am going to tell you now. You will follow Franz. You will count slowly to fifty once Franz is gone and when you finish counting you will go.'

Fantastic, I thought, they *are* taking me with them!

'Do you know how to run zigzag?'

I nodded.

'Those clogs of yours, you will hold them firmly in your hands. Make sure you don't drop them. You will run zigzag to the junction. At the junction you will turn sharply to the left and run or walk fast until you come to the main road. You will cross the road and enter the forest for a depth of fifty steps or so. I will be there and I will find you. You must not call us or shout or turn back.'

He told me to take my place close to Franz. 'Do everything I just told you, as quietly as a mouse.'

We were given hot soup and chunks of bread. Most people ate the soup and kept the chunks of bread for the following day. We were counted and allowed to choose our spots under the two roofs. The Boxer whispered to me, 'No goodbyes to anyone!'

It was hours later when we began our escape. The SS on guard stood together between the two sheds, smoking and chatting. We waited in the corner, quite out of sight. Apart from us, everyone else seemed asleep. I was dying many a death, rehearsing in my mind all the instructions Moniek had given me.

The Boxer went first, together with his woman. They simply walked away, quietly and fairly slowly it seemed to me. Others followed a few seconds later, then Franz and his woman, and I began my count. No one else heard us – they were blissfully asleep on the dry straw after our gruelling three days and two terrible nights.

As I began to run zigzag, I felt sure that any minute a bullet would fly through the starry night and hit me between the shoulder blades. That I would hear 'HALT!' and then gunfire, but nothing happened.

I reached the junction and turned sharply to the left. I began to walk then run, run and walk until I came to the road. I crossed it and entered the forest. My feet hurt. I sat down and wrapped them up and put my clogs on. I was now engulfed in total darkness. Seventy-five of my paces would be just about fifty of Moniek's steps, I thought, staggering from tree to tree. Maybe they left without me and went on, I worried, still counting. Tomorrow when the SS take me back they will split my skull open and spear me with their bayonets!

A big hand grabbed my shoulder. It was the Boxer.

'Got your clogs on?'

'Yes,' I replied, 'but I have to adjust them.'

'Do everything quickly now... pee, shit... there will be no stops on the way.'

The Boxer and Franz decided that we should walk along the main road – reasoning that if we were caught in the forest we would be shot immediately. Also, we had only a few hours in which we had to reach Dresden. In the forest we would have to advance slowly and we might easily lose our way. We began to walk fast. The Boxer estimated that we had about twenty-five miles to cover. I brought up the rear. Franz led the way: it was all planned out between him and the others. There were nine of us in all, including three women. The Boxer's woman was by far the weakest. Two men took turns helping and supporting her.

At one point walking along the road by the forest, we came upon a couple of home guards who stood by their sentry box with anti-tank guns. There were posts lodged in the ground at the edge of the road and tree trunks scattered nearby ready to fit on the posts to halt advancing vehicles. Franz gave them a Heil Hitler salute and said something about going to load corpses (I never managed to find out what he actually said to the two home guards). The Boxer and Moniek the Testicle were ready to deal with them if they refused to let us pass or attempted to arrest us. But Franz in his perfect Austrian-German must have sounded very convincing because they chatted to him enjoyably, gave him a couple of cigarettes, told him the time (2 a.m.) and waved us on.

By daybreak we were close to Pilnitz Castle, well beyond Pirna. Explaining that he had to shift this little group of prisoners, Franz somehow got us all onto the first tram to Dresden. Apart from us, there were only some three or four people on the tram. It was really touch and go, and if the SS had spotted us in our concentration camp garb, they would have taken us and shot us against some wall. We had no trouble finding the factory. The Boxer knew his way around and made all the decisions. He didn't tell us what his plans were, he just gave orders.

His woman wasn't doing at all well and he laid her on the back seat of an abandoned car in the factory forecourt. With the other Moniek, he went to look around and when they returned we all climbed to the top of the burnt-out floor and lowered ourselves by using a rope, one by one, onto the glazed roof of the courtyard. To one side were the painted-out windows of the cigarette factory and we all squeezed through one of them to get inside. The cigarette factory had not been reopened since the bombing, and the part we had entered was locked shut. There we climbed up onto the top of enormous vats, which reached just below the level of the ceiling. And so we hid, spread-eagled, as quiet as corpses.

Moniek the Testicle, who was lithe and strong as a cat, was sent to cover up our tracks. He also thought he might be able to bring the Boxer's woman back with him from the abandoned car. Not long afterwards, he returned alone. There was no time to get her, he explained, because a truck full of SS men had arrived.

But he had brought the rope back with him, and shut the window. Now, he said, there was no trail leading to our hiding place. We heard the sounds of the SS next door. Some time later we heard the screams of the Boxer's woman. The Boxer wept – we heard his sobs but lay silent where we were. The SS searched for hours but they only searched the metal factory side. Then all was still. The Boxer told us to remain very quiet because they may have left one or two of their men behind to hide somewhere and listen for any sound of movement. He told us to be prepared to lie like this for many hours. He would tell us when it was time to speak, to move or to lower ourselves down. We peed where we were.

'The SS will come back again this afternoon and again tomorrow morning. You'll see.'

I could not understand how he had managed to keep such a cool head after the loss of his beloved. When we heard her screams, I thought he might do something wild, jump down and run to her rescue.

Just as he had foreseen, the SS men did return, and this time they searched for us with dogs. We could hear barking and shouting and a few gunshots. The Boxer explained that the search dogs could not sniff us out because the tobacco smell is very strong and dogs hate it. And in any case, they could never tell them how we had slid down from the roof, he said, reassuring us and giving us courage.

The following day the SS came again and searched the metal factory side. When they had gone the Boxer allowed us to lower ourselves to do our 'essentials' in the corner; meanwhile, Moniek the Testicle had found us water to drink. It tasted peculiar but no one got sick from it.

We stayed there three days in all. Early on the morning of the third day I was ordered to go down with Moniek the Testicle.

I was feeling weak and dizzy, but Moniek was extraordinary: when we reached the perimeter of the glazed roof I watched him scale the wall along a corner pipe with the rope wound around him like some human fly. When he got to the top, he attached the rope and lowered himself back to me again. I found it hard to twist the rope around my leg, grip it, and pull myself up this way, but I managed somehow. Then Moniek came up.

'If they catch you inside the factory, don't give us away. Just give one loud scream and keep your mouth shut for ever after.'

I understood him fully.

'And if you don't get us the clothes, the Boxer will do exactly as he promised.'

I nodded. I understood that too.

I got into the office through the factory door and waited. I heard someone coming and I hid behind a filing cabinet. It was the Dutchman. I didn't know whether I could trust him or not because I remembered that when I had once received a parcel from Mr and Mrs Podlawski, he had approached me and said, 'Did you get nice things in your parcel?' I had pretended I didn't know what he was talking about, fearing he would denounce me to the SS. He said he was not a spy or an informer and that he knew all about the parcel.

I put my hand out and greeted him. I felt I had to risk it. He was really pleased to see me. He said the SS had been there and searched the place a number of times. I asked for some food and he gave me one of his sandwiches and a cup of soup from his thermos. I told him about the lie I had told Moniek the Boxer about being able to get clothes for all of us. I didn't mention that he had threatened my life if I failed to get the clothes.

'I'll go and get Mr Braun. I'm certain that between us we will manage to find you all the apparel you need.'

I told him how hard it was for me to know whom to trust – our lives were at stake.

'I understand, I understand,' he said. 'Mr Braun is no Nazi; he will help you all he can and of course so will I.'

I sensed that he meant this and I was overjoyed. He went to

fetch Mr Braun and I climbed back up to tell Moniek the Testicle what was happening. But the rope was gone. He was neither above nor below. I didn't want to shout and as I stood looking down at the courtyard well with the glazed roof below, someone put his hand over my mouth and grabbed me from behind. It was Moniek the Testicle.

'What's happening?' he asked.

I was speechless for a moment, paralyzed by the shock of what he had done. Then I told him everything.

He asked me to repeat it, and I did.

'Did you tell him where we are hiding?'

'No,' I replied. 'He didn't ask me.'

We watched from the top of the building to see whether the Dutchman would return with the SS. Eventually we saw him with Mr Braun, both carrying wrapped parcels. I went alone to rejoin them.

Mr Braun fitted me out with a pair of galoshes (he had no shoes my size), socks, and a Tyrol jacket and trousers. To get rid of the shaven strip down the middle of my head the Dutchman cut all my hair short and gave me one of his own shirts.

'Think of a good Polish name,' said Mr Braun.

'Roman Podlawski,' I replied.

'Type this out for Roman Podlawski,' said Mr Braun to the Dutchman, handing him a piece of paper with handwriting on it.

And while the Dutchman was typing, Mr Braun got hold of some clothes for me, gave me some food for the journey and told me to go to Oberpoyritz on the outskirts of Dresden, to the house of a Mr and Mrs Fuchs. The note he gave me said that I was a Pole who had been working in Chemnitz and had lost all his documents in the bombing, and that I wished to continue working on the land for Germany and the Third Reich... something along these lines. I was given the address of Mr and Mrs Fuchs, and then told to memorize and destroy it. He showed me how to get there on the map and said that if anyone stopped me on the road, I should show them the paper the Dutchman was typing and explain that I was a factory worker from Leipzig on my way to Dresden, because I didn't want to be captured by the 'Yanks'; that I was now going to work for a farmer in Oberpoyritz.

'When they question you, say you don't understand and keep repeating the same story over and over again. Don't tell them anything about the factory or any of us.'

'Shall I go now?' I asked.

'Before you set off, tie some string around your galoshes and your trousers and remember, when you're stopped and questioned, say you're a Pole who wants to work for the Reich and repeat what I just told you. Good luck, Roman Podlawski, put this typed paper in your pocket.'

'Will you help my friends?' I asked anxiously. 'They also need clothes and food, and help to escape...'

'Yes, yes, don't worry about that...'

'They're on the roof,' I said.

All seemed to be going well, though I didn't have a chance to say goodbye to the others. In fact, I was really terrified of Moniek the Testicle, so I was glad not to have to face him just yet. The provisions Mr Braun had given me were delicious. As I walked I ate them all. I felt unafraid, filled with good food, and was quite enjoying my stroll in my new outfit. I checked to see whether I had the document with the address of Mr and Mrs Fuchs in my pocket. Yes, it was there. I sauntered happily towards the Elbe taking the route Mr Braun had shown me on the map.

As I walked along, I grew increasingly aware of the devastation all around from the bombings in February. I hadn't known Dresden before the bombings, because we were never allowed out of the factory, except for the four who went under SS escort twice a week to load a cart up with food and push it back to the factory. The Dresden I knew was the area between the railway station and the factory we had marched along when we first arrived. Now I saw rubble everywhere and the remains of buildings sticking out of the ground.

Once again I came to the River Elbe, where soldiers, not SS, were checking the papers of those who wanted to get onto the boats that were ferrying people across. I showed them my paper and they began to talk to me. I repeated what Mr Braun told me to say, and then added, '*Ich mo'chte Arbeit. Auf wiedersehen.*' I kept repeating this and when I had the chance I took the document out of their hands and said, '*Danke, auf wiedersehen,*' and got on the boat. They all laughed, and when we got off on the other bank I asked them which way to Oberpoyritz.

•

When I got there, the locals pointed out the home of Mr and Mrs Fuchs, but they were not in. A young woman with a toddler invited me into the kitchen to wait for them. She offered me a cup of soup and a piece of bread and we talked. I told her I had run away from the Americans to work for the German people.

'You poor thing, you shouldn't have run away,' she said. Then she took out an album and turned the pages to the photos of her wedding, of her little daughter as a very small baby, of her husband smiling, and then again in uniform with a death's head insignia on his jacket.

Startled, I exclaimed, 'But he's in the SS!'

She shut the album and put it in the next room. When she returned her eyes were red and moist.

'He's been fighting in Russia and I hope he is all right and will soon come back home to us,' she said. 'Would you mind waiting outside now? I have to leave and lock up the house.' She gave me a stool and showed me where I could sit and wait in the passage.

Before leaving with her child she asked me whether I had been ill-treated by the SS. I asked her to repeat the question and tried to think up a good answer. She asked again and I replied. 'I am afraid of them.'

'So was the whole world,' she said and left.

Soon after, Kurt and Herta Fuchs returned. They had been expecting me. I looked at their faces. They looked as if they were in their late-thirties, and seemed nice. They studied me too for a while, and then took me out to their garden shed, which was a kind of greenhouse with windows, where a bed had been made up for me with blankets and a pillow and a long warm nightshirt. Mrs Fuchs said that I could have a bath in their bathroom that evening, but otherwise I would be staying, sleeping and living in my garden shed. They would bring me food and water, and I should use the two buckets that were there. They would come each day and instruct me as to what work needed to be done in the kitchen garden. If I was to hear voices in the house, I should make my way quietly into the shed. Only in special circumstances should I come to the house. If I ever did, I should knock quietly on the door and wait.

The following day the Fuchses told me that in order to stay with them I would have to register at the village hall and get a ration book. They instructed me as to what to say, and feeling myself to be utterly Roman Podlawski, I foresaw no problems whatsoever.

At the village hall I spoke to a friendly woman who took me to the office where a man began to question me. I am a Pole; I kept repeating, and gave him my name. I told him that I wished to work for the German people.

'Say a prayer in your language,' he suddenly demanded. At my school in Chodecz, we Jewish children could either stand to attention silently whilst the Christian pupils recited their morning prayers, or wait outside the classroom until the prayers were over. I had stayed in class and knew the Roman

Catholic prayers as well as I knew the *Shema*, and I now began to reel them off in Polish.

'That's fine, that's fine, come back tomorrow to collect your papers and your ration book,' said the man.

All through April I worked in the vegetable garden. There was a lot for me to do there and I enjoyed the work. Every day either Mr or Mrs Fuchs would outline my chores for the day and when I completed them, they would come out and tell me what to do next. Sometimes they would work beside me but mainly I worked on my own seven days a week, with an occasional break whenever Mr Fuchs invited me to accompany him on his wife's bike and cycle to the village. In relative safety, away from the SS, working in the fresh air, with enough food to eat and a good bed to sleep on, I felt I was putting on weight and getting stronger and fitter with each day that passed.

One day, as I was going into my shed, I heard voices. From behind a tree, I spotted Czarnulla at the back of the house! This occurred twice. And once, when I knocked on the door of the house after hearing voices, Mrs Fuchs opened the door and said I could come in. As I was taking off the huge garden shoes Mr Fuchs had given me to wear for work, I thought I recognized the voices... could they be those of the SS guards? I froze inside and I peered through the open door before entering. There stood Avraham Sztajer and Adam Szwajcer, two of the group of 500 metalworkers whom I had thought were hiding out in Dresden.

I was delighted to see them, and they seemed pleasantly amused to see me. They seemed relaxed and spoke quite freely. They were working for another farmer who lived nearby, but they said that they came to the Fuchses each night. (But I think that they must have slept on the farm where they worked.) Before returning to their farm, they came out to the vegetable garden with me and I showed them where I lived and worked. They told me that Mr Braun had also written them a letter of recommendation with the address of the farm. They had been told that I was at the Fuchses.

I asked Sztajer and Szwajcer what had happened to the others in the factory with whom I escaped, Moniek the Boxer, for example. Adam Szwajcer said that Czarnulla told them – and at this point Sztajer interrupted him and said: 'Oh, you'll meet up with them in Heaven.'

Towards the end of April, soldiers cut wedges into the poplars that lined the road to Oberpoyritz and stuck dynamite into them. The villagers decided to remove the sticks of dynamite because it was known that those who tried to defend themselves would be bombed, looted, raped and murdered when the Russians arrived.

From the second of May onwards, the entire village began to move into shelters and cellars. Mr Fuchs on his bicycle and I on his wife's rode over to the farm where Sztajer and Szwajcer worked. They were overjoyed with the news. 'It's only a matter of hours now and then we will be free men...!'

On 4 May we heard shots in the distance and Mr and Mrs Fuchs invited me to join them down in the vegetable cellar for safety. Just before midday, a Russian soldier was seen cycling towards our village. When he got there, he jumped off and shouted, '*Davaj czasy*!... Give me your watches!'

I asked Mr and Mrs Fuchs whether I could leave my shed now that we were liberated, but they gave me a strange look. I went back to my garden shed and wept.

Return to Chodecz – Journey's end

That night Grandfather came to me in a dream. 'Get up, go straight back to Chodecz,' he urged. The dream was so vivid I jumped out of bed and began to dress. Only then did I realize it was a dream.

Next day I kept thinking about the dream, trying to understand it. Perhaps Iccio had returned from Russia by now; and perhaps Zosia somehow escaped from the Warsaw ghetto, hiding with a Polish family, and had made it back to our home in Chodecz? Maybe we would all meet up there. Just thinking about it made me long for my family and home.

I told the Fuchses that I had decided to return to my town in Poland as soon as possible.

'When do you think that will be?' asked Mr Fuchs.

'Tomorrow.'

'But tomorrow we've invited Avraham Sztajer and Adam Szwajcer to the house,' said Mrs Fuchs. 'You must stay and celebrate the end of the war with us. And how will you get home?' she added.

What a strange question, I thought. 'I'll walk until I come to a railway station and catch a train, and if there is no train, I'll just keep walking.'

'Do you know the way?' asked Mr Fuchs.

'Yes,' I replied, 'of course I know, I go north east or east and then north.'

The next day Sztajer and Szwajcer and I joined Mr and Mrs Fuchs for a festive dinner to celebrate the end of the war. We had baked potatoes, sauerkraut with sausages, and two bottles of wine. Mrs Fuchs was quite animated as she served the food. Mr Fuchs told us he had been a welder in the 1930s but a serious illness left him unfit for army service so he drove an ambulance instead. He was never a Nazi, he said. He whispered this for fear someone outside might over-hear...

Mrs Fuchs told us she had known Mr Braun from the factory in Dresden for many years and that he was not a Nazi either. I had never been told how my staying with the Fuchses came about. Braun had called them at the Oberpoyritz post office about a young Pole who wanted to work as a gardener, and they had agreed to take me in. They had even thought of adopting me if I turned out to be a fine young person, and now they were hoping I would stay on a bit longer.

'Of course he'll stay!' said Adam Szwajcer and they all laughed, quite merry with wine by now.

'It's time to correct an untruth,' I declared. 'I am a Jew, not a Roman Catholic.'

They all laughed till the tears ran down their cheeks. When they stopped, I told the Fuchses that I was grateful to them for giving me a job and feeding me, and for all their kindness to me, but now I had to start my journey back to Chodecz. One day, soon, I promised, I would come back to visit them.

Mr Fuchs took me to his study and showed me where Chodecz was on the map. He measured the distance as the crow flies which came to about two hundred and fifty miles.

'Here, take this map with you,' he said, and cut the pages out of the atlas for me. 'Aim first for Bautzen and if there's no train there, go on to Görlitz. I will give you my little compass and my bicycle.' Bicycle! I was overjoyed with the gifts. If I could do something like twelve miles a day on foot, I could easily do twenty-five to thirty miles on a bicycle. I could be in Chodecz by 20 May, almost in time for Zosia's birthday.

Mrs Fuchs seemed concerned about my optimistic impulsiveness, my setting off so soon after the end of the war on such a long journey.

'But where will you sleep?' she asked.

'Oh, in the fields or woods,' I answered. 'It's May, it will be getting warmer every day.'

She nodded. 'I will give you a blanket with rubber backing, the one my husband used in the ambulance service.'

'*Danke, Frau Fuchs.*'

I had thought about a blanket, but didn't want to ask her for one. She and Mr Fuchs had done so much for me already. And now she was giving me this wonderful blanket with a rubber backing to keep out the moisture… this really was all I needed. She also gave me a food parcel, some clean, warm underwear and a good pair of lace-up boots she had managed to procure from her neighbour, the young woman who had the little girl.

I tucked the bottom of Herr Fuchs' trousers into my thick socks, and wearing my clean new shirt and Tyrol jacket, considered myself smartly dressed. My hair was longer now and had turned quite blond during the time I had spent working outside in the garden. The thought of home – of finding Zosia and Iccio and perhaps Peccio and his family – made me feel quite giddy.

'I'll come back. I'll visit you in Oberpoyritz one day, you'll see.'

She gave me her hand. I shook it warmly. A German lady shaking hands with a Jew, I thought. How quickly things have changed. Mrs Fuchs' eyes looked sad. For the first time I noticed the darkish hair on her upper lip.

'Do you expect to find your mother when you get back to Chodecz?' she asked.

'No, Mrs Fuchs, not my mother!' I said emphatically.

Mr Fuchs shook hands with me too. 'We and the garden will miss you,' he said, and seemed on the verge of adding something, but then changed his mind and said, 'You worked well… thank you.'

I waved at them and mounted Mr Fuchs' bike which now

belonged to me and cycled off to say goodbye to Avraham
Sztajer and Adam Szwajcer.

They both thought I was crazy to be making my way back
now.

'We can have a nice time here for a few weeks, let things
settle down and then go back to Poland or to Palestine... Stay
with us!' said Adam Szwajcer.

'No, I must go back to Chodecz.' We embraced and they
wished me good luck. 'Good luck to you both,' I shouted from
the distance... I could still see them standing there, waving
to me.

They didn't understand my urgent need to return to
Chodecz, to see my family. Who was still alive? If I had to crawl
on my hands and knees I knew in my heart I would get there. I
stopped to wave at them again but they were gone.

Why had I told Mrs Fuchs that my mother would not be there?
Why was I so emphatic about it? Miracles happen. I never actually saw her dead. She might have, somehow, with the help of
God, survived. As I cycled on, it continued to bother me that I
had spoken with such certainty. Who knows? Perhaps she
would not be in Chodecz when I arrived but maybe she would
get there some time later. Supposing the officer in charge of
the SS in the Lodz ghetto had been a German from Chodecz,
supposing he recognized Mother and sent her to a hospital and
ordered that she be given special care and extra rations. After
all, I had heard stories from men in the Auschwitz group about

inmates with smashed bones who were given six to eight weeks of medical care and good food to see how well they recovered, and when they did, they were transported from Auschwitz to various work places.

I stopped cycling and got off to shake these thoughts from my mind, to force myself, physically, to remember other members of my family and happy times in the past.

As I rang the bell on my handlebars, I thought of my Cousin Misio who had composed a piece for violin and bicycle bell. Whenever he played this piece and nodded his head, I was supposed to ring the bell. He thought my timing rather poor, but when we played the piece for our families after Shabbat, everybody thought highly of it. Misio, I was certain, would return to Chodecz, if only to visit us. I thought of his mother, my Aunt Sabina. She would definitely come back from Kiev, and so would Uncle Ignac. There would be music once again and joy and laughter…

On and on I cycled. That first day of my journey home I must have covered sixteen miles. I could have cycled further but I came across a large shed with lots of straw inside, and took my bicycle inside. I made myself comfortable, ate some of the food Mrs Fuchs had given me, went out, found water, drank and washed, said my prayers, asked God not to fail me on this journey home, covered myself with the blanket and fell soundly asleep. It was light outside when I awoke and began the next stage of my journey.

A signpost indicated the direction to Görlitz. Fortunately, I was on the right road, but it was full of potholes and metal scraps and things that looked like sharp stones. Suddenly, I had a puncture in my rear wheel. Since I had no repair kit I had to cycle on the rim but the wheel became so warped after a while it was easier to walk the bike. No one passed me from either direction. The sun came out and I took off my Tyrol jacket and strapped it to the blanket on the crossbar. Then a little later I took off my shirt and vest. I enjoyed feeling the sun on my body. It brought back memories of being with the other boys in Chodecz, playing naked in the shallows of the river, our backs turning bright red from the summer sun.

I pushed the bike and felt hot and good. There was a smell of spring all around. An open lorry full of Russian soldiers passed me, dodging the big holes in the road. They were singing and I waved to them and shouted *Zdrastvujte*, one of the few words of Russian I had learned from Father who had served in the Czar's army. But they didn't hear me above the din of their singing. One or two waved back to me and within seconds they were merely a speck on the horizon. I tried to ride again, but it was no use. When I looked down I found that my front tyre was also flat. I walked on, pushing my bicycle. There were bigger holes in the road now and more of them, too. I will not be parted from this bike, I resolved. In Chodecz I will have it repaired.

The sun was high above me when I sat down for my first meal of the day. I ate the bread with the cutlet inside it and it tasted so good I had another one and then realized that I had only one left and a very long way to go.

I walked on, my back felt very hot. I saw some wild rhubarb. I tried a stalk. It tasted sour and good, my body seemed to need it. I picked a large quantity and strapped it to the bundle on the crossbar. There was a bullet-riddled building ahead. I called out but no one answered. There was a pump in the grounds. I pumped the handle a few times and water came out, good water, cold and clean. It tasted like Chodecz spring water. I drank some more and then lay down to sleep. When I awoke I gulped more water from my cupped hands. The sun was still hot so I undressed and stood there splashing myself. The sun dried me and I put my clothes on. I was about to leave when a very old lady came out of the wreckage.

'Are you Russian?' she asked in German.

'No, I am a Jew and the war is over.'

She turned round and went indoors without another word. I knocked on the door to ask her for a bottle or container to fill with the good water but she would not answer or open the door.

I began to walk again and came upon a partly broken stone with the word *Bautzen* clearly visible on it but the number of miles was illegible, so I took out my compass and reassured myself that I was going in the right direction. A few miles further on, the landscape changed. Here the trees were broken and the ground was ravaged. Auburn-faced corpses were strewn about the fields along with horses, swollen and stiff, their legs in the air. The air reeked of them. I was sickened and frightened, surrounded by death. I too could be caught and killed in this battle-scarred landscape. I could be accused of looting.

I saw a farmhouse in the distance. There were holes in the walls and part of the roof had been shot away. I lifted my bike over my shoulder and made my way towards it. My plan was to go there and hide till early morning. Everywhere around me cows and horses lay dead. A narrow lean-to ladder led to a loft. I climbed up and had a look around. Part of the roof was missing. A straw-filled mattress lay in the corner. I turned the mattress over. It looked firm, fairly clean. I checked the seams for bugs and lice. I was quite an expert on vermin by this time, as an alumnus of Stutthof. I was clean now and I very much wanted to remain clean.

I went down to get my bike. Slowly I struggled up the ladder with it, my treasure with the two flat tyres. I went down again to look for food but found nothing. I chewed on a couple of rhubarb stalks, then pulled up the ladder and lay it on the floor. It was still too light out to sleep, so I went to the corner where the roof had been shot away and looked down at the dead scattered across the spring fields. I could not understand this waste of life, this murder. Grandfather had once told me that God wants us to be good and happy. I lay down, pulled the blanket over my head and prayed. I felt my back burning and went on praying until sleep overtook me. I awoke at the break of dawn.

Before leaving the farm, I searched for food again. There was nothing anywhere, nothing to eat. As I was heading out, walking under a porch with a pitched roof, I heard a hollow sound under my feet. I walked over it again and again and each time I heard the same hollow sound. I picked up a spade and began to dig. Just below the surface I found a kitchen cupboard with the doors facing upwards. Inside, neatly stacked, were hermetically-sealed jars. I pulled the 'tongue' of red rubber of one jar and tasted the contents. Inside there was meat – delicious-tasting pork.

Very occasionally the Jewish leadership in the Lodz ghetto would receive a small ration of tinned meat. Once when I was collecting such a ration for Leon Chimowicz and his family I tasted a tiny bit of it and imagined the 'goodness' and strength flowing directly to my muscles. I felt better instantly and for days after thought about the meat. It would be my daydream. Under my agreement with Leon C. any meat I received on my ration would go to him and his family.

Now, I sat down and ate the whole jar in one go. I had no utensils to eat with so I broke off a piece of wood and used it as a spoon. I arranged the blanket under the crossbars of my bike as a kind of pouch and put the seven meat jars into it with straw between them. I shut the cupboard doors and covered them with earth and headed off. I crossed the fields of the dead as quickly as I could. Half an hour later I was back on the road to Bautzen.

As I pushed my bike, I felt contented with the food inside me and the thought of having seven jars of meat packed inside the blanket. The sun rose, here the road was no longer full of potholes and most of the trees were intact, not crippled by the war. How good it is to be alive and free, I thought. I had walked for three hours by now, judging by the sun. I took out my compass and found that I was heading east. No one passed me or approached. There was no one anywhere. I couldn't understand why, and I walked on.

Some time later I heard a motorbike in the distance. A Russian soldier drove up. I was pleased to see him. Disliking the SS and the Nazis, I thought of Russians as friends and liberators. *'Ruski ja cie Lublu,'* I said and added, *'Zdrastvuj towarish!'* All learned from my father.

He began to speak in Russian very fast. I smiled and said in Polish that I could not understand him. Then he said, *'Davaj czasy'* ('Give me watches') and showed me a forearm full of watches and repeated the two words again. I told him that I had no watch and showed him my thin, bare forearms. He pointed to the bulging blanket suspended from my bike's crossbars. I took out one jar and handed it to him. The meat was visible through the glass. He looked at it and then at me.

'Tovarish, you have it, please, take it and enjoy it,' I said in Polish. He raised the jar, held it above his head for a second or so and then let it smash to the ground.

'Trousers down,' he said in Russian. I pretended I didn't understand what he meant. He repeated his command and showed me with gestures what he wanted me to do.

I put the bike on the ground carefully so as not to break the jars in the pouch and began to lower my trousers. Why was he making me do this? I couldn't understand. As I was undressing I told him in Polish that I was a Jew, returning to his home town, Chodecz, after spending the war years being punished, tortured, starved, and imprisoned by the SS. I searched my mind for words to convey the German brutalities in the Polish. '*Ja Jevry.*' I hoped he would understand. I looked at him and he stood there unmoved by my words. I repeated again, '*Ja Jevry.* I am a Jew.'

'*Ja Jevry, ja tovarisheh.* I am a Jew, I am a friend.' I stood there naked from the waist down. Instinct told me not to take off my good lace-up boots, lest he grab them and leave me there, bare-footed, so I let my trousers hang down over my socks and boots. I glanced at his eyes. They were indifferent, vacant like a murderer's. He took his revolver out of its holster, pointed it at my head and pulled the trigger. There was a loud click. He put the gun back in the holster, restarted his motorbike and drove off without another word.

I stood there with my trousers down, looking at the jar of precious meat splattered on the road and mixed with broken glass. I thought of picking it up and carefully checking it for slivers of glass. A few weeks earlier I would have done this but now I had other jars in my pouch and the war was over. Why had the Russian soldier done such a thing to me? The Russians were our liberators, they were supposed to be our friends.

I stood there baffled, shaken by the incident, still staring at the meat and glass on the ground where insects now swarmed and I thought, 'All that lovely meat… What a waste, what a terrible waste!'

Finally I reached Bautzen and headed for the railway station. Near the station, in an area cordoned off and heavily guarded by Russian soldiers, there was a crowd of a few hundred civilians, men as well as women. They were standing with their suitcases and bundles. Naturally I assumed they were waiting for a train.

I went up to a Russian guard but he motioned me away so I approached another one who did exactly the same. Then I saw an elderly woman outside the cordoned-off area, walking slowly up the road. I caught up to her, all the while pushing my broken down bike with the pouch of precious jars under the crossbars.

'Excuse me,' I called out in German, 'are these people waiting for the train?' She looked at me and walked on without a word. A man, also elderly, stood in a doorway, peering out. I went up to him and said, 'Are these people waiting for the train?'

'For a special train,' he replied.

'Are they going to Poland?' I asked.

'They are Russians and they are going to Russia,' he answered and turned back into his house.

But that's marvellous, I thought, they'll have to pass through Poland on their way. I went back and tried to push my way into the guarded area where the lucky Russian civilians were waiting for a train to take them back to their homeland, but the guards at the flimsy wooden gate only laughed and waved me away. I went up to them again and began to speak in Polish. I pleaded. They stopped laughing and regarded me stony-faced. 'Niet,' they said, barring my entry.

I was trying to sneak in again when all of a sudden someone

from behind began pulling me. I clung to my bike, trying hard not to drop it with the meat jars in the pouch. This Russian holding me was an officer. He had dark hair and smiling dark eyes and a broad handsome face. Instinct told me that, although he was dragging me away by the collar, here was the person who might be able to help. I began speaking in Polish. I told him about myself. He listened attentively and heard me out. He then answered in fluent Polish, 'Speak faster and tell me everything you want to say.'

I told him I wanted to get back to Chodecz, and asked if he would please help me. He told me to follow him and took me to every guard in the cordoned-off area where Russian civilians and what turned out to be POWs were waiting for the train. He told the guards not to let me through. 'You wait there.' He pointed to a spot some distance away and added, indicating the cordoned-off area, 'If you sneak in and hide among those people I will personally seek you out and shoot you. Do you understand?'

I told him that I did.

'All right. You wait here.'

I set my bike down carefully on the ground, and sat at the appointed spot to wait for him. 'Why is it,' I thought, quite puzzled, 'that even the Russians want to shoot me? Is it because I am a Jew? Perhaps I made a mistake by telling him that I am a Jew?'

I still had one more sandwich left. I had saved it and put it out of my mind. It was now three days old. I took it out and sniffed the meat cutlet inside the bread. It didn't look or smell very fresh. I really wanted to open another jar of pork. I got rid of the filling and kept the bread. It was quite a wrench to throw out the filling but I reasoned that I must do it, because if I spoiled my stomach and became ill I would not be able to get to Chodecz. I opened a jar and with a piece of wood began to eat the meat. Mrs Fuchs' bread still tasted good.

As I sat there absorbed in my bread and meat, an open lorry filled mostly with men guarded by Russian soldiers arrived at the gate of the cordoned-off area. I waited outside until the same officer who had told me he would personally shoot me if I sneaked in, came over and inspected the list and called out the names. One by one they descended from the lorry. Sometimes he would stop people, question them, or chat and laugh, and then let them join the others in the compound. They all carried bundles, sacks or suitcases. How I wished I could be one of them.

I put my food back in the blanket and ran across to tell him I was still waiting.

'Get back,' he shouted. 'Wait where I told you to wait.'

I went back to my place and continued eating my delicious food and watching the people get off the lorry. I drank some water and waited. Some time later the officer called me over and told me to get on the empty lorry. It was the same vehicle that had brought the people to the station.

'Leave the bike here,' he ordered, but I pleaded with him and he asked a soldier to put it on the lorry.

'Where are we going?' I wanted to know.

'Not all the way to Poland. Only as far as Görlitz,' he said. One of the soldiers on the lorry would look after me, he explained, and when we get to Görlitz he would put me on a train bound for Poland.

I thanked him and wanted to give him a jar of meat, but he only smiled and said, 'Hold onto it, your town is many miles away and you'll need this food.'

Six soldiers with guns climbed onto the lorry and two joined the driver in the front cabin. The officer brought one of the soldiers who had sat next to the driver to the rear of the vehicle, pointed towards me and said something to him. Then he went somewhere and brought me a big loaf of bread. I thanked him with all the Russian words I knew: *Pozalsta, spasibo, ja cie lublin.* The other soldiers laughed and so did the officer. I reached out to shake his hand but he motioned to the driver to move out and we were on our way to Görlitz.

We stopped somewhere along the way and more armed soldiers climbed onto the back of the lorry. There was not enough bench space for them so I had to strap my bicycle outside on the back of the lorry. Naturally I put the blanket with the food under the side bench where I sat. The lorry rocked and shook. Some of the soldiers sang *'Moskva moja'* and other songs. They rolled cigarettes with thick black *Machorks* and a few hours later we arrived in Görlitz.

There were hundreds of people waiting outside the railway station. Russian soldiers walked up and down between them.

The soldier assigned to look after me asked me to follow him. Instead of taking me to one of the queues, he took me into the station where a loaded train stood, patrolled by more armed soldiers. My guardian called two of them over and spoke with them, pointing to me. He didn't seem very different from the ordinary soldiers but they sprang to attention when he spoke to them and they treated him with special respect, listened to him attentively. When he finished speaking he gave me a tap on the head and said something I couldn't understand. Then he left. The two guards asked me to follow them.

The train was not unlike the one that had carried us from the Lodz ghetto to Auschwitz, only here the wagons were uncovered and the doors were closed. There were people perched precariously on top of the wagon, looking down and making remarks I failed to catch. The soldiers found a ladder, and one held it while the other climbed up and peered down from the top. I stood by, with the bundle of food slung over my back, holding onto the handlebars of my bike. I had the feeling they would not allow me to take the bike onto the wagon.

'There's space for you but without the bike,' shouted one of the soldiers from the top of the ladder. 'Not the bike,' he repeated, but I pretended not to understand. He pointed to me, ordered me to climb up, shook his head and said 'Niet,' when I asked him whether I could bring my bike up too. The soldier holding the ladder told me to lean the bike against a wall. An officer approached and the soldier quickly told him what it was all about. I asked the officer in Polish if I could take my bike with me. He said it would be too crowded and that I had to leave it behind.

I lowered myself into a corner of the train wagon. A soldier helped me pass down my blanket with the loaf of bread and the jars bundled inside. I sat down on the straw beside a man and woman who looked to be in their late twenties. It was clearly a nuisance for them to move over and rearrange their bags and suitcases. I made myself a snug little nest in the straw and introduced myself to them in Polish. They had been working on a farm, they told me, and were not yet married. When I opened a jar of meat and offered them some, the smell of it was too delicious to refuse. They became more friendly then and produced a spoon with which I scooped out the meat and spread it on three pieces of bread. We ate and talked. Where was I heading, they asked, and I told them.

They passed me a bottle of something that tasted like cold tea with fruit juice, watered down. They were surprised when I told them that I was a Jew.

'But you've just eaten pork!' exclaimed the man.

'Where I worked in Germany,' said his girlfriend, 'I heard that all the Jews in Poland were killed off by the middle of 1944.'

'Well that can't be true, because as you see, I'm still alive,' I said.

I watched them now as they drank from a bottle of alcohol. The man, Zbyszek, had blond hair parted in the middle, revealing a broad forehead; his buxom girlfriend Krysia wore her hair in a single braid. They made some more room for me and I curled up and went to sleep.

It was dark when I awoke. The train was still standing. I tucked the food under my arm, covered myself with the blanket and went back to sleep. The next time I woke up Krysia was sitting on Zbyszek, rocking and laughing. The train was moving.

'What time is it?' I asked them. I wanted to remember the time we left Görlitz.

'It's rocking time,' said Krysia and they laughed again.

When I next opened my eyes it had begun to drizzle. I turned my blanket over to the rubber-coated side, and Krysia and Zbyszek took out a rubber sheet and covered themselves with it.

'We got this and our other things from the hospital where we worked,' explained Zbyszek.

'But Krysia said you worked on a farm,' I said.

'Towards the end of the war we worked in a hospital.'

We sat in silence as dawn was breaking.

'You have so little... Did the Russians take your belongings from you?' asked Krysia.

'They took my bike,' I replied.

'You must have had some lovely things, a pity they've taken them away from you. But you'll be rich again; the Jews know how to get rich,' she said.

Zbyszek said, 'My mother worked for a rich Jewish family before the war. They treated her very well. She sometimes brought home Jewish food... gefilte fish, *kugel*... We liked it a lot.'

•

The train often halted and we were shunted to one side for long periods of time. While we waited, people began lowering themselves to the ground in search of food or drink, to attend to their needs, and if there was a water pump, to take turns washing. One of us took it in turns to remain on guard, to look after our possessions. Although I had only my blanket, jars and a piece of bread, these items were vitally important to me. When it was my turn to go down I learned that the train was going as far north as Lodz.

One night as the train sped on, I was awakened by a pleasant sound – Zbyszek, leaning back against his bundles with Krysia's head on his lap, was whistling the beautiful Polish songs we used to sing in school before the war. I wanted him to go on and on… the music seemed to signify the end of the war.

Zbyszek and Krysia asked where I had been during the war but when I began to talk about Auschwitz, I could see in their eyes that they thought I was inventing the horrors of the place. So I told them about Chodecz instead: about the lake, and how I had been the first in my class to swim across it, about fishing with my friends, and the seasons of the year. As I spoke, I felt such a longing to be back there with my family that tears streamed down my face.

When we arrived at Lodz station I said goodbye to Zbyszek and Krysia. I still had one jar of meat and a crust of bread left. It was 13 May. So many partings, I thought, so many people had come into my life for a matter of days or even hours, and with one goodbye they were gone, probably for ever. It seemed as if I had known Krysia or Zbyszek for much longer than this journey.

Here I was in Lodz again. I was familiar enough with the ghetto but not with the rest of the city. What should I do, where should I go? I wandered aimlessly around the station area in a daze. A man came up to me and asked if I had anything to sell. I walked away without answering. The man followed and again said, 'If you've got something to sell, go to the main Lodz market. If you try to sell it here, you'll be arrested. Where are you from?'

'From Chodecz.'

'Where's that?'

'Near Wloclawek.'

'This is Lodz. Where do you want to go?'

'To the cemetery,' I said.

'Which one?'

'The Jewish cemetery in Marysin.'

'I'll show you the way.'

We walked towards a tram stop. On the way he drew very close and said quietly, 'I'll help you dig the stuff out and we'll split it fifty-fifty. If you want to sell it, I know people who will buy or swap it for other things… What have you got buried there?'

'My father and grandfather.'

He stopped and said, 'You're lying to me.' He took a knife out of his pocket.

'No, sir, I'm not lying. I am going to visit their graves and pay my respects to them. They died in the Lodz ghetto. I was in the Lodz ghetto, too. I don't know these parts of Lodz, but once I reach the ghetto…'

He didn't wait to hear me out but spat on the ground, cursing, and went back to the station.

I took the tram, telling the conductor that I had no money for a ticket. 'You're not the only one,' he replied, waving his hand to indicate that I might as well stay on. I got off when I recognized the ghetto. The barbed wire and the sentry boxes were gone, and so were the wooden bridges, and all the people wearing yellow stars. The well-fed faces I now saw didn't seem to belong to these parts, somehow. It all looked so different to me.

By the time I reached the Jewish cemetery, the day had turned very warm. After so many hours of inactivity on the journey from Görlitz, cramped up in a tiny space, this walk of a few miles utterly exhausted me and I felt weak and faint. I didn't want to take pork meat into the Jewish cemetery, so I hid my last jar somewhere along the outer wall, washed my hands inside, and drank some water. Now I felt better.

First I went to Grandfather's grave, but I couldn't find it. A few years had passed since my last visit to the cemetery and the whole area looked different, as though someone had ploughed it up. My father's grave, further on, was still intact, with the metal plate on which I had engraved an inscription affixed to it.

I stood there and thought about the lovely years with him at home in Chodecz. I began to say the Mourner's *Kaddish*, the prayer for the dead, but couldn't remember the words, so instead I said the *Shema*. Father, I called inwardly, I will pray for you as often as I can, and you too, Grandfather. And may the *Shema* I have just recited elevate your souls and the souls of Szlamek and his son Danus, and those of all members of my family who have died and my friends who were murdered – I will remember you always!

I no longer felt faint, only tired, so very tired. The sun shone on the grave. I put my blanket on it, and lay down and fell asleep. When I awoke the grave was in shadow. I found a stone and placed it on the middle of the grave. I felt strangely happy and well. In Chodecz the men used to wash their hands before leaving the cemetery; so I went back and washed mine and then drank some more water. It tasted good.

'This isn't drinking water,' said the man by the exit.

Outside, I collected my glass jar with the meat inside and began making my way back to the station.

Where the main wooden bridge used to be, near the church, I ran into Miss Rosa. She was helping a small hunchback push a pram with a kitchen cabinet perched on top.

Miss Rosa had been one of the women whose job it had been to serve soup at the metal factory. It was everyone's dream to get a ladle full of the thick soup with potatoes from the bottom of the cauldron instead of the thin liquid from the top, and we would beg Rosa for it with our words or with our eyes. The extra nourishment could spell the difference between life and death. It all depended on whether Miss Rosa liked you or not. I liked Rosa but she neither liked nor disliked me. She ladled some of the soup from the top and some from the bottom. To her I was just a thin, well-behaved but starving youth who had been adopted by Leon Chimowicz.

Rosa was thirty years old. We all knew her birthday, and the birthdays of the other kitchen assistants and soup ladlers who were so important to us. I made her a brooch once out of a piece of aluminium wire, with 'Rosa' written in script.

'Oh, how sweet of you,' she had said as I passed it through the soup kitchen window and put it in her apron pocket.

And now, here she was in Lodz. I was very pleased to see someone from the ghetto still alive.

'Hello, Miss Rosa!'

'Of all the people in the factory, you're the last person I expected to survive. Where did they take you?' she asked.

'To Auschwitz, Stutthof and then Dresden. And you, Miss Rosa?'

'I hid, here in the ghetto.'

I helped her and the little hunchback who had strapped himself to the front of the pram to push it and hold the cabinet steady. We walked and talked about the people we had known at the factory. When I told her I was making my way back to Chodecz, she invited me to stay at her place overnight and catch the train in the morning. I was delighted.

The three of us carried the cupboard up the stairs to the first floor and into her small flat. We sat and talked and she boiled some potatoes for us. 'We can also have some home-brewed vodka a friend gave me,' she said. 'If a *klapsedra* like you could survive the concentration camps, there's hope for others… This is an occasion to celebrate!'

I was touched and told her that I had a jar of pork meat and I carefully drew it out of my blanket. Miss Rosa opened it and tried a spoonful.

'It's heaven!' she exclaimed, giving me a meaty kiss. 'You're an angel!'

Later, after a bath, I got into bed and slipped under the sheets next to Miss Rosa. Her body was warm. Tired out from the train journey and my walk to Marysin and back, I felt I was falling blissfully asleep. But Miss Rosa had other plans. As her hand roved over me, I remembered an incident in Chodecz when I was eight. Podlawski was taking our mare to a stallion and I was allowed to ride her the two miles there. When the stallion was brought out, Podlawksi took me off the mare and led her towards the stallion. She began moving her hind legs apart in an agitated way; and meanwhile, the stallion was positively fierce. He neighed and reared up on his hind legs. His owner, holding him, said to Podlawski, 'Put in the stick, he's ready.'

Miss Rosa's breath reeked of vodka fumes and my under-nourished body didn't respond to her stimulations. I told her how, in Dresden, the chief SS woman would kick us boys in the groin, and how I was often singled out for this – as she really seemed to hate me more than anyone else.

Miss Rosa stopped doing what she was doing, 'Why didn't you tell me straight away? You poor thing – now I understand it all.'

The following morning, she saw me off at the station. It was chaotic: people were lying on their bags everywhere, asking for tickets, pushing their way through, accompanied by Russian soldiers. Miss Rosa told me to wait, and some moments later came back and handed me a paper to sign. 'Do you have some sort of identity card?'

I looked at her in bewilderment, 'No, nothing like that.'

I followed her into the station master's office.

'This is my young cousin,' she said to the station master, touching his face. 'You're a sweetie,' she cooed, as if she had known him for years. We came out with a signed, countersigned and stamped document, allowing me to travel by train from Lodz to Chodecz and back again.

She waited with me at the station for a long time, and when the train pulled in there was a terrible scramble, and once again she told me to wait right where I was. She returned with a man wearing a railway uniform. He helped Rosa put her 'cousin' on the train. This time the train had proper compartments and carriages, although there were no more seats available.

I waved to her from the window and she blew me a kiss and her lips formed words I could no longer make out. It was good to be on this train, going back to Chodecz. I made myself comfortable in a corner near the corridor, sitting on my blanket.

At one point, the train stopped for about half an hour and Russian soldiers came aboard and questioned people and searched their bundles. They prodded the bulge in my pocket.

'What's this?' they asked.

It was my crust of bread. I showed them the travel paper, but it didn't interest them and they moved down the compartment.

I kept thinking of my family, praying some of them would still be alive. The day before, at Father's grave, when I named all those I knew were dead, I had intentionally left out Mother, Sala and her two children, Zosia, Iccio, and Peccio and his family. Since I never actually saw them dead, I could continue to hope against hope that they were still alive and would be waiting for me in Chodecz when I arrived...

Towards evening, the train arrived at Chodecz station, some four miles from the town. I decided to sleep in the waiting hall until first light the following day. Other passengers got off and faded into the darkness. I looked closely, but I didn't recognize anyone. A man wearing a railway worker's cap came over and asked me to leave because it was his job to lock up the waiting room. 'Where can I sleep until early morning?' I asked him.

'Have you got something valuable on you to give me?' he asked.

'Not really.'

'Well, how about your lace-up boots? I'll find you a room with a bed for them.'

'No, I need my boots, but thank you.'

His face did not look familiar to me.

'So what else can you give me if I let you sleep on my bed?'

All I had were the two pages of the map, the compass Mr Fuchs had given me, and the blanket. 'Either the compass now or the blanket tomorrow, when I wake up.'

He examined the compass with childish interest, as if it were something he had always wanted. He pocketed it and asked me to follow him. We entered a small room where there were brooms, buckets and tools. 'You can sleep here,' he said, pointing to a cot in the corner with a straw mattress on it.

'Are you hungry?'

'Yes, I am.'

He unlocked a rather lovely wooden cupboard, and took out a round loaf of bread from one of the shelves. With a hacksaw-like blade he cut me a slice of it and smeared it with a brown, gravy-like substance, then wiped the blade with his thumb and index fingers, licked them, and said, 'Here, that will settle your stomach. There's drinking water in here.'

He pointed to a bucket with a lid, took out the compass, looked at it again, and smiled.

'It's a nice piece, this... I've got to lock you in from the outside, but I will be here around five o'clock tomorrow morning.'

Before leaving, though, he locked the cupboard, and added conversationally, 'This is an old piece of furniture. It must have belonged to some pious Jewish family. That's where they kept their prayer books. The books were no good to me so I burned them. No one could understand the mumbo-jumbo inside.'

There were no windows in the store room, but I slept well. When the man came to wake me before dawn, I was in the middle of a dream. In it, I was carrying an enormous sack full of prayer books on my back. Grandfather, who walked beside me, picked up the books that kept falling out. He stuffed them back in the sack and said, 'You have to bring them to a proper burial.' Jewish prayer books and 'holy' books which contain the name of God are given a burial similar to people.

'But Grandfather, they're too heavy, I can't carry them any more.' I was bent to the ground and could hardly breathe.

It was a relief when the man opened the door and announced loudly, 'It's five a.m. There's a *doroszka* to Chodecz you can catch in about an hour.'

'I don't have any money. I'll walk instead. It'll only take me an hour or so.'

'Hey,' he said. 'Those are nice boots.'

'Yes,' I said and began to lace them up. He stood there wondering what else he could get from me. 'All right,' he said, as if outdone, 'I'll slice you another piece of bread for the road.' This time he didn't spread fat on it.

I thanked him, folded the blanket, and put the bread in my pocket. Just as I was tying the blanket in a bundle over my shoulder, I noticed initials scratched on the cupboard doors. I knew this cupboard: it was the same one we children in *heder* had kept our books in. Seeing it here now saddened me.

'*Dziekuje i dowidzenia* (thanks and goodbye),' I said.

•

It was not quite 6 a.m. on 15 May 1945, when I set off on the last leg of my journey back to Chodecz, with nothing but a blanket, the travel papers no one had bothered to inspect, two pages of an atlas, a piece of bread and a heart full of hope and longing for my family.

I strode briskly, like a marathon walker who knows the finish line is just around the corner. The air was fresh, the sun shone brightly. Every tree, every bend in the road, every ditch and field and house I saw looked dear and familiar. I even recognized some of the dogs that barked in greeting though they were old now.

I decided not to call on anyone until I had first seen the Podlawskis at their house on Lesna 1, the house Father had built for them.

I wondered how they were. I wondered how his sister-in-law's family – Mrs Lewandowska, my lovely wet-nurse – all were. My heart beat faster as I thought of my family and our home, of Lewandowska and the Podlawskis.

I passed the house with the wheel on the roof where the storks would nest. I had arrived before the storks, before the swallows. The houses I passed looked smaller to me. Will the lake still be as big as I remember it, I wondered.

I walked on and eventually came to Lesna 1. Mrs Podlawska opened the door.

'Romek! Come in, come in, my boy! Oh how thin you look!' She turned and shouted, 'Stasiek!'

Mr Podlawski, for as long as I could remember, had been an early riser. He would arrive at our barn to groom the horses just after 5 a.m., day in, day out. He had even worked on Sundays and would then go to church with his wife and daughters.

It was now nearly seven. Podlawski emerged from the kitchen wearing only the vest and long johns in which he had probably slept. He said nothing when he saw me, but only stared at me in disbelief. Then he embraced me and held me like this for a long while. There were tears in his eyes when he let me go. I was in Chodecz again, the war was over.

Mrs Podlawska embraced me too, and as she did, she felt me all over with her hands as though purchasing a goat at the market. 'You're all skin and bones, child.'

It had been almost five years and a thousand worlds since she last saw me, and I did not feel like a child any more.

'Come here, have a plate of *zur*.' This was the sour soup with potatoes they ate for breakfast. 'But first, drink a glass of water.'

I had forgotten about her morning glass of water. She was convinced that a glass of water, first thing in the morning, helped to regulate the system and remove impurities.

Podlawski asked about Mother and Father... what was the news? Where were they?

'Leave the lad alone, Stasiek, let him eat his soup first!' I ate and listened to Podlawski and answered an occasional question.

'So, he died of starvation, you say? He was only eight years older than me... and Grandfather, such a good and clever man.'

Father was clever too, I thought.

Podlawski screwed up his eyes, as he did when he had something profound to say. 'Do not mention to anyone around here that your father is dead,' he added.

'Why not?'

'It may not be to your advantage,' he said, tapping his nose with his index finger. 'You'll have time to tell the bad news later on. Most of them are not your well-wishers. Hold out, my boy, be wise, tell them only as much as is good for you.'

I sat opposite him and listened, enjoying Mrs Podlawska's sour soup and the slice of bread with pork dripping. I found myself nodding approval to everything he said. 'And Mother, what happened to her?' he asked.

I told him what I knew, and added, 'But one hopes, perhaps...' I couldn't finish the sentence. Mrs Podlawska sat resting her elbows on the table, holding her face in her hands. She didn't say a word.

'The Nazis were a bad lot,' said Podlawski. 'They must have sent your mother to Chelmno where most of the Jews from Lodz went. Your aunt and cousins from Izbica were all sent there.'

It was the first time I had heard of Chelmno and asked him whether it was a concentration camp. 'No, just a place where the Nazis murdered Jews by the thousands, seven days a week, around the clock... Oh, they were a bad lot, those Nazis.'

I told him about Sala and her children and about my cousin Szlamek Halter who had arrived in the Lodz ghetto in 1943, looking so well and fit. Podlawski just repeated, 'And poor Sala and her children... and poor Pan Szlamek from Izbica...'

Mrs Podlawska suddenly interrupted, 'Did you get that parcel we sent you?'

'Yes, *dziekuje*, thank you... You can't imagine how much it meant to me, not just the food, though it was delicious and I was so hungry, but to know that you cared... It was like a message of hope; it made me feel stronger and more determined to survive...'

We sat in silence for a while after my long recital of thanks. I went back to my soup and wiped the plate clean with a piece of bread, watched in silence by the Podlawskis. And then, as if talking to myself, I said, 'You were angels to send that food to me. I will never forget it, never!'

'You know, I helped your father and Szlamek bury a big oak chest,' said Podlawski. 'He filled it with things he bought from your Uncle Ignac and Aunt Sabina's shop, like tea and soap and tobacco. The chest is padlocked and I have the key to it.'

I said that my father had told me about the chest and how to find it – a certain number of paces beyond the last shed.

'Did he tell you about the possessions your parents left with us?'

'No, I don't know anything about that.'

Mrs Podlawska began to point heavenwards, and then I realized that it was actually towards the ceiling. 'Wait, woman! Let me tell him in my own time!'

Podlawski considered himself the boss with our plough and horses, as with his wife and their three daughters. Though he tended to think and speak slowly, he hated being interrupted.

We now sat in silence while he cooled his temper and found a way to continue. Mrs Podlawska stood up, took my empty plate away, and without asking, ladled more soup into it and set it in front of me. 'Go on... enjoy it.'

Podlawski reached for a tin box, opened it, took out tobacco, and began to roll himself a very thin cigarette. Then he licked the tissue paper, put the cigarette in his mouth, and continued.

'Your father stored a heap of tobacco in the oak chest. He guessed that there would be a shortage of it after the war, and that other staples like tea and coffee would also be in short supply. If you want to make me happy, please save some of the tobacco for me.'

'Of course I will.'

'Some tea would be nice too, for when the girls come to visit,' said his wife. Podlawski tapped his tobacco tin and said, 'They only sell it nowadays in exchange for meat or sugar.' Mrs Podlawska added, 'We can't afford the meat, but Stasiek cannot give up his smokes.'

I clearly remembered how men at Stutthof would trade a vital bite of bread for a puff on a cigarette.

Mrs Podlawksa raised her head from her hands and said, 'I think that you ought to open the chest now and bring the stuff back here.'

'All in good time, all in good time... When Zosia and Iccio return,' said Mr Podlawski. 'Didn't he just say they're coming back?'

From the moment I entered the Podlawskis' house, I had

been waiting to hear news of my family. I wanted to ask: 'Has anyone been in touch with you recently?' But I was afraid to be told: 'No, we haven't heard from anyone.' So I said nothing, filled though I was with expectation and longing – for my mother, my sisters and my brothers...

I continued putting away my second helping of *zur* as I listened to Mr Podlawski. I realized that what he had said a few moments before about the people of Chodecz not being 'well-wishers' was probably true, though I had hoped otherwise. After all the suffering in the ghetto and the camps, Chodecz and its people had acquired a kind of heightened reality for me – or was it an unreality? I had been so eager to go out and see them, but that was before Podlawski's warning. Now something inside prompted, as if a voice were whispering the words: There's no hurry, Romek, this is the journey's end.

Podlawski went on talking about tobacco and the way people mixed it with impurities nowadays, even dry potato leaves. As he spoke, I returned to my thoughts: here I was with the people who had known me since birth, people who had seen me every day of my life until I was twelve years old – kind, affectionate people I could trust. The word 'love' I reserved for my wet-nurse, Mrs Lewandowska... but she had so many children of her own. How would she feel towards me after so many years? Still, the war was over, I would soon go to see her. Hitler and his SS were defeated; no need to hurry now.

Podlawski was now telling me about the clothes my parents

had asked him to keep in the loft. Mrs Podlawska did not interrupt him.

'You see, my boy, when Hitler's armies defeated Poland, they
started confiscating things from the Jews, so your mother and
father asked me to hide their fine clothes. They're all up there,'
he said, pointing to the ceiling, as Mrs Podlawska had before. I
felt I was expected to say something in response.

'Neither my father nor my mother mentioned the clothes, so
maybe they intended you to keep what they gave you to hide.'

'No!' said Podlawski emphatically. 'These things belong to
the Halter family and I shall only keep what they give me.'

Mrs Podlawska shifted uneasily in her seat till she could no
longer contain herself.

'Romek needs the clothes, he needs shirts and things. We
need a plough and a couple of piglets. If we ask Celina, she'll
get everything we need and more in exchange for one of your
mother's fur coats. Stasio, should we wait and wait? Romek told
you that Mr Halter is dead and he himself needs so many
things...'

Now that she had spoken her mind, we all sat in silence for a
while.

'How are Celina, Marysia and Genia?' I asked. Mrs Podlawska told me that all three daughters had left Chodecz and
were living in the city. Celina, the middle and brightest daughter, was married, but had no children yet. I asked after Mrs
Podlawska's sister, my lovely wet-nurse Mrs Lewandowska.

'Yes, she's still in Chodecz.'

We talked on and on, and then Mrs Podlawksa warmed some water for me in a huge pot on the stove and rolled the tub out from behind the screen. I scrubbed myself from head to toe. Then she gave me one of her husband's clean vests, a pair of long johns, and some trousers, which she altered for me on the spot with the old Singer sewing machine my mother had given her. I watched her as she cut a wedge of material from the back, and tucked in the waist to make the trousers fit me, looking like she used to when she sewed for us before the war. Then she gave me a clean, collarless shirt and a pair of socks. The lace-up boots and the Tyrol jacket looked fine, she said. Clean and fed and spruced up, I went off with Podlawski to greet the town of Chodecz.

No one recognized me.

'They don't expect you here; they think you're dead, like all the other Jewish people in this town and in all the other towns in the region,' said Podlawski.

I wanted to see our house first. It looked neglected and small. Three families were living there now. The woman who opened the door did not invite me in; her parting words to me before she closed the door were, 'You Jews built this house with our money and our sweat. Now it's our turn to live here!'

'But how can you say such a thing? The house belongs to my family and to me.'

'I can say anything I like… Get out, go away!'

We didn't see the other two families, but went into the

timber yard instead. It was neglected and completely empty. We walked over to where my father had told me that the chest was buried. Podlawski confirmed that this was the spot. The whole place looked shabby; the fence boards over which I had called to Karol Eszner were either loose or torn away.

'It's only been this way since the Germans were chased out,' said Podlawski.

'Are the Eszners still alive?' The Eszners were *Volksdeutsche*.

'Only Mrs Eszner. She lives in one room facing the street,' said Podlawski.

I made a mental note to return to visit her, but it was too sad to see our house. I wouldn't return just yet.

As we walked down the street, we met Marysia Giewis. She was a year older than me but had been in the same class at school before the war. Now she was a grown-up, well-developed woman, yet I pictured myself standing in front of her like the same twelve-year-old boy I used to be. She didn't recognize me at first. I said it was nice to see her, after so many years... and I enquired after her parents and sisters. They were all well, she said. We went on chatting for a while, though she seemed tongue-tied and didn't ask after my family.

'Please do come and see us. I run the shop almost single-handedly now.' Her father, Mr Giewis, had been the Polish butcher and sausagemaker before the war.

We headed for the market square and Podlawski told me about what had happened there in 1941. 'They got the Jews here – they were probably from Izbica, or Kowal or Klodawa. The SS made them lie face down on the cobblestones, and beat them till they bled. *Juden, Juden*, they said. And the SS told us that anyone who gave them food would be rounded up and punished. We knew what 'punished' meant. Witek Bog took food out to the Jews in the forest. His mother had to hide him in a pit under the floor for the rest of the war. She would take him out for air at night. You'll see – he looks like he's made of wax and his mother must have aged twenty years.'

My eye rested on some paving slabs with Hebrew and Yiddish on them. They were tombstones from our Jewish cemetery.

'Could we please go and see Mrs Lewandowska?'

'You go,' said Mr Podlawski. 'I'll show you where she lives now and make my way home. I won't come in. We'll eat at six o'clock or whenever you get back.'

Podlawski had been engaged to marry Lewandowska at one time but something happened and he married her sister instead. Now he was always a bit awkward around his sister-in-law and distanced himself from her. Mrs Lewandowska, on the other hand, was as easy and natural towards him as she was towards everyone else.

The walk through town saddened me. The Jews I remembered so well were no longer in their little homes… I could see them in my mind's eye going off to synagogue or to market early in the morning. I remembered their faces, the way they walked, and the way they dressed.

'Do you still work?' I asked Podlawski.

'During the war I had to work for a German farmer. Now I work the land that belongs to your parents. I claimed it back for them with the paper that your father gave me at the beginning of 1940. There will be enough food there for us all.'

When the Germans were driven out of Chodecz towards the end of 1944, he said, he and his Celina had taken the deed my father wrote out for them to the town hall. They had spoken with some workers there who agreed to stamp and date the document with the pre-war stamps they had hidden in their homes during the course of the war.

'There were German stamps there too, but I didn't want German stamps on your father's document,' he said. 'Of course we need a horse and stable and a plough, but we'll manage.' And then he added. 'I hope other members of your family get back to Chodecz, but if they don't, would you mind our sharing the land? It will feed us and it gives me something to do.'

'Of course I don't mind,' I said as we walked, feeling his happiness. 'Maybe one day soon you'll be able to buy a horse of your own.'

'This war has left us all on crutches. You can't expect a man with crutches to run a race.'

I had forgotten Podlawski's old sayings.

'But soon you won't need crutches any more.'

'We'll see, we'll see... it all depends on the Bear...' he said before leaving me to go to see Mrs Lewandowska, while he made his way home. The Polish peasants called Russia "the Bear".

•

Mrs Lewandowska lived on the upper level of a house that had belonged to a Jewish family before the war. The front door was slightly ajar so I walked past the kitchen and knocked gently on the sitting-room door. Inside I found Mrs Lewandowska hand-sewing something. She wore glasses. Her hair, gathered in a bun at the back, had gone grey. She was forty-six, I knew, because she was two years younger than my mother. I had not seen her for five years, and though she still looked lovely to me, she seemed to have aged quite a bit. There was a young woman sitting at the table with her back to me. My knock on the door and entrance went unnoticed. I stood there looking at Mrs Lewandowska and the young woman's back. Mrs Lewandowska peered over her glasses.

'No, I don't believe it… my little hero is back!' she shouted, and rushed towards me still holding her sewing. She pressed me to her bosom. Her glasses fell off. She kissed me on the forehead and on the cheeks and I kissed and hugged her.

'Is your father alive?'

'No, he died,' I said.

'What about your mother?'

She went through the names of every member of my family.

The young woman got up from the table and stood close by, watching us and smiling. It was Jadwiga. I saw her now as if for the first time. She was lovely. Did I detect my father's features in her face – for she had his mouth and his grey-blue eyes? She embraced me and I felt like a child beside her. She was in the full bloom of her womanhood, as developed as Marysia Giewis, whom I had seen earlier that day.

'I work in Wloclawek,' she said. 'I just arrived.'

'And I've also just arrived,' I said.

We both laughed. Mrs Lewandowska told me there would be a family gathering the following day because Jadwiga, who worked for the government, had heard that settlers from Poland could get land virtually free in the newly-acquired parts of East Germany that were now annexed to Poland.

'We're thinking of settling there.'

'Are you sure?' I asked.

'Jadwiga and I think it's a good idea.'

Jadwiga was in fact filling in the forms she must have brought with her from Wloclawek.

'When did you arrive in Chodecz?' asked Mrs Lewandowska.

I told her I had gone directly to the Podlawskis.

'About the territories, it's still a secret, so please don't tell my sister and brother-in-law or anyone else in Chodecz.'

Jadwiga went to the kitchen to prepare something to eat. I followed her and we chatted there. She avoided questioning me about my family and our life during the five years of the war. We talked about our pre-war Polish classmates and she told me that most of them had gone to look for work in Wloclawek, Lodz, Warsaw, Poznán and Torún. When we came back from the kitchen, Mrs Lewandowska was sitting on the stool, tears streaming down her face. I put my arm around her.

'You will come with us, Romek, we will all go to the new territories and begin a new life. There is nothing left for you here. No one will care for you,' she sobbed.

'But someone is bound to be alive. Iccio may come back from Russia. Or Peccio and his wife and child or my sister Zosia... who knows, even my mother may still be alive somewhere. You'll see, other Halters will show up soon... I was the first one here, that's all.'

'Please God, please God, let it be so,' said Mrs Lewandowska, heaving a great sigh, not raising her eyes from the sewing.

Jadwiga said that a number of Jews had returned to Wloclawek, and that she would go to the new Jewish registration office there the following day and put up a notice that I was back in Chodecz and looking for my Halter relations.

We talked about the old days. Mrs Lewandowska remembered the time I went to play with Karol Eszner wearing my best synagogue suit. I was about to set off for the synagogue with Father and Grandfather, and Karol and I were walking along the rim of the bog when suddenly I fell into the stinking slime. I hurried home to Mrs Lewandowska who poured buckets of water over me, and had me changed in time for services.

Mrs Lewandowska sighed again.

'Your father and mother left some belongings with me. Your father had a false bottom made in the chest and only I know how to take it out. You will need these things to set yourself up.'

'What I really need is for my family to get back to Chodecz right away.'

•

'You'll never guess what's in there,' said Mrs Lewandowska, pointing to the chest.

'Your family silverware, the Passover silver and the goblets, your father's manuscripts and his collection of gold coins... and other things... they're all in here, this innocent-looking coffer.'

'You're not leaving for the new territories just yet and I'll be here for a while, and other Halters are sure to return... Dear Mrs Lewandowska, there'll be plenty of time later to take the things out of the chest.'

Mr Lewandowski worked in Kowal, she said. Every day he would come home, and then immediately set off again to fish.

'Fishing is his life. I am only the mother of his children,' she sighed.

'I'll come back tomorrow,' I said.

'Yes, come and spend some time with us all tomorrow. We'll eat and drink and talk, and you'll be part of the clan.'

She stood up from her sewing stool, embraced me and said, 'May God send them to you, my boy. We must live in hope that some of them are still alive and will soon return.'

She paused and then looking me in the eye added quietly, 'We will not leave you all alone here. You will come with us to the western territories of the new Poland.'

When I returned to Lesna 1, Podlawski had taken all the clothes down from the loft and spread the coat and the furs out on the bed, the table and floor. The whole room stank of moth-balls.

'There's nothing here for me to wear, really,' I said. 'This was Mother and Father's stuff. You should keep it.'

'We could buy a couple of piglets and a plough in exchange for that,' said Mrs Podlawska, pointing at Mother's fur coat, 'plus some things for you.'

Podlawski was angry with her. 'Wait, woman, didn't you hear what he said? Someone else in the family may turn up before long… Don't start dancing on their empty graves.'

'But I'm sure Mother would like you to have her coat to buy whatever you need now. Later… when she returns… if she needs a coat, I'll buy her the finest one in the world.'

Mrs Podlawska took the fur coat and carefully wrapped it in a sheet, and without so much as a glance at her husband, she put it in the huge chest that stood against the wall.

'Celina will help me sell it well,' she said. 'This is a job for us women.'

That night I couldn't fall asleep. The dreams and longings that had given me strength over so many months had now ended with my return to Chodecz. I felt completely alone. Out of all the Jewish people of the town, I was, so far, the only one who had returned. How many others would come back? Chodecz seemed so different without the Jews, without their shops and businesses. It was unreal: no longer my home town. As I lay in the corner of Mr and Mrs Podlawski's room, I wept and prayed. I felt lost. I didn't know where to go from here.

•

The following day I walked around the town on my own. There were no traces of our synagogue. The spot overlooking the lake, where it once stood, had been ploughed over. From there I walked to the cemetery on the outskirts of Chodecz.

I said the few verses of *Kaddish* that I could still remember, adding my own words of prayer in memory of my relatives and friends and all the Jews of Chodecz who had died. The wind blew in my face, and I felt like the only human being alive. In my mind's eye, I saw the field at Bautzen, with all the dead lying there, and then I saw before my eyes the murder of my Jewish friends at the quarry outside Chodecz in the spring of 1940…

Looking up, just beyond the cemetery, I could see the knacker's yard, and next to it the strange little house where the town's dog-catcher lived. He had been feared as much by the children of Chodecz as by its dogs.

'If you don't finish everything on your plate, the dog-catcher will get you,' people used to say.

From time to time the dog-catcher would come to our house to buy timber, and from my hiding place, I would watch him talking with my father, studying his bushy eyebrows and his one round eye.

I took another route back to town, past the tree where they used to set the stretcher with the corpse on the ground while the rabbi delivered his eulogy. Women were not allowed to go beyond this point in the cemetery. As the corpse lay there, its face uncovered for all to see, people would sometimes fall upon it, kissing it and weeping and shrieking until the rabbi began his speech with a short prayer.

Once I had run ahead of the cortège together with the other boys and I had climbed this tree. From here I had the best view of the corpse, that of a toothless old woman who used to come to us every Friday, when Mother would give her food for the Shabbat and money for her family. As I handed her the 'goodies' she would open her mouth three or four times like a fish and eventually say in Yiddish, 'Thank you and blessings on your family.'

I knew what she was going to say but Mother told me that I must wait and listen and answer her, 'And blessings on you, Mrs Moskowitz, and on your family.'

And she would wink at me and depart.

As I sat on my branch, listening to the most dramatic moment of the rabbi's speech, when his voice reached a crescendo and the women howled and the men sobbed, I clearly saw Mrs Moskowitz open her mouth and give me a wink. At that moment, I shouted at the top of my voice, 'She's alive, she opened her mouth and winked at me!'

The rabbi stopped speaking, the women stopped howling, and the men looked up angrily. Someone pulled me off the branch and gave me a few smacks. At home I got another hiding.

'You certainly put your foot in it there, didn't you,' said Zosia. 'How can an old woman, who's completely dead, *wink* with her *mouth*!'

As I stood there remembering this, I decided to climb to a higher branch. The tree seemed so much smaller now. I closed my eyes and tried to envision the funeral.

The dog-catcher drove by slowly in a cart pulled by an emaciated horse. I was glad he didn't see me; otherwise the whole town would soon have known that Romek, nearly eighteen, had been sitting on a branch of the 'funeral' tree. I climbed higher and looked across the fields towards the edge of the forest where our land was; where Mrs Lewandowska had once led the potato pickers in the last hours of her pregnancy. The field had been ploughed. Podlawski must have planted a new crop of potatoes there.

From there I went off to visit my old school, Szkola Powszechna. It looked much as I remembered it, an elegant three-storey building in the classical style. In front of the façade there was a large courtyard area with some trees and a playground where we would spend some time in the breaks. I saw the window on the second floor in the centre of the building, above the steps leading to the entrance, where the headmistress would sit, watching the children come in, occasionally summoning some of them to her office to be reprimanded if they had come late, or behaved badly on the way to school, which she could clearly see from this window. I asked a youth standing outside whether he knew Mrs Wisniewska who used to teach there before the war. He led me to the adjoining building where all the teachers used to live.

I knocked on Mrs Wisniewska's door and waited. There was a

sound of bolts and locks and through a small gap, I saw Mrs Wisniewska peering out at me behind the chained door. 'It's Romek Halter,' I said and asked if I could come in to see her. She opened the door and let me in.

'Sit here,' she said, looking me over from top to toe, and as she did, a thought ran through my mind. In Chodecz when older pupils or ex-pupils visited a teacher it was customary to bring a gift. I explained that I had come empty-handed because I had no means at present to buy anything. She waved my remark aside.

Mrs Wisniewska was now in her forties, still pretty, with a round face, blue eyes, a small, typically Polish nose and a nicely-shaped mouth. She was short and still blond. Mrs Podlawska, I had noticed, had rotting teeth, but Mrs Wisniewska's were still lovely. I remembered the way she smiled the day Mother brought me to school for an interview when I was six. I had fallen in love with her at first sight.

'Tell me, Romek, when did you get back to Chodecz and where were you during the last five years?'

I began telling her about the years of starvation in the Lodz ghetto and mentioned in passing how helpful it had been to record my daily experiences there in writing, and that my mother had always said I had been very fortunate to have a good teacher like Mrs Wisniewska... and that perhaps now I ought to become a writer.

'Your mother was a dear friend. But remember, Romek, only the craft of writing can be taught, not the art of it. I tried to teach you grammar, structure, spelling... perhaps I taught you to think clearly so that you could write clearly. But in the end, a writer is an artist, and no one can tell you how to become an artist, how to breathe life into the characters you write about. I hope you haven't come to me to ask whether you should become a writer or not because I couldn't possibly tell you that.'

I had come to see her without a plan, without wishing her to tell me anything. I just had to tell someone I liked that I was alive, that I had returned to Chodecz.

'How is Mr Wisniewski?' I asked. Mr Wisniewski had taught us Maths and Physical Education, but since he disliked P.E., he would always take us marching instead.

'He's dead,' she answered. 'He was an officer in the Polish army. The Russians killed him.'

She was extremely blunt and matter of fact, so much so that I found it difficult to talk with her, to ask her more about Mr Wisniewski or about her son, yes, her only son.

She sighed. I told her very briefly the rest of my story while she sat there looking at me with an expressionless face. From time to time she shook her head as if to the rhythm of my words, but all the time her blue unblinking eyes looked into mine.

'So what will you do now?'

I told her I was waiting for members of my family to come back; surely, some of them had survived. When they returned we would move back into our old house together.

'Did you speak with the people who are living in your house?'

I told her that there were three families living there now and that I had spoken to one of them.

'The woman I spoke to was nasty and shut the door in my face,' I said.

'You should not have talked to her. They may come after you now. Law and order haven't been restored yet, and they could easily murder you rather than argue or give up a room to you.'

I sat there, stunned by her words.

'To them you are a Jew worth this much,' she said snapping her fingers. 'No one will protect you here... Some Poles think that what the Nazis did to the Jews was right. Listen carefully, Romek, if you should see something that once belonged to your parents, don't claim it, just say, "How nice that you have this now. Mother and Father would be glad..." Romek, I'm glad you came to see me. You need my help to think out how you're going to survive here on your own.'

We sat there in silence for a while and sipped herbal tea.

'You have relations abroad?'

I told her about my aunt in Switzerland and Mrs Wisniewska said, 'Go see her. And keep a low profile while you wait for your brothers or sisters to return. Don't wander around too much on your own and don't talk "big" to anyone.'

I kissed her hand the way she had taught us to in the first year of school. She smiled.

'Come and see me soon the way you did today... You used to draw so nicely, draw me a flower and bring it to me.'

•

I went directly to my parents' house to speak to the woman I had seen the day before. Either she and her family were out or they saw me through the window and decided not to come to the door, so I went to the back of the house and knocked on the kitchen door. The man of the second family that now lived in our house opened the door in a friendly manner. He must have been expecting someone else because when he saw me his expression changed. His eyes became piercingly cold.

'What do you want here, little Jew?' he said.

I began with the words Mrs Wisniewska had suggested.

'I have news for you. I will soon be leaving Chodecz for good, and going to live with my aunt in Switzerland. I was wondering if you'd like me to sign any sort of document renouncing my claim to your part of the house… Of course the same goes for the other two families living here.'

'What's the catch?' he asked.

'No catch. I'll be here living with Mr and Mrs Podlawski for a couple of weeks and then I'll be off for good. If you and the others would like me to sign a document, write one out and I'll come and sign it. We'll shake hands and drink a glass of vodka and that will be that…'

He studied me, his eyes narrowing, and finally said, a little suspicious still,

'Come in then and have a glass of vodka with me.'

He opened our kitchen cupboard and there on the bottom shelf were many bottles of different shapes and sizes, all filled with a murky liquid. He opened a bottle and poured out two glasses.

'*Na zdrowie*,' he said and then added, 'to good health, to this house – yours yesterday, mine today.'

He nearly emptied the glass with a single gulp. It was a deadly drink and it numbed my mouth.

'A cousin of mine in Przedecz makes this stuff. My wife helps him brew it… Someone in the family has to earn a living.' He gave a laugh, relaxed and happy now.

'I tell you, my friend,' he added, no longer addressing me as 'little Jew'. 'It's the best vodka in the whole world… A Russian would give his balls for a bottle of this stuff.'

'Oh absolutely,' I said. 'When I leave you I'll have to go sit a while out past the sheds to clear my head. I'm not really used to drinking.'

Then I pulled myself up and added, 'I haven't tasted such great vodka in years. Could you sell me a bottle perhaps? I'm going to the Lewandowski family from here and I'd like to bring them a present. I'll pay you as soon as I have some money.'

'Sure, my friend,' said the new owner of this part of our house, handing me a small bottle and then immediately snatching it back again and exchanging it for a bigger one.

'This part of the house is worth a big bottle, my fine little friend, so enjoy it. It will dry up all your tears.'

With this he gave me a friendly slap on the back that sent me flying across the kitchen and almost made me drop the deadly bottle. My host tipped back another glass with a single gulp, wiped his mouth, reached out to me and began to pump my hand. '*Dowidzenia, Dowidzenia*. Go, sit on your land and let your childhood memories clear your head. This was your house once and we all want you to enjoy it for as long as you're in Chodecz. So come as often as you like, my dear little friend, as often as you like.'

I left him there.

'I don't believe it,' said Mrs Lewandowska to her family. 'Yesterday he turns up with only the rags on his back, and today he brings us a bottle of vodka more precious than gold dust!'

'How did you manage that?' asked Mr Lewandowski, slapping me good-naturedly on the back. But he did not wait for me to explain. He took the bottle out of Mrs Lewandowska's hands and began to open it. This brought on a flurry of excitement. Jadwiga put glasses on the table – I was relieved that they were tiny – and Mr Lewandowski began filling them.

'To a good life in the new territories,' he said raising his glass, and without further ado, he threw back his head and emptied the glass.

'I think Romek should definitely come with us. He'll help us become the richest landowners in the territory and keep us in vodka, too,' said Mr Lewandowski after two drinks and more laughter.

To avoid having to drink I went over to the Lewandowski 'boys' and shook hands with them. We started reminiscing – the time we climbed the fence and stole apples, or the time Mietek Kowalski was shot in the bum with salt pellets, or that autumn night we made a bonfire and roasted rooks on a spit and baked potatoes in the ashes, or the time we uncovered a bees' nest and had to jump into the river and duck under the water to escape their fiery stings, or the time one of us let a bull out of Mr Werner's pen and it wreaked havoc among the cows...

Suddenly, I needed a piece of bread, something to soak up the fat of the meat and the awful taste of the vodka. I went to the kitchen; Jadwiga came along too and gave me a piece of bread. I told her about my visit to Mrs Wisniewska.

'She let you in?'

'Yes, why are you surprised?'

'Because ever since the incident, she refuses to see anyone.'

'What incident?' I asked.

After the Russians liberated Chodecz, she explained, some of their soldiers had been billeted in the teachers' block. Mrs Wisniewska was climbing the stairs to her flat one night when a group of drunken soldiers pulled her into their room. Mr Wisniewski heard her screaming. He threw on his Polish officer's jacket and ran to her rescue with their ten-year-old son.

'All we know about what happened after that was that the soldiers killed Mr Wisniewski and the boy. Mrs Wisniewska hasn't recovered yet,' said Jadwiga.

I suddenly felt sick and had to vomit.

•

For the next three days I stayed mostly indoors and in bed. Jadwiga came to see me next morning before setting off for work in Wloclawek.

'It was a bad war, you're mentally and physically exhausted, Romek, and you need feeding up… Let Aunt Podlawska spoil you, just rest in peace and quiet here,' said the wise Jadwiga.

'I'll find the names of the Jews who returned to Wloclawek and if there's someone related to you, I'll let you know.'

Now I understood why Mrs Wisniewska had been so frightened and had all those bolts, locks and chains on her door. Fear, I had learned, could render a person unable to behave rationally or logically. One terrible explosion could instil a sense of fear that some people could never shake off. I, who had lived under the SS, knew that I had to take chances in order to survive. I trained myself to shake off the effects of punishment and fear as quickly as possible. This did not mean that I was not afraid, only that I learned to adapt to fear and to carry on with life.

Mrs Wisniewska's world had changed after her experience; but would I be right to take her advice when it came to what I should do? Would those people now living in our house really murder me? I needed a few days of quiet rest under Mrs Podlawska's care.

After three days of rest, on the fourth day, I awoke feeling better. It was a warm and sunny morning. After a breakfast of *zur* and bread, I drew a flower and wrote beneath it a note to Mrs Wisniewska thanking her for her advice and telling her that

I had acted on it. I also told her how wonderful it was to see my dear teacher whom I regarded so highly and for whom I had the deepest affection – all the nice phrases Mrs Wisniewska had taught us, but here they were appropriate because I meant them. I headed to her house and dropped the letter in her mailbox. From there, because it was sunny and warm, I decided to go for a walk by the lake.

I crossed the town in the direction of Huta-Chodecka, followed the stream and took the forest road for about a mile to the lake. I sat on the shore, skipping pebbles and watching the herons glide across the water or perch on the tree stumps. I followed the reflected light of the rippling waves. Every bend in the lake held some memory for me. This was where Mother and I and Aunt Sabina and Cousin Misio used to come swimming, where at the age of five I learned to float. Soon I was paddling in circles around Mother and Aunt Sabina who stood in the water up to their shoulders while Misio stayed in the shallows. I remember shouting with glee, 'Misio, I can swim, I can swim…!'

I was here now. I had truly returned to Chodecz.

Water. The flat surface of the lake mirrored the sky. I hadn't been swimming in nearly six years. I wondered if I still remembered how. It suddenly struck me that in the ghetto and in Auschwitz I missed hearing birds. I now sat and listened. Another sensation I had missed: the fresh scent of the forest. I breathed in lungfuls of good air until my head started spinning. Then I remembered the stench of rotting flesh brought back to our cramped dormitory by those who had been sent out to collect corpses after the bombing of Dresden.

The factory in the Lodz ghetto also had its unique smell of metal and machine oil. Then I thought of those two and a half days on the way to Auschwitz-Birkenau, packed in a cattle car with eighty others, and the way the train carriage had reeked with the pungent smell of fear mingled with urine and excrement.

I sat thinking of the ever-present past, of the loss of my family and all the Jews of Chodecz, Izbica Kujawska and other towns in our region. I began to tremble uncontrollably all over. To stop the spasm I undressed completely and slowly waded into the lake. I floated a while. I told myself: *I still remember how to swim.* I wasn't in the water long. I came out still shaking. I curled up naked, trying to dry off in the sunlight. What would become of me? What should I do? Where should I go?

I asked myself these questions in a whisper, and then out loud. I asked Grandfather why had he urged me in my dream that night to return to Chodecz immediately? I had no answers to these questions, and all the time, other incidents from the past kept coming into my mind. Then my thoughts turned to the fact that apart from having no family, I had nothing in other senses: I had no schooling, no knowledge of the world or how things worked; I was ignorant about life outside the ghetto and the camps. Any day now Podlawski might say, 'Romek, as you know our house is very small and our daughters will soon be coming home for their summer holidays. I would like to ask you to move out.' What would I do then? Where would I go? There had been no news from Zosia, Iccio and Peccio. Aunt Sabina, Uncle Ignac and Misio who went to Kiev were probably dead as well.

Thinking about this made me shiver even more. Mrs Lewandowska, her husband and their many children would be going to the new Territories. She told me that I should go with them, but did she truly mean it? Mr Lewandowski had said in jest, 'We could do with a Jewish brain. Your task would be to make us all rich.'

As I sat there naked, arms around my knees, thighs pressed to my stomach, head bent, I wanted to pray. I covered my head with my shirt and then recited every prayer I knew. My body was still shaking as I uttered the Hebrew words. I was sitting there, the shirt still on my head, shaking a bit less now when suddenly a hand touched my shoulder. I turned slowly and looked up. A woman in black was standing over me. She was collecting kindling. The wood was beside her, tied with rope.

'You haven't been swimming, have you?' she asked

I nodded.

'You know it's forbidden to swim until after the Saint's Day on the twenty-fourth of June. That's when the priest blesses the lake and it's safe to swim again!'

I didn't recognize her – she probably came from the outskirts of Chodecz, from Huta-Chodecka.

'You could have drowned,' she said, crossing herself, and then packing the kindling expertly on her back, she walked away into the forest.

•

A little while later, I got dressed and gathered myself together. I walked into the forest and saw more women gathering kindling. Among them was our former neighbour, Mrs Eszner. In the old days, Mrs Eszner wouldn't have been caught dead doing such lowly work among the poorest of the poor. Now her hair had gone completely grey. She looked so old and withered I could hardly believe this was the same woman, her hair swept high and a black ribbon with a glittering pendant around her neck, in the oval photograph that used to hang in the Eszners' living room. Then I remembered my own mother, with her swollen eyes, her wasted body, and the metamorphosis that she and all the other Jews in the ghetto had undergone.

Mrs Eszner was not surprised to see me. Perhaps the word had gone round that I was here.

'How are you, Romek?' she asked.

'I'm well, *dziekuje*,' I heard myself say. We walked back together.

'What is Karol doing?'

'He hasn't returned yet.'

'Returned from where?'

'None of my sons are back from the war. They are serving with the SS.'

I was angry with myself. Why did I ask her these questions? I had seen the SS in action, murdering my people. I felt saddened and confused. I didn't want to know any more, so I carried her kindling in silence.

Suddenly she spoke to me, 'Romek, do you remember how I punished you once?'

'Yes, I do. I had been pilfering your plums from your plum tree right next to our fence, and suddenly I felt a hand grab my hand. I nearly died. You told me to come to your home the next day and receive my punishment – otherwise you'd tell my parents, and they'd punish me.'

'Yes, and do you remember how I punished you?'

'You gave me a whole bucket of potatoes, and you told me I had to peel them.'

'And do you forgive me for that punishment?'

'Yes, of course.'

There was another pause in our conversation.

'Are you waiting for your family, Romek…?'

'Yes, I am. I feel that Zosia may come back, or Iccio from Russia.'

She did not ask about the fate of my parents, my grandfather, my brothers and sisters. Given that all her four sons had served in the SS, I suppose that she was in a good position to know what might have become of them.

'Yes. I'm also waiting. One of my sons may still come back from Russia.'

We walked along a little more. She told me that her husband had been killed by the Russians when they entered Chodecz. Everyone had been in the main square as the Russian tanks rolled in, and her husband was spotted among the crowd. Jealous Poles from Chodecz shouted out to the Russian 'liberators' that here was a man whose four sons had been German soldiers, that they had fought against the Russians at Stalingrad. He was pushed by the crowd into the path of a Russian tank, and crushed to death. Others now occupied their house, she added. She had been allotted one small room that faced the road...

I left the wood outside her door. We parted by saying the customary *Dowidzenia* – 'See you again' – to one another. And I left. I never saw her again.

On my way back to the Podlawskis, I decided to go and see Marysia Giewis, the local butcher's daughter who had been in my class at school. I had promised to call on her and her family. Marysia was not home. Mrs Giewis and Jadzia, the older daughter, received me warmly.

'The three Pinczewski sisters turned up yesterday,' Mrs Giewis told me.

'The Pinczewski sisters are back in Chodecz?'

I was excited – the Pinczewski sisters had also been in the Lodz ghetto. I wanted to run off to see them. 'Where are they now?' I asked.

I found the sisters living in the attic of their old house. Like many Jewish houses, it had new occupants, but the sisters had been allowed to stay there. The new owners were also feeding them. They were afraid to go out for fear of being raped.

The sisters were sitting on a straw-covered floor with a sack and a suitcase in a corner of the room. We embraced and smiled, and again embraced.

'You survived,' I said.

'And you did too.'

We talked about the camps and about all those who died and then we sat in silence for a while. I told them what Mrs Wisniewska had suggested regarding our house, adding that I was uncertain whether I had done well. It seemed pretty silly to give away a part of one's house for a bottle of vodka.

They thought I had done right to act on her advice. They considered themselves lucky to have been allowed to stay where they were without trouble. They had heard that their two brothers who were officers in the Russian army were on their way back to Chodecz.

'When they get here we'll leave Poland, maybe even Europe,' said the eldest sister. They asked me what I would do a week or two from now if no one in my family returned.

'Someone will,' I replied. 'Zosia, or Iccio, who went to Russia like your brothers... and Uncle Ignac and Aunt Sabina and Cousin Misio, surely they'll be in touch soon...'

I went through the list of family members I hadn't seen dead, ending with Mother who had been taken from the Lodz ghetto during the *Aktion* of 1942.

'She may be alive...' I added.

Nadzia, the middle sister, looked at me quite angrily and spoke words I shall never forget: 'Romek, after all that's hap-pened to us, you're a fool to go on deceiving yourself. Hitler's men didn't play around on the transports. They murdered everyone. We were all doomed to die. Face it, your mother is dead; in fact most of your family is dead, otherwise they would be here by now or like our brothers they would get a message through to say they're alive. You should go to Wloclawek and find out. There may be some good news waiting for you.'

'But what about Iccio, Aunt Sabina, Uncle Ignac, Misio? They all went to Russia.'

'The Germans invaded Russia. Hundreds of thousands of people were killed there. If your brother Iccio were alive, he would surely have contacted Podlawski... as you did. If you want to survive – be strong, be clear-sighted about the past.'

I fully understood what Nadzia was saying but I hated it. I refused to believe that all my family had died. Getting back to Chodecz was all I had thought about. Without my family, now that I was here, I realized I was nowhere.

I went to Mrs Lewandowska to ask for Jadwiga's address in Wloclawek. I wanted to take some of my parents' things to sell in Wloclawek.

'That's not a good idea,' said Mrs Lewandowska. 'Someone could snatch it from you or knife you first and then take it. And there are always drunken Russian soldiers hanging around the black-market areas.' She gave me some money instead.

Podlawski accompanied me to the station. I got on the train with the paper Miss Rosa had helped me obtain, signed and stamped by the station master in Lodz.

In Wloclawek a policeman told me where the Red Cross office was. They had no news of any Halters. I wrote to my

Aunt Sarah Wiener at 8 Chemin des Cèdres in Lausanne, Switzerland, telling her that I was alive and in Chodecz.

Dear Aunt, would you please send me a parcel of clothing – shirts, sweaters etc, and food to Lesna 1, Chodecz.

On the wall I hung a notice: 'Romek Halter of Chodecz, age 17-plus. I am alive.'

The man who worked at the Red Cross office said, 'If you're a Jew, go to this address. They serve soup there and also have lists of people who've returned from the camps or from Russia.'

I found the place. It smelled of cooked vegetables. Thin, pale, poorly-dressed people were eating soup. 'What's your name? What's your name?' they said in Polish or Yiddish. A woman who didn't stop eating said aloud, 'He must be Szlamek's brother.'

Szlamek was well known in Wloclawek where he had worked as the manager of the plywood factory.

I was given a plate of soup with bread, barley and potatoes.

'Romek,' said a voice in the corner. It was Zurawski the butcher who had lived in Chodecz till 1937, when he moved to Wloclawek. I sat next to him and he told me he had been in Chelmno and had survived by cutting open people's stomachs. I stopped eating and looked at him. He had a mouth, a nose and eyes but how could a man who cut open people's stomachs as a way to survive – how could he carry on living?

'Your cousin from Izbica Kujawska, Szlamek Halter. I recognized his face in 1943. He was dead of course.'

He went on talking but I didn't take anything in except the

words, 'People from the Lodz ghetto were sent to Chelmno.'

I decided not to go to see Jadwiga. Instead, I turned back and went to Chodecz.

Back at the Podlawskis' house, I found Mrs Podlawska in tears. Eva, my half-brother Szlamek's wife, had come by with a Russian officer, and had taken away my mother's fur coat, the one that could have bought the Podlawskis a couple of piglets and perhaps a plough. Eva, the wife of my dead brother Szlamek is alive. How wonderful, I thought.

'Why did you give it to her?' I asked. 'It was my mother's coat.'

'I didn't, the Russian searched our room and found it.'

Mrs Podlawska said that Eva was going to come back later that night. Sad and tired after my journey and the talk with Zurawski, I wanted to sleep.

Eva arrived with the Russian officer. She embraced me and I was very glad to see her. Only now did I realize how small she was. The Podlawskis were terrified of the Russian. Eva introduced me to him. He spoke Polish to me. I had a feeling he was Jewish, but it was only a hunch. We spoke a little about the past and then Eva asked me where Father had buried the oak chest. I hadn't realized that she knew about it. Perhaps Szlamek had told her before he was taken away.

Eva wasn't looking at or addressing Podlawski, but he interrupted to say that he had no idea where it was. He had heard something about a buried chest but he did not know where it was. Then he wanted to go out for a walk, but the Russian ordered him to stay.

'You and I are the only surviving Halters,' said Eva.

'How can you be so certain?' I said. 'I didn't know you were alive until just a few minutes ago. Other members of the family may yet turn up in the course of time…'

I was about to tell her where the box was. I thought perhaps that with the Russian soldier who spoke Polish it would be safe to dig up the chest and bring it back to the Podlawskis to divide up the goods amongst ourselves. I would keep a little extra for those who might turn up later, Zosia or Iccio or Aunt Sabina and Uncle Ignac…

Just as I was about to speak these thoughts, there was a split second's hesitation. In that silent space, the Russian officer grabbed me by the neck the way Moniek the Boxer had before we escaped that night, and then he squeezed it till my eyes nearly popped out, and shook me so hard it hurt and I felt my head would fall off. He didn't know me. I wasn't easily frightened. I stood facing him while Eva and the room and the Podlawskis in the corner all swam before my eyes. He let me go. After what he had done to me, I would never speak to him.

Again he shouted at me, 'Speak up, speak!'

Eva pleaded with me but I lay face down on my bed and said nothing.

Before they left, the Russian officer said that he would find the chest if it took him a whole month of digging. If Podlawski and I tried to get it, he threatened, he would shoot us both.

The next day, apart from some marks around my neck, I was feeling fine. Mr Podlawski and I discussed the incident at length, and he concluded that we had better forget about digging up the oak chest, at least for the time being. If Eva's Russian found it, he reasoned, it would be his good luck and our bad luck, that's all. If he didn't find it, we still had a chance. The chest had been in the ground so long that another few weeks would make no difference. Iccio might still be alive and when he returned from Russia wearing his officer's uniform he could help us. The oak chest wasn't worth being shot over now. This Russian clearly meant what he said. 'Oh, no, there's no doubt about this! No doubt at all!' said Mr Podlawski.

I told Podlawski that I intended to get up early – at 4.30 a.m. the following morning – take a spade, a crowbar, the keys, a pickaxe and a sack with me, dig up the chest and open the lid. I would take the stuff out and put it in my sack and then bury the chest again and carry the sack back to the Podlawskis'. I could see that Mrs Podlawska approved of my plan; but Mr Podlawski said, 'Count me out. I don't want to be shot.'

I told them that after much thought I had arrived at the conclusion that Eva, who lived in Wloclawek most of her life, had gone back there with her Russian. They would certainly return, but not before 4.30 or 5 a.m. I would have to dig up the chest tomorrow morning before they returned, when it would be totally safe.

Mrs Podlawska nodded in agreement. Mr Podlawski said that

apart from lending me the tools he would have nothing to do with the plan.

Later that day I visited Mrs Lewandowska and told her about Eva and the Russian officer and what had happened the night before.

'I have a better plan,' said Mrs Lewandowska. 'I'll speak to Eva and suggest that you marry her. You will be strong and fit before long and she knows you come from excellent stock. Together the two of you might be able to get the house back and all your belongings. She'll have herself a young husband and you'll have a clever wife.'

'But, but, but,' I heard myself sputter. 'I must be half her age... and I don't love her!'

'Love has nothing to do with marriage,' said Mrs Lewandowska. 'Love is something people write about in books. Listen to me, I've lived much longer and I care about you.'

I couldn't imagine what had come over her.

'But the other day you said I could go to the new territory with you.'

'I know I said so – but what will you do there, dig potatoes, plough the fields?'

I was suddenly aware that I was totally alone.

'Eva will make a good wife,' Mrs Lewandowska continued. 'She can teach you things. She managed Szlamek's business in Wloclawek. And she's Jewish. Your father and grandfather, and your mother too, I'm sure, would wish for you to marry a Jew.

Eva may not seem young enough to you, but she's only a little over thirty, not too old to bear you children. I really think this is something you should consider.'

I remembered my visit to Szlamek and Eva's when I was eight. They were newlyweds and living in Wloclawek. Eva took me to a shop where she bought me coloured pencils, paper and a book about butterflies. She was a curvaceous little woman, no more than five feet tall. I remembered that my father had taken objection to her short stature. One day, on our way to the best cake shop in Wloclawek, Szlamek walked with such big strides that Eva laughed and said, 'Don't you grow to be a giant like my husband because then I'll need wings to keep up with you both.'

As Mrs Lewandowska tried to convince me of the advantages of marrying Eva, I thought of something else.

'But do you know what Eva did to us in the Lodz ghetto?' I asked. 'Mother and Father and I were starving and so were Sala and her children. Mother took a small packet of sugar cubes out of the box Eva kept under the bed. Then Eva brought along a huge man and he beat Mother up and wanted to strangle us both.'

'Romek, Romek that's enough, put all those horrid yesterdays out of your mind and think of life, of a better tomorrow...'

She pressed my head to her.

'Come with us to the new territories then. You will be one of us... but something tells me you wouldn't be happy there.'

'I could marry Jadwiga,' I said with a laugh. 'She's my age.

She's good looking and I've known her for years. We always got on well together, even when we were babies.'

But Mrs Lewandowska didn't laugh. 'No, Romek,' she said, 'not Jadwiga.'

There was a long silence. I waited for my dear Mrs Lewandowska to explain. She sat facing me, calmly and lovingly.

'Why not?' I asked.

'Because your parents and your grandfather wouldn't want you to marry a non-Jewish woman. I worked for your parents before you were born. I was close to them, and I know what they would have wished for you. Do you see what I mean?'

I saw it clearly. When the daughter of one of my father's friends fell in love with a Polish officer, she had to choose between never seeing her parents again or breaking off with her beloved. The entire Jewish community of Chodecz was in an uproar about it. In the end, the young woman drowned herself in a well and was buried outside the cemetery.

Mrs Lewandowska said that she had thought of three possible plans for me: the first, that I would marry Eva; the second, that I would leave for the new territories with her and her family; and the third, that I would join my aunt in Switzerland. Since my mother had not returned yet, she would fill in as my mother and give me the attention and advice I needed so much more than her other children right now.

'They know where they are,' she said with a smile. 'You don't have anyone else in Chodecz who knows you the way I do, who loves you and cares what becomes of you.'

'I have the Podlawskis too,' I said.

'My sister cares about you to a certain extent but her main concern is feathering her own bed. My brother-in-law is a narrow-minded, stubborn home-spun philosopher who treats you no better or worse than he would treat his own son, if he had one. Look at his children: all three have left him. They only come home for Christmas or maybe a few other times during the year. But let's talk about your Aunt Sarah now.'

I told Mrs Lewandowska that Father had made me memorize her address, and that I had written her a note the other day from Wloclawek.

'Once your Aunt Sarah came to Chodecz with her eldest daughter Fanny. That was a couple of years before you were born. She got on well with your father and mother. From time to time, she would send them parcels. She must be well-off because the things she sent were very beautiful, very expensive. Switzerland is a rich country and hasn't been ruined by the war. It would be a good place for you. You could get a fine education there. Who knows – you might even qualify as a doctor.'

For people in Chodecz, 'to qualify as a doctor', was the ultimate achievement.

'I'll wait,' I said, 'in case other members of the family show up. Then maybe we'll go to Switzerland together.'

Mrs Lewandowska sighed deeply and said, 'I think that the third plan is by far the best. You have an aunt and uncle and cousins in Switzerland, and they'll give you the new start in life you need. Here the war has destroyed so much. The Nazis murdered not only the Jews but our own Polish leaders as well. Do you remember the night in 1939 when forty men and women were taken away? We found the spot where they were shot and buried. If it hadn't been for Hoffmann, your father and Szlamek would have been shot as soon as the Germans came.'

Two of Mrs Lewandowska's younger children came into the room and said that they were hungry. She cut them each a hunk of home-baked bread smeared with pork dripping. They each took a bite and ran out to eat the rest outside. All my thoughts fled. I was back in the days of starvation when nothing mattered as much as food. Without asking, she cut a big hunk of bread from the loaf, spread it with the dark crunchy bits of meat from the bottom together with the pork fat, and handed it to me.

'I never gave you *treife* to eat when I worked for your parents, except my own breast which you suckled as an infant,' she said.

I was completely absorbed in the food. I shut my eyes each time I took a bite to savour the taste and concentrate on the act of eating, which seemed almost sublime after the years of starvation.

Mrs Lewandowska sat in silence pretending not to watch me. When I finished my last bite she said, 'This box you're sitting on was designed by your father. It holds some of your father's precious manuscripts. There are more books in that other box,' she said, pointing to a coffin-sized chest. 'Would you like to see them? They'll all be yours one day if no one else returns. I'll keep them safe for you.'

Mrs Lewandowska turned the wooden box upside down, unscrewed the pegs and removed the wooden lid. I washed my hands and covered my head out of respect for the Hebrew and Yiddish manuscripts I was about to handle. The first one I unwrapped had densely handwritten pages either in Yiddish or Hebrew. I felt ignorant and realized that the war had robbed me of the learning I might have had by now, at age seventeen. The beautiful illuminated Haggadahs must have been in the second box which, according to Mrs Lewandowska, contained Father's coin collection and other things.

'We'll open the big box another time. You're not leaving for Switzerland right away, are you?' she asked with a laugh. I had told her how saddened I felt by finding Chodecz empty of Jews, and had also told her about my plans to go to Switzerland to my aunt.

'We'll open it then when Zosia, Iccio or Peccio get here.'

After my talk with the Pinczewski sisters I no longer spoke of Mother as though she might still be alive, although I never stopped hoping that she had survived by some miracle.

'Yes, we'll all open it together,' I added.

Back at the Podlawskis', Mrs Podlawska said her husband had left. He'd gone to see his cousins in a village a few miles from Chodecz because his 'nose warned him that Eva's Russian officer would be sure to catch anyone who tried to dig up the oak chest'.

'Do you believe that?' I asked Mrs Podlawska.

'No,' she replied, 'but Stasiek is daft that way. His nose tells him one thing one day, another thing the next. He had visions of this Russian dragging him outside and shooting him. He even imagined the exact spot where he would die if he stayed to help you dig up the chest.' Mrs Podlawska gave a laugh. 'It's hard to talk sense with a man like my husband.'

Hearing this, I too began to feel my courage failing me, but I told myself that Mr Podlawski was superstitious. The Russian was probably in Wloclawek with Eva now and the safest time to dig up the oak chest would be tomorrow before dawn. That's when I would do it.

I asked Mrs Podlawska to wake me at 4 a.m. the next morning, and she promised she would. She put the spade in a sack and handed me the keys to the oak chest.

'What about a crowbar and a pickaxe?' I asked her.

'The spade is enough, you'll see. The ground is fairly soft now. Remember to spit on your hands so you don't get blisters.'

Mrs Podlawska told me the latest news from Chodecz. There was a Russian colonel quartered on Werner's estate who was in charge of the whole area and had a man and a woman working for him as translators from Polish to Russian and Russian to Polish. Rumour had it that the woman was Jewish and that the Colonel liked her very much.

My mind was elsewhere. I kept imagining myself digging up the oak chest. I felt anxious. I have to do it, I thought, and I will do it, but how I wish that Podlawski were here to help.

When we finished eating I washed my hands and went outside to say the *Shema*. I asked my parents and grandparents to shield and protect me, and felt a little calmer. I would will myself awake at four, I decided, just in case Mrs Podlawska overslept. I was just about to undress and go to bed when Mrs Podlawska came in and said, 'Jews are supposed to know about the future... Will tomorrow work out all right?'

I looked into her worried eyes and found myself saying: 'Yes, everything will work out all right.'

Mrs Podlawska woke me before the clock struck four. She fed me a breakfast of curds and dark bread. I picked up the sack with the spade and walked out. Except for the occasional barking of a dog, the streets of Chodecz were completely deserted.

I reached our house, and went into the garden, counting out the paces beyond the shed. When I reached the spot I paced it out and began to dig. The ground really wasn't very hard and the digging went well. I took Mrs Podlawska's advice and spat on my hands and rested from time to time. After about an hour I touched the wooden top of the oak chest. I felt elated. Soon the whole top was clear and I dug around the sides. A little more digging and I realized the chest must be buried upside down: the padlock was nowhere to be found.

I took a rest. As I stood there gazing at the chest, thinking how to go about opening it, I became aware of a presence behind me. I veered around. Standing over me, legs astride and revolver in hand was Eva's Russian officer.

In that split second when my eyes met his I pushed the revolver away with the spade handle and said, 'It's all yours, you win. I don't want anything. Take the spade.'

The Russian muttered curses first in Russian, then in Polish, and then said, 'I should really now shoot you,' adding a few expletives for good measure. As he spoke I began to walk away, silently counting my steps because Father, who had a permit for a Luger in the days before the war had told me once that it was hard to hit a target at more than twenty-five paces. Twenty, twenty-one, twenty-two, I counted... and still no shot was fired.

I ran all the way back to Mrs Podlawska's house. I sat down on the bed and wept, less from fear than a sense of failure. Eva's boyfriend had outsmarted me and seized my birthright, and I was helpless against him.

I told Mrs Podlawska what had happened. For the first few moments all she could say, wringing her hands and crossing herself was 'Jesus Maria! Jesus Maria!' Then suddenly she said, 'But you brought the spade back, didn't you? It's the only one we have.'

I explained why I hadn't brought the spade back but she went on about how precious it was to them, and why they could not afford to lose it. Mr Podlawski would be very angry; he would never forgive her. We should have listened to her husband, his 'nose' had been right... and the Russian might still show up and shoot us all.

Eventually she pulled herself together and said, 'Go quickly to the Werner estate and see the Jewish woman who works as the colonel's interpreter. Ask her to help you.'

I thought Mrs Podlawska's idea was brilliant and instantly became animated.

'What time is it?' I asked.

'Twenty past six.'

'All right, I'll go now.'

Mrs Podlawska went with me.

The Jewish interpreter at the Werner estate questioned me in great detail. Mrs Podlawska was told to wait downstairs in the corridor.

'Soap, tea, coffee – what else is in the chest? Any gold or jewellery?'

'No, I don't think so,' I said.

Someone woke the Colonel, who walked in wearing a long night-shirt and looking like a character straight out of a children's book. He had a round face and pig-like eyes under bushy eyebrows. The interpreter addressed him in Russian. He looked me over a moment and then gave orders I could not make out, outside of a word here and there.

Two officers, two soldiers and a man who spoke Polish climbed into the lorry with me and we drove out to our place. We found Eva's Russian there standing beside the still-unopened chest. He seemed surprised and angry to see us all. The two officers apprehended him and drove him away and the two soldiers, the Polish-speaker and I, waited till the truck returned and then all together picked up the oak chest and loaded it on. It seemed miraculous to me that Father had managed to carry something so heavy with only Podlawski to help him. Szlamek must have helped them.

When we got back to the Werner estate I handed the key to the interpreter. She unlocked the chest, which gave off a musty smell. Inside, I recognized the stuff Father had bought from Uncle Ignac and Aunt Sabina, mainly laundry soap and tins of tea and coffee.

The Colonel, fully dressed and now looking more authoritative, entered the room with a younger, slimmer and taller officer. They both ignored me as the Colonel said something to the interpreter who then enquired once again whether there was any jewellery, gold, silver, china or suchlike in the oak chest.

Again I replied that I didn't think so.

The Colonel said something, and the interpreter walked out and returned with an old blanket. She spread it on the floor and proceeded to set out the contents of the chest for the two soldiers to examine. With corkscrews, knives and nails they prodded every single bar of soap, while the interpreter searched through Mother's Singer sewing machine cover, under the wooden lid of which she found packets of needles. The Colonel looked at me as though I were playing some sort of trick on them. This made me angry and I felt I'd had enough.

'These are all my things,' I said aloud. 'Please arrange for them to be sent to Lesna 1.'

The woman translated what I had said and the Colonel said something in reply and everyone laughed except for me.

'These are all my things,' I repeated, pointing at the oak chest and the items spread on the blanket. The Colonel looked at me and I looked back into his pig-like eyes as if to say, 'Enough of this, take a bar or two of soap for your trouble and send the chest to Mr and Mrs Podlawskis'.'

He motioned me to follow. The interpreter said, 'Come along with me, I'm also going with the Colonel.'

We entered a small adjoining area away from the others where he began to stroke her hand, ignoring me and speaking tenderly to her. When he left I said, 'Surely as a Jew you can understand that I who have just returned from Hitler's concentration camps would like to have back what is rightfully mine. Everything in the oak chest is mine. It belongs to my family. I am the only member of my family who has come back to Chodecz so far and...'

She interrupted me and said, 'Because I look different, people assume I must be either a Jewess or a gypsy, but in fact I am neither. Still, I understand you, I sympathize with you. I've seen concentration camps. I know what those places were like. Now listen, you must leave Chodecz right now, without delay. You had a narrow escape from that Russian officer. He could have broken your bones. Stay away for six weeks or so, and I'll arrange right away for a horse-cart to take you to the railway station. Don't worry, you'll get some soap and some tins of tea and coffee.'

'Some!?' I exclaimed

'Don't interrupt,' she said. 'You're lucky the Colonel is such a kind-hearted man, otherwise you wouldn't get a thing.'

And that was that.

All this time, Mrs Podlawska was waiting downstairs. The interpreter had a sack of 'some' of the goods sent out to a horse-cart with a driver from the Werner estate, beside whom sat a Russian soldier. Mrs Podlawska and I sat in the back. First we drove to their home, where I gave Mrs Podlawska more than three-quarters of the contents of the sack.

'Please share this with your sister,' I said. 'I should be back in about a month. If anyone from my family returns, tell them to get in touch with my aunt, Sarah Wiener, at 8, Chemin des Cèdres in Lausanne. I'll write to my aunt and let her know my whereabouts.' Then I told her what the interpreter had said.

While waiting for me at the Werner estate, Mrs Podlawska had managed to recover her spade. That, together with the soap, coffee and tea, plus the sewing needles, made her quite happy. She embraced me. 'See you soon,' she said light-heartedly. I looked at the smooth round face with the peasant kerchief tied around it and tried to memorize her lovely image. I had a feeling I would not be seeing her for a long, long time.

Adrift in Europe

I decided to go to Lodz. I couldn't think of anywhere else I could go, and that's where Miss Rosa was. I had some soap in my sack to repay her kindness in putting me up and having used some of her precious soap on me. I felt confident that the contents of my sack would enable me to live anywhere for a time, how long exactly, I couldn't say, but I didn't allow it to worry me. Tomorrow was tomorrow, but meanwhile, the war was over and I was free.

What did worry me was the thought of missing family members who might turn up in Chodecz in my absence. I resolved to write about my plans to Mrs Podlawska, trusting that she would find someone in Chodecz to read my letter to her since she herself was illiterate, and also to Mrs Lewandowska, whose daughter Jadwiga could read. But where would I live if Miss Rosa was no longer at the address I had? Where would I sleep?

It was getting dark when I arrived at Miss Rosa's apartment. A man opened the door and invited me in. He told me his name was Aaron, and he had also been in the Lodz ghetto during the war. He asked me where I had worked.

'On Lagiewnicka,' I replied. He was a few years older than me, and insisted on engaging me in a conversation where he would name people and ask me whether I knew them. 'No, don't know him,' I kept answering. 'No, not him either.'

Eventually he said, 'Are you sure you were in the Lodz ghetto?'

From time to time he would go to the mirror and comb his hair, which was still quite short. He wore a sleeveless vest and kept examining his rather small biceps.

'Rosa loves me,' he remarked out of the blue. When I didn't reply he asked if I was related to her. I told him we had worked together in the ghetto and that on my way back to Chodecz a couple of weeks ago Rosa had been good enough to put me up for the night. 'And I hope she'll let me stay tonight, because I have nowhere else to go,' I said.

'We'll manage,' said Aaron.

When Miss Rosa came home she welcomed me warmly.

On the train to Lodz I had made her a little parcel of soap and tea. When I presented it now, she was overjoyed. 'Soap!' she exclaimed. She took out a piece of it and some tea and hurried to the door. 'I'll be back soon,' she said, 'and then we'll have a feast!'

I lay down on a blanket on the floor. I told Aaron I'd had a long day and that I was very tired. I fell asleep instantly.

The next thing I remember Miss Rosa and Aaron were trying to wake me, laughing drunkenly and handing me a plate full of food.

When I awoke early next morning I had no idea what time it was. Rosa and Aaron were still fast asleep. They had covered me with a heavy coat and there was a pillow under my head. I felt hungry and began to look for food. In the frying pan, covered with a plate, I found some cold fried potatoes with egg and sausage.

'That was the feast,' I thought, helping myself to the delicious-smelling food. I washed it down with water and wrote a note to Miss Rosa saying I would return later. I took my sack of goods and left for the black market.

Passers-by directed me to the main trading area of the market. Even now, in the spring of 1945, with the war over and the hope of a better tomorrow in the air, Lodz looked grey and weary. It sullen inhabitants were huddled in their worn-out clothes. After the murderous cruelty and the suffering and privation they had known, there was no joy left in them. In the market everyone spoke in whispers: 'What have you got to swap?' and 'Show me your goods.'

I decided to get the 'feel' of the place first. I was still afraid to show anyone what I had in my sack for fear that they would take it away. I found an old rag and tied it diagonally around the sack so that it hung in front of me where I could see it.

More people began to mill about, but without any bundles that I could see. I looked for stalls, for carts and horses – that was how I remembered the market in Chodecz before the war. Could this really be *czarny rynek*, the black market? I thought I must be in the wrong place. Most of the people I asked didn't bother to reply, but only looked at me as if to say, 'What are you doing here?'

One woman studied me a while and then said, 'Why d'you ask? Did someone say he'd meet you at the black market? There are several of them here...'

There were Jews wandering about, searching rather than selling, buying or swapping. They would approach and say, '*Bisdee an iyd? Rets-too maame looshen?*'

When I answered in the affirmative, other questions would follow, preceded by the usual: 'What's your name and where did you live? In which camp were you? How old are you?' Then the searching questions began: 'Did you know X or Y or Z, have you met up with him?'

Then, if my answers were still in the negative, they would shrug their shoulders and saunter away. Perhaps I, too, should be looking for members of my family this way, I thought... or at least for the familiar faces of those who may have known the Halters and might give me a lead, a sign of hope that this or that member of the family was alive...

I walked around, staring at the faces, and then, feeling in need of a rest, squatted next to a woman with a basket. She was not Jewish. She told me she had hard-boiled eggs to swap. I told her I had soap. 'Soap!' she exclaimed. 'Real soap?'

She lent me a knife to cut the bar of soap into eight. 'You

really need a thin wire to cut this, otherwise you'll make soap flakes,' she insisted. Eventually she took an eighth of the flakes and soap chips in exchange for four of her eggs. I ate one on the spot. It tasted good. I made certain not to drop the tiniest morsel. I ate it slowly, resting against the wall as I squatted, thinking about the potatoes, eggs, and sausage Miss Rosa had left in the frying pan. Perhaps she hadn't meant all of it for me. Too late now... Eating this hard-boiled egg was rousing my appetite and more thoughts of food. Perhaps I should buy another four eggs and eat one more... Apportioning the weekly starvation ration into seven equal parts in the ghetto had taught me not to be guided by my stomach.

'No, one egg will do,' I told myself, and continued ambling around the market.

Suddenly somebody sprang up behind me and covered my eyes with his hands. In the camps there had been bread-snatchers who worked in pairs doing that. One of the men at Auschwitz had taught me how to defend myself and protect my bread. I reacted instinctively now, sliding my hip to one side, and 'pumping' my arm up with all my might and digging my elbow in the belly of my assailant. His hands dropped from my eyes as he doubled over in pain. The next move was to kick him before he had time to hurt me. I was about to do this when I thought I recognized the figure, crouching in pain before me. I couldn't believe my eyes: it was Leibel Zylberszac, the youngest of the three Zylberszac brothers. His eldest brother, Wolf Zylberszac, whom we called Willie, a brilliant and creative mechanical engineer, had been my section boss for a time at the metal factory here in Lodz. He had been good to me. The other brother was Zalman – rather crude and ordinary. Leibel, who was four years my senior, had also been in the section that his brother Willie headed. The Zylberszac family belonged to the infamous Jewish underworld of Lodz. Leibel was wild and daring. He had been one of the boys who managed to sneak out of the ghetto and slip back in under the heavily guarded barbed-wire fences with smuggled food. The three brothers had all been with me in Dresden and on the march from which I escaped.

I felt terrible seeing Leibel now, crouching in pain. I squatted beside him and begged his forgiveness. I stroked his face and whispered that I had some hard-boiled eggs with me.

'Now you're talking – how many?' he said in Yiddish.

'I almost kicked you when you were crouching there just now,' I said.

'Ahh,' said Leibel, 'I know that little trick from the camps; it's kids' stuff.' He pulled out a huge, sharp knife. 'Now, *this* is what I call defence!' he said, strapping it back behind his leg.

Leibel and I sat down and leaned against the wall. He ate the two hard-boiled eggs I gave him and I ate the last of the four. I asked him what had happened on the march after I ran off. Apparently the SS had told the group at roll call next day that they had caught all of us who escaped hiding in the factory and shot us all bar one. The only person brought back alive was Moniek the Boxer's woman. When she gave herself up from her hiding place in the car in the factory courtyard, they brought her back to the transport. She also believed that all of us who escaped had been shot because she heard the sound of gunfire coming from inside the factory. The march had continued to the Theresienstadt ghetto and many from the Dresden group who struggled or could not keep up the pace the SS set were shot on the way.

Leibel had come back to Lodz to collect the jewellery his family hid in the ghetto, jewellery which in fact belonged to him, he said, because he was the one who had procured food outside the walls in exchange for gold, watches, rings etc, always keeping the best pieces for himself. Now, though, he wanted to bring the treasure back to his two brothers in Theresienstadt and share it with them. Many others from our metal factory might still be there if we could get back to Theresienstadt quickly. (Theresienstadt had been a 'showcase' camp, and had been used until 1943 to deceive the Red Cross into believing that Jewish life under the Nazis was civilized and humane.)

Leibel suggested that I accompany him to Theresienstadt. I explained that I still hoped someone from my family would turn up and that I wanted to stay around to meet up with them.

'Oh, come on, we'll travel to Prague, to Budapest… We can get almost anywhere by train. I know how.'

I told him I still had some soap, tea and coffee left in my sack. 'Wonderful!' said Leibel. 'The world is ours.'

We bartered some of my soap for more food and drink and

went off to Miss Rosa's place together. Leibel knew her too and she was happy to learn from him that some people from the Dresden transport had reached Theresienstadt safely. 'Is X alive? What about Y?' she asked.

Aaron and Leibel remembered each other from their days in the ghetto; clearly, there was no love lost between them. At one point Leibel whispered to me, 'Aaron's always been a bit of a *potz*,' which means he seemed rather half-baked.

There was also another man at Miss Rosa's place called Shimon, who had been with us in Dresden and was related to the Kleszczelskis. He was overjoyed to hear from Leibel that Dr and Mrs Kleszczelski had both survived and were now in Theresienstadt. Feeling livelier now, we ate and drank and Shimon told us how some members of his family had paid in gold and silver to be smuggled out of the ghetto. He explained that three members of his family had crawled into a metal drum which was fixed to a horse-cart and were smuggled out in 1940. The plan was that if this turned out to be a 'safe' way to escape they would get a message back, but if the message contained the words 'Praise the Lord', then on no account should the Kleszczelskis follow. The message had come back with the words 'Praise the Lord'.

I remembered that Peccio had also written to us at the beginning of 1940 when we were still in Chodecz that he, his wife and child were planning to get out from the Lodz ghetto. And this was the last we heard from him.

Sala, who lived in Brzesc Kujawski, had received a more

detailed letter from Peccio telling her that he thought it was possible to get out of the Lodz ghetto and that a group of Poles were willing to smuggle people out in circular drums mounted on a horse-drawn cart in exchange for jewellery and gold, and that he and his wife and son were going to do this. Peccio said that they would pay to be smuggled out and then try to make their way south. He begged Sala not to tell us yet since we were bound to worry. That as soon as they were safely out he would find a way to communicate with her so she could let us know. The second letter never came. Sala told us all about this when we were all together in the Lodz ghetto.

Shimon, like Miss Rosa, had hidden in the Lodz ghetto and had been liberated only a few months previously by the Russians. Ever since, he had been trying to find out what happened to his family and trying to trace the Poles who had smuggled them out at the time. He knew that one of the Poles who brought the message with the words 'Praise the Lord' had mentioned that he came from Pabianice. Shimon had searched for him there and in the adjoining villages but found nothing. He felt sure he would recognize these men if he ever came across them. He talked to everyone he could, and even offered rewards, not that the rewards amounted to much. Then he went to the Polish police who worked closely with the Russian militia. They told him that the smugglers were Polish-speaking Germans who had been brought in especially from the area around Danzig to try out an early method of gassing in metal drums, later improved for use in Chelmno. Shimon said he wanted proof of what they said, but they answered, 'What we told you is true and you have to accept it.'

The fact was, that no one who was smuggled out in a metal drum at the beginning of 1940 from the Lodz ghetto was alive to tell the tale.

I told Shimon that if I heard anything about Peccio I would get in touch with him through Miss Rosa and that he should do the same if he heard anything. At this point, Miss Rosa told us to stop talking about the past and simply be happy that Leibel had brought us the good news that so many of the people from the metal factory were in Theresienstadt.

Later that night Leibel and I left Miss Rosa's and went to his room, a squalid little place he had rented for a month in exchange for potatoes, half a sack at the beginning of the month and the rest two weeks later. As we both lay on the rags that covered the floorboards, threadbare blankets over our backs, I fell asleep wondering whether I would catch lice again. It had been so nice to be clean and rid of them. Leibel was already asleep; I said the *Shema* in silence. Then I said a prayer asking my parents and grandparents to guide me.

Since my return to Chodecz my family had been constantly on my mind and in my spirit. During the war I only prayed for the war to end and to be able to return safely to Chodecz where I would meet members of my family who survived and everything would be all right again. Though I could laugh, smile and even sing, in the evening before going to sleep, I would feel very much alone. The years before the war seemed like a golden age.

In the morning Leibel showed me the padded underpants in which he hid the jewellery. 'Why do you want me to know where you hid the stuff?' I asked.

'Because,' he said, 'I'm going off to spend some time with women and I want you to wear the pants or keep them under your head when you go to sleep. Here, I'll lend you my knife too.'

Leibel spent most days at the black market buying and selling, and seemed to be enjoying himself. I would make my rounds to the Red Cross office to enquire whether there had been any messages for me from Chodecz, any news of Zosia or Iccio. Instinct told me not to return to Chodecz. Eva's man would surely 'snuff the life out of me' as they used to say in the black market. Every day I would go to Miss Rosa's place to ask if any card or letter had arrived and each time she would answer, 'Sorry, Romek, there is nothing for you.' It was time to move on. There was no point in hanging around Lodz any more.

After some days, Leibel too had had enough of Lodz and wanted to get back to his brothers. I resolved to get across the border to Czechoslovakia, which I imagined was near Switzerland where my aunt lived; it had been many years since my geography lessons. There I would part from Leibel.

For the next two days we traded on the black market to buy eggs, bread, *speck* and smoked bacon for the journey. Before we left, I insisted on saying goodbye to Miss Rosa. Leibel had no time for Miss Rosa now so I went alone. We shook hands. She wished me luck and gave me a kiss on the forehead. Then, looking deeply in my eyes, she said that we might never see one another again, that I would be making my way to Switzerland and that she would probably end up in Palestine or the USA.

We boarded the train for Czechoslovakia but had not been travelling long when the Polish border police told us to get off the train at Wroclaw because we didn't have the proper documents. Leibel had bought them on the black market in Lodz and was convinced that they would do the trick, but the border police only tore them up and escorted us off along with many other travellers who simply squatted on the platform at Wroclaw and waited for the next train. This was how one travelled in those days after the war.

Suddenly Leibel spotted a dark-eyed, dark-haired woman in her late twenties making herself comfortable on the platform. He addressed her in Yiddish and she replied in Yiddish: her name was Frania, and she came from a small town in Poland, and had been in two concentration camps with her sister, but there they had been separated and she had been sent to work in a factory near Chemnitz. When the Russians liberated her she had gone back to her home town in Poland. There, two men who lived near her parents' home took her out to the forest one morning… Here she broke down and wept.

Leibel put his arm around her and encouraged her to go on. She said she had been made to dig a pit and that they were about to murder her but decided to rape her first. After the rape she pleaded with them to spare her life and they raped her several times more before putting her on the train for Warsaw with the warning that if she ever returned they would not spare her life. Leibel took out his knife and said he felt like murdering those men. I asked her whether she ever got to Warsaw, hoping to find out if she had come across someone called Zosia Halter.

'No,' she said. 'I was in Warsaw but I didn't come across her.' However, through the Warsaw Red Cross, she had found out that her sister was alive and in a hospital in Prague. The Red Cross had given her a document which she thought would enable her to cross into Czechoslovakia, only the border police had told her it was a worthless piece of paper anyone could have bought and so, like us, she had been thrown off the train.

When I heard that the Warsaw Red Cross found Frania's sister for her I began blaming myself for squandering my time with Leibel in Lodz and for not going to Warsaw in search of the members of my family...

Suddenly Leibel became interested in the Red Cross paper the police had returned to her. He passed it to me. I had been certain that Leibel could read but now he said, 'Read it out loud and not too fast': and then, 'Read it again.' This was the paper that would get the three of us across the border, he said. It was a marvellous document, a piece of paper straight from heaven. Leibel's mood now changed from vengeful anger to exhilaration over some plan that he was obviously hatching.

He came up close to Frania and gently stroked her face. He told her that we would look after her, protect her and take her across the border. That she shouldn't worry herself about anything, not even about what had happened to her. 'Your anatomy is not like soap,' he told her, 'it doesn't wear out with use.' If it turned out that she was pregnant the doctors in the Prague hospital where her sister was would be able to take care of it.

'Czech doctors are good and kind people.' Leibel knew because he had met many of them in Theresienstadt when they came to help the Russians treat the sick and the dying. One of his brothers had been looked after by a Czech doctor. Frania cheered up. We ate eggs and black bread and Leibel outlined his strategy for crossing the border.

He insisted that first we must think of a good, Russian-sounding surname. We all sat and racked our brains.

'Zukow,' I suggested. I must have heard his name at one time during my short stay in Chodecz. At the mention of 'Zukow' the other two looked blankly at one another: but none of us knew the names of any other Russian generals. I decided to ask the people on the platform. 'Excuse me, but can any of you name two or three Red Army generals who fought against the Nazis?' Most of them told me to get lost. A few said that Stalin himself had led the entire Red Army. A grey-haired man asked me why I wanted to know. When I replied that I merely wished to find out who had commanded the liberation forces in the east, he mentioned several generals, including a certain Konin.

It was a name that appealed to me because 'kon' in Polish

means 'horse'. Leibel and Frania liked it too. To this we affixed the name Igor. Igor Konin was just the Russian name we needed.

Leibel and I left our belongings on the platform with Frania and went off in search of 'our cousin, a Russian army captain who might be in Wroclaw'. We ignored the ordinary soldiers, approaching officers only, and asked them in Polish whether they knew a Captain Igor Konin. Most of them couldn't understand Polish and simply brushed us aside. Some shot us strange glances, asked us to repeat the question and went their way without answering.

Eventually, a Polish man pointed out a building being used by Russian officers. Since we were not allowed inside, we waited in front of the door and stopped every officer on his way in or out. One of the officers happened to speak Polish, and was willing to listen to our story. We told him that I was Leibel's cousin, that Leibel had a sister Frania who was waiting at the station with our belongings (Frania and Leibel did indeed look like brother and sister, with their dark eyes and dark hair), and that their sister Haya was lying ill in a hospital in Prague.

The officer smiled and blinked; yet we still pressed him. Leibel decided that it was time to show him the marvellous piece of paper Frania had been given by the Red Cross in Warsaw (despite which we had been thrown off the train by the Polish police). The officer read the document and handed it back to us. We told him we were Jewish survivors of the concentration camps. All we wanted was to get across the border into Czechoslovakia. The officer answered that the border was a little over sixty miles away – weren't we aware of it? We weren't, and the news came as a shock.

'So why did the Polish police make us get off the train?' asked Leibel. The officer shrugged his shoulders. Leibel and I looked at one another in dismay. 'My sister Haya might be dying all alone in Prague. I want to see her alive... please help us.' Leibel, I felt, was overacting a bit.

The officer asked who this Captain Igor Konin was, and Leibel was ready with the answer: Konin was a cousin of ours who had left Lodz in 1939 and gone to Russia, where he must have changed his name because on the list at the Red Cross in Lodz it said that Josef Zylberszac, now Captain Igor Konin, was currently somewhere in southwest Poland, searching for members of his family.

'I,' said Leibel, 'am Leibel Zylberszac, a cousin of Josef Zylberszac.'

I thought Leibel had done very well but by the look of him, the officer had heard quite enough of our story. He told us to wait outside, that he would be out in half an hour or so. Leibel played another card now, his ace, he later told me. He was confident that if anything would do the trick, this would. 'My sister is a beauty, a real princess!' he shouted after the officer. The officer stopped, turned and smiled. He had heard Leibel clearly but all he said was that if he met Captain Konin inside he would tell him that his cousins were waiting for him by the door and send him out to us.

Leibel and I felt that it was necessary to reward the Russian officer with a gift of some sort. 'Give him one of your rings,' I suggested to Leibel, but he dismissed the idea. 'What about a watch? The first Russian I met was riding a motorbike, and when he stopped to ask me to give him a watch, he nearly murdered me...'

'Ah well – nearly – we've all "nearly" been murdered every minute of the day for years... nearly!'

Leibel fell into deep thought. I could tell he was deep in thought because of the way he shut his eyes and lightly tapped his forehead.

'What we need is vodka and *machorka*, tobacco. All soldiers drink and smoke and when I tell him that we have good provisions for the journey, *speck* and bread, and *machorka* and vodka, he will surely come with us.'

We calculated that it would take about two hours to reach the border by train, another hour or so to cross safely into Czechoslovakia, plus the officer's travel time back to Wroclaw, roughly eight hours in all.

'He'll only do it if he can enjoy the trip, if we make it worth his while. We must tell Frania that we'll need to find some vodka and tobacco if we want to cross the border,' said Leibel.

Leibel decided to return to the station and I waited for the officer and brought him back with me. The station had become the scene of a lively black market, thronged with townspeople bartering food and drink in exchange for goods. Leibel winked at me as if to say, 'I got the vodka and the tobacco,' though I soon found out that he had decided not to buy tobacco because it was too costly. The officer took one look at Frania and it was clear to us that he liked her. He told us that the train was not due for an hour and a half and that he would be back before it arrived.

Some time later he came back with a junior officer who was instructed to take us across the border. He gave us a friendly pinch on the cheeks, winked at us and said goodbye. The train pulled into the station, and our junior officer helped us find seats. Russian soldiers came around to check our documents, and our officer showed them a piece of paper. They saluted and moved along and we were on our way to the Czech border.

The young Russian officer didn't speak Polish or drink vodka or smoke. He sat there quietly studying us as if he had never seen human beings like us before. He neither frowned nor smiled but kept to himself at first. We had the compartment all to ourselves and began to feel like important people or prisoners under escort. We took out our food and offered vodka, *speck* and bread to the officer. Leibel and Frania drank some of the vodka, and Frania grew tipsy and started waving her arms around and singing first in Polish and then in Yiddish. Her voice was not very pleasing or musical. Leibel was a better singer. I too joined in, but Frania said my voice was even worse than I imagined. They asked the officer to sing them a song. 'La, la, la?' and he replied 'Da, da,' and sang a song, the words of which sounded to us like '*Kalini, Kalini, Kalini, Kalina…*' He had a fine voice. Then he sang '*Moskva moja*' and Frania was transfixed as she listened to his voice. Suddenly she jumped up on his lap and wriggled her bottom from side to side. Although the officer was younger than Frania, he treated her like a child.

Forgetting that Frania was supposed to be his sister, Leibel winked at him as if to suggest that he could have her.

I was feeling very full from the meal of bread and *speck*. After so many years of starvation I was not used to eating this much and I curled up on the seat and fell asleep. When they woke me, the officer was just about to get off the train and we were on the Czech side of the border, not far from Prague.

The train pulled into Prague, and from the station we made our way to the hospital. The cobbled streets were strewn with the makeshift graves of German troops who had resisted the advancing Russian army. When we arrived at the hospital we found Frania's sister looking perfectly recovered. She approached us with a blanket around her shoulders and as the two sisters wept in each other's arms, my tears too began to flow.

Later that day, Leibel and I said goodbye to Frania and her sister and started back to the railway station. When we found out that the train for Theresienstadt wouldn't be leaving for some hours, I decided to search for the Red Cross and Leibel went to look for the black market.

When I eventually found the Red Cross office and began to speak in Polish to the two people at the counter, I was unable to make myself understood. I could have used my basic German with them but did not want to be taken for a German.

Eventually they gave up and called a woman who spoke several languages. She took me aside and asked me to tell her very slowly in Polish what I wanted to say and if she still couldn't understand me, to help her out in French or English or perhaps in German. She was kind and had a gentle face.

I told her a little about myself, that I was hoping to hear from members of my family, that I was sure they must still be alive. She asked me questions and wrote down the answers. I gave her the names of my brothers and sisters, the dates of their births, our address in Chodecz and explained that I had been to the branch of the Red Cross office in Wloclawek looking for them. We chatted some more. She asked where I was going from Prague. I said I hoped to join my aunt and uncle in Switzerland eventually but that my immediate destination was Theresienstadt. She asked me why I wanted to go there. I told her that I knew that some of the people I had been with in the Lodz ghetto, Auschwitz-Birkenau, Stutthof and Dresden had made it to Theresienstadt, so I would now try to find them. The Red Cross woman asked me for my aunt and uncle's address in Lausanne and told me she would write to them on my behalf in French. I remembered the address and she laughed when she heard my pronunciation of *chemin*. To make sure that I had given her the correct address she asked me to write it down for her. 'How nicely you write,' she said, and I told her that I had had a good teacher named Mrs Wisniewska. The woman said she would ask my aunt and uncle to send their reply to the Red Cross office in Prague, and that I should keep in touch with the office and let them know my whereabouts. Then she wrote down her name, Mrs Karlov, and the full address of the office on a piece of paper. How did I propose to get to Lausanne, she asked. I hesitated a moment and then shrugged my shoulders and said, 'By train, I guess, the way I travelled to Prague.'

'But what about papers... permits, visas... do you have any?'

'No,' I replied, 'I am travelling without papers.'

On a map of Europe she pointed first to Prague and then to Lausanne. 'You see, it's over six hundred miles from here to there, and you'll be crossing a number of frontiers on the way.'

This came as a surprise to me and I didn't know what to say. We looked at one another. 'The Swiss border is heavily guarded and they will not let you through without a visa. Switzerland is a rich country that tries to keep out the poorer Europeans.'

I was disappointed because I had imagined Switzerland to be a kind of extension of Czechoslovakia. Why I should have thought this, I don't know.

Mrs Karlov invited me home for supper. When I told her I was with a friend, she said I should bring him or her along. 'Meet me later at the office,' she said.

When I got back to the railway station and told Leibel that we had both been invited to supper by a Red Cross lady he said that he could not come along. 'I forgot to bring my dinner jacket,' he joked. 'How can I show up at this dinner party without one?' Besides, he was eager to join his brothers as soon as possible.

We decided to part. I had made up my mind to go back to the

Red Cross office and Leibel wanted to catch the train for Theresienstadt. I told him that I would be seeing him there either the next day or the day after.

'Perhaps,' said Leibel, and we waved goodbye to each other.

I returned to the Red Cross office with a few flowers that I had exchanged for three hard-boiled eggs. (Mother had taught me that a guest should always bring flowers.) Mrs Karlov was happy to see me and very pleased with the flowers.

'I knew you would return,' she said, and asked me where my friend was. When I told her he was in a hurry to find his brothers who had all survived, she said something like, 'You never know, one day you too may hear that members of your family survived.'

I sat in the corner of the Red Cross office and waited for Mrs Karlov's husband to collect us on his way home from work. He was a doctor.

On the table before me there was a book with pictures of mountains. I stared at the pictures and tried to make out what the captions said. I had been taught in school that the Tatra and Carpathian mountains were part of Poland. In this book they were Czech mountains. Who was I to believe? Mrs Wisniewska was no liar surely.

I remembered how I had learned to lie. In the camps when you sneaked up and fished a potato out of the cauldron and someone caught you, the rule was never to admit to it, because if you confessed, the punishment could cost you your life. The force used to extract a confession was often less severe. Perhaps lying is a thing people normally learn to do later in life. I had learned it in the camps at an early age. Dr Kleszczelski once said to me, 'If we survive this and you are lucky and able enough to continue studying, say you've already completed one university, the University of Auschwitz and Stutthof, and that you have graduated with honours in some very difficult subjects.'

I gazed at the picture of the mountains and pondered over what Dr Kleszczelski had meant by that. Suddenly I felt a presence looming before me, a very tall man with a thin and gentle face, his grey hair combed back.

'So you're the young Pole my wife told me about. How do you do? I am Dr Karlov.'

Something like that. I don't remember it word for word, only that he greeted me in German. I answered that I was a Pole but a Jewish Pole, or Polish Jew. He smiled and asked whether there was a difference. At first I didn't know what to say but then I replied that in Chodecz there had been about seven hundred Jews, and that most of them were murdered. He nodded. Because his nose was long I asked him if he too was Jewish.

'No,' he said. 'Do I look Jewish to you?'

'Oh yes,' I answered. 'Because you have a large Jewish nose.'

He sat down next to me and told me that while we waited for his wife to finish her work he would tell me something about large noses. Napoleon, he said, chose his officers on the basis of their eyes and facial traits, and most of his generals had large noses. And it was a much-feared and very large-nosed English general who eventually defeated him at Waterloo. I asked him if he too was an officer and he told me that not all men with large noses are officers. No, he was a doctor. He had a nice laugh.

When we got to their home, Dr Karlov examined me. 'Where and when did you get these boils on the back of your neck?' he asked. In the Lodz ghetto in 1942, I explained. I was a little scrawny, he said, but fairly fit.

As we ate soup, they asked me about my family and how we lived in Chodecz before 1939. Would I tell them a little about Auschwitz-Birkenau, they asked, and I did, but only a little, as the experience was still too raw to touch. I merely described my arrival in Auschwitz and how I had felt when out of a whole trainful of Jews in cattle cars only we metalworkers escaped the ovens. The Karlovs did not quite grasp what I meant by the ovens or they may have just been stunned by what I said. They looked first at each other and then at me and Mrs Karlov asked me if I would like to have a bath.

The bath was blissful and afterwards Dr Karlov gave me a pair of socks and a vest three times my size that came down to my knees and underpants I had to knot in front, and a clean shirt and trousers: a completely new set of clothes. He showed me how to tuck the trouser cuffs into my socks to make plus-fours of them. Mrs Karlov said she would throw out my old clothes and give me some more of her husband's things. I said that it was a pity to throw them out because I could sell them on the black market since I didn't have too many lice...

In Stutthof we used to say that during the day we were tortured by the SS and at night by the lice, bed bugs and fleas. They hadn't heard of Stutthof.

They asked me to try on the shirt. First I tried on Dr Karlov's trousers and then his shirt, and when I reappeared they burst out laughing, but their laughter was so contagious I couldn't help laughing with them. Tears of laughter were running down Mrs Karlov's face.

That night I slept in a clean bed between clean sheets. I awoke in the morning thinking I was back home with my parents and feeling so good that the days of the ghetto and the camp seemed unreal, like some horrific nightmare.

I stayed with the Karlovs for two nights. During the day I walked around the streets of Prague. After Chodecz and even Lodz, Prague was amazingly beautiful, and when I reached the River Vltava and looked across it, I saw buildings such as I had never seen before. This must be the most beautiful city in the world, I thought, and said so to the Karlovs in the evening. They said it was probably one of the fifteen most beautiful cities in the world. How wonderful and interesting the world must be, I thought.

'Come back to us again soon and we will teach you Czech,' smiled Mrs Karlov when we were saying goodbye. Dr Karlov shook my hand and told me to be sure not to lose my new trousers. 'You are our adopted son, if only for a few hours. Take good care of yourself,' they said.

A short while later I was in Theresienstadt. The Russian soldiers at the gates of the city would not let me through. I stood on the outside, looking in. After a time I spotted a woman from the Lodz ghetto who had worked in the metal division and had been in our transport to Auschwitz, Stutthof and Dresden. I shouted to her and she walked over to have a closer look at me. 'So you *are* alive!' she said from the other side of the fence. She spoke to me in Yiddish. 'They told us when they brought back the Boxer's woman that they had shot all of you.'

I learned from her that the Boxer's woman was in Theresienstadt, still alive, though sick; and that the Russians guarding the ghetto were a nice lot, but were under strict orders not to allow anyone in or out because of the contagious diseases that were so rife inside.

'Don't worry,' she added, 'there are a lot of holes in the fence further on, and it's easy to sneak in. And if you're caught all you'll get is a smack or two.'

Used as I was to the severity of the SS who would hang, shoot, or mercilessly beat anyone who disobeyed their orders, to be punished with a smack or two was truly laughable. That would certainly not deter me from getting in, I thought. Not even typhoid will stop me.

Inside, I located others from our transport. What interested them most of all was how we had escaped that night from the death march. They had believed the SS men who told them that we had been caught and shot. I began to realize that none of them really cared about me, they were so preoccupied with their own problems, their own lives and plans for the future.

I searched for Leibel and learned that he and his brothers were no longer in Theresienstadt. No one knew where they had gone. Leon Chimowicz had also left, together with his brother Alfred, and the rest of his family. In fact all the enterprising members of our group were gone.

I searched for Dr Kleszczelski. I brought greetings for him from Shimon, who I had met at Miss Rosa's place in Lodz. He was not in the barracks where I was told I would find him. I had missed him by a couple of days. He too was gone.

I felt tired and sad. It was Dr Kleszczelski, I remembered, who had worked out a way for us to sit zipper fashion in the cattle cars that transported us from Auschwitz to Stutthof. He had taught me many practical lessons of survival and had always spoken nicely to me.

And then there was the time, I recalled, when the Podlawskis had sent a parcel to me in Dresden, addressed to the plump German woman who worked in the office. She had written a letter on my behalf with her own return address. When the parcel arrived she brought it to the office and opened it in front of me. It contained *speck*, a slab of butter and a loaf of home-baked black bread. She took the butter and the *speck* herself and gave the bread to me.

A little later, she called Dr Kleszczelski into the office. He was escorted by an SS man. The doctor had been summoned this way many times before. Once inside, the SS man would sit down and smoke a cigarette whilst the plump German woman would pretend to be going over blueprints with Dr

Kleszczelski, though in reality she was consulting him about medical problems, of which she had many.

For a Jew to prescribe medicine to a German was a punishable offence – but he could whisper words of advice. And on that day she rewarded him with a piece of butter and some *speck* which he quickly slipped under his jacket. She told him it was from a parcel I had received, that I had kept the loaf of black bread myself and had given her the *speck* and the butter.

Later that day Dr Kleszczelski led me out to where the wire coils were stored and questioned me about the parcel. Why, he asked, had I given the German woman the *speck* and the butter? I told him that she had simply taken it.

'You must never again ask Podlawski or anyone else in Chodecz for food parcels,' he said, 'because if the SS find out, they will be punished and so will the German woman in the office, and you will be shot for asking a German woman to do what is *verboten*. I will write to the German woman telling her that no one must find out about the parcel. I will explain this to her as delicately as possible and put in some medical advice at the end of the note. The war will be over shortly and some of us may survive. It would be foolish to take risks that could get you shot. As a runner, you must be particularly careful.'

He then told me to bring the bread. I crawled out from the wire coils and brought him the bread from my hiding place. With the knife he had made from a broken saw blade, Dr Kleszczelski cut a few slices for his wife, himself and me. Then he buttered them and put some *speck* on top for each of us. He gave the rest of the loaf to me. We ate and whispered quietly together, savouring every morsel. It had been years since I tasted butter. The *speck* on top made it even more delicious. Fat on fat – to us it was bliss.

We talked about lying, I remember, because he had told me not to tell anyone about the parcel, and if I were confronted with it, he said, I should either be silent or lie. Lying in our circumstances was not a crime, if we did it to save lives, our own or others, or to avoid suffering. But if I survived, I would have to be re-educated because life after the war would require a different code of behaviour, a different way of doing things.

I wished I could see him, now, here in Theresienstadt. I wished I could greet him and ask him what I should do next. I felt lost.

I found my way to the infirmary, where the sick and dying lay. I managed to catch a glimpse of the Boxer's woman but the Czech doctor attending her told me not to touch anything or come close to the patients. I told the woman Moniek was still alive but she didn't seem to react. In fact, I knew that Moniek was probably dead but she was in such terrible pain that I wanted to give her some hope by telling her that I had seen him alive. I repeated the news and went on to describe what happened when we returned to Dresden. Nothing I said made much of an impression on her. I told her that I would go back to Oberpoyritz and try to find him, and tell him that she was alive. At this she nodded and I think she said, 'Will you do this for me?'

As I was leaving the infirmary the doctor told me to get some food. He gave me directions to the soup kitchen, where I found more people from my transport. That night they put me up in their barracks. The place was overrun with fleas, but I must have either been immune to them or utterly exhausted because I slept till morning without waking once.

I decided to return to the Fuchses and so the following day I went to Litomerice where I exchanged a bar of soap for some eggs and a piece of *speck*. I found out that there was a train going to Dresden. People at the station were not sure when it was due to arrive, but they were certain it would be hours yet.

Instead of waiting there I knocked on a door nearby and asked the Czech lady of the house in Polish and broken German if she would please hard-boil the eggs for me. It took a bit of pantomiming to make her understand, but when she did, she laughed heartily and invited me in. Other members of the family arrived and I told them a little about myself. They nodded to one another in confirmation as they grasped my words. I told them that I had vowed to return to the Fuchses who lived near Dresden and that I wanted to bring them something in gratitude for all their help.

Then I told them about Avraham Sztajer and Adam Szwajcer and Moniek's girlfriend but this was too complicated for my rudimentary Czech, so I returned to the story of the Fuchses, explaining that the butter and the *speck* I bartered for my soap was for them. The lady of the house was puzzled that I, a Jew, would go all the way back to Dresden with butter and *speck* for a German family…

She hard-boiled the eggs for me, and served me a bowl of soup. As I ate, the children whispered amongst themselves and one of the daughters asked me where my father and mother were.

When I told them they looked baffled and a long silence followed, eventually broken by the lady of the house who told me, half in mime, that the train for Dresden is always full and that sometimes people have to sit on the roof. Her husband gave me a length of wire and a rope so I would be able to strap myself to the train if necessary. In addition he gave me a rag to use as a mask to keep the soot out of my nose and mouth, in case I had to ride near the engine.

I offered the lady a few of my eggs in return for her help and kindness, but she declined them. Inside my bag was the rest of the precious bar of soap, so I cut off a piece of the chunk I was going to give the Fuchses, and this she willingly accepted. I thanked them for the soup and they patted me on the back in a friendly farewell. The father accompanied me to the station and waited with me there until the train arrived.

The train was full to bursting, just as they had warned me, with people crammed into every possible space. With the man's help I joined the passengers on the roof. A man sitting beside me said in German that the train would be passing under many bridges so I should strap myself to the horizontal running cable. He asked me whether I had a belt and I showed him that I was fully equipped with a rope and a wire and proceeded to fasten them around and under the cables. The man sitting behind the engine gave a loud blast on a horn every time the train approached a tunnel or was about to go under a bridge. He was black with soot and soon I too was covered in it. The engineer also sounded warnings on the train whistle, and every time I heard the trumpet and the whistle blowing I would lie down flat till we had passed through the tunnel or under the bridge. At first it was fun, but soon I saw how dangerous this mode of travel was; it required constant alertness and because I couldn't nod off for a moment, it was extremely tiring.

When the train made its first stop, I lowered myself into one of the compartments through the window. My sudden appearance provoked fierce resentment. The passengers punched and hit me but I refused to be ejected. Compared to the SS transports in jam-packed cattle cars this was only mildly uncomfortable. Soon I found myself, or rather made myself, a place to squat and when I became hungry I ate an egg and a piece of black bread.

I dozed in this position. When I awoke I felt elated at the thought of meeting up with Sztajer and Szwajcer again and telling them about the survivors I had met from our transport and the good news that Moniek's woman was still alive... and all the news from Theresienstadt and about my travels to Poland.

At what we all thought was the German border, the Russian soldiers simply let the train pass. It was all strangely simple and uneventful compared to the difficult crossing Leibel and I had had from Poland into Czechoslovakia. The passengers on the train were mainly adults and those near me spoke German to each other, but they spoke it in whispers, no longer the confident class of only a few weeks before.

By this time I had a place to sit, if only on the floor. I kept to myself. No one spoke to me. The only thing I had forgotten to bring along for the journey was water; it was hot in the train and I was thirsty, very thirsty. So when the train stopped in Decin, I stepped off with my bag, found the lavatory, drank some water and washed my face, in time to get back on the same train.

We were travelling along the river now. The countryside was beautiful. I stood at the window, admiring all I saw. Wouldn't it be nice, I thought, to return one day with my family and sail down the river?

'Is *das die Elbe*?' I asked the strange woman next to me.

She looked me up and down.

I got off the train at Pirna, where our transport had been taken after the bombing of Dresden. I knew the name. Oberpoyritz must be somewhere nearby, I thought.

It was growing dark. If I had to find a place to sleep, I told myself, better a small place like Pirna than the big station in Dresden.

An elderly man was sweeping what seemed to me a perfectly clean floor. In Poland, I thought, people say, 'The floor will wear out if it's swept too often. What's the point of cleaning a floor that isn't dirty?'

This old boy at Pirna station did not philosophize – he simply got on with it, painstakingly sweeping every inch of floor in a steady rhythm.

I asked him where Oberpoyritz was. He put down his broom and took me into the adjoining room where he showed it to me on the map. 'Three or four miles from here,' he said.

'Can I sleep here in this hall?'

'Ja, ja, natürlich.' He motioned to me to follow and led me to a small store room. There he took a blanket out of a trunk and said in German, 'In the morning, just put it back on top of the trunk. No one here will take it.' Fantastic, I thought. No thieves in Pirna. So soon after the war, and not one German soldier or SS man in sight. All of them vanished. Nothing more to fear. I felt safer here at the railway station in Pirna than I would have felt anywhere in Poland.

I found a clean, working toilet and a basin with running water. The water tasted good so I drank some. I asked the old man for a small towel. He unlocked the trunk and fished out a big clean rag. 'Just put it back with the blanket in the morning,' he said. I noticed that he had a book sticking out of his pocket; very few Polish railway waiting-room cleaners would have been literate.

I took out one of my eggs to give him, but he only smiled and said, 'You eat it.' So I ate it for dinner, drank some more water, washed myself and recited the *Shema*, and curled up in the corner of the room where I slept like a log.

The following day I rose early. I went to the toilet and enjoyed this clean public place. There was no one at the station so I stripped naked and washed myself all over, making full use of the facilities and the rag the old man had lent me.

I put the rag and the blanket back in the store room on top of the locked trunk, drank some more water and set off towards the River Elbe in the north. If I followed it I'd eventually reach my destination. It was a lovely June morning. I was cheerful and it felt good to be alive. Soon, I thought, I would be seeing Sztajer and Szwajcer and the Fuchses. I reckoned that it would take me no more than a couple of hours to cover the few miles.

The sky was blue with fluffy white clouds and the light was so beautiful and bright that even the bomb-shattered buildings didn't look too bad. It was a warm morning, I remember, not too hot. My eighteenth birthday was approaching. Would I spend it with Sztajer and Szwajcer and the Fuchses?

As I walked on, I thought about my family: Zosia, Iccio, Peccio and his wife and child – those who might still be alive. Maybe I would hear something soon.

I walked on, checking with passers-by from time to time to make sure I was on the right road to Oberpoyritz. After I crossed the river I found a nice spot with a view and stopped there to eat a piece of bread and an egg. I ate slowly, taking small bites and chewing for a long time to get as much pleasure as I could out of the good food. A little butter and *speck* would have been delicious but they were presents for the Fuchses and I controlled myself.

Suddenly I realized that I had nothing to give Sztajer and Szwajcer. What a pity. I will give them each a tiny piece of soap, I thought. Surely they will understand that this is all I can offer.

Now I began to recognize my surroundings. I was on the outskirts of Oberpoyritz. Once the Fuchses had taken me cycling along this road. But those passing me by were all strangers and no one took any notice of me. Their faces looked troubled and preoccupied.

I decided that I would first take a look inside the garden shed where I had been sleeping only a few weeks previously. Why, I don't know. It was a simple impulse, curiosity to see if it still looked as I remembered it. I went around the back and climbed over the fence. The garden looked neglected. Strange, I thought, it is not like the Fuchses to let the weeds grow. The shed was unlocked. I walked in. Nothing much had changed except that there were boxes lying around where I used to sleep. Inside the boxes were Mr Fuchs' belongings, along with some cobwebs and dust here and there.

I took out my presents and prepared myself as I walked to the front door. With a pounding heart I knocked and waited. There was no sound inside. I knocked a few more times. Then I knocked louder. Mrs Fuchs opened the door. She looked wizened, terribly aged. She stood there and stared at me and her eyes grew wild. She was dressed in black.

I greeted her and began to say that I had kept my promise to come back with gifts for her and her husband, just as I had rehearsed it so many times when I imagined meeting them face to face again. But before I could finish my little speech, she emitted a piercing shriek, a raw animal cry that astounded and frightened me. Then she shouted 'Gie wek wek... Go away, go away!' and slammed the door in my face.

Her neighbour, the young German woman with the baby who had shown me a photo once of her husband wearing a uniform which had skulls on the collar, the insignia of an SS unit, hurried out when she heard the noise. I approached her and she beckoned me to follow her into her house. Inside she told me what had happened.

'Although the war was over by a number of days, the hatred of the Jewish people by the Germans was still very great. When some Oberpoyritz men who had served in the SS found out that these two Jews, Szwajcer and Sztajer had been hidden by Mr and Mrs Fuchs and that now with Mr Fuchs they were becoming active in searching out SS men and organizing the citizens of Oberpoyritz, they came armed one day and took the three of them into a nearby field. They bound their arms behind their back and also bound their legs, made them kneel, and shot Mr Fuchs and Szwajcer through the head. They took Sztajer – who told them something – away. Mrs Fuchs dragged her husband to the yard and buried him under the cherry tree. Szwajcer was buried in the field where he was shot. Nobody knows what happened to Avraham Sztajer.'

We sat in silence. I was stunned. She put a cup of soup in front of me, and I ate it.

'Go now! It isn't safe for you here.'

I asked her to give the presents to Mrs Fuchs and left. I didn't ask her whether her own husband had returned or not.

I started back, not to Pirna this time, but to Dresden. It seemed safer to take the route through the fields. Although Dresden was further away than Pirna, I thought I had a better chance of getting a place on the train to Litomerice from Dresden. I thought of Sztajer and Szwajcer and Mr Fuchs. I was hot and thirsty. I knocked on someone's door and asked for water. They gave it to me, and I drank a great quantity and rinsed my hands and face.

A little further on, I said the *Shema* three times, once for each of them. I lay down on a patch of grass and looked up at the sky. Fluffy white clouds floated above me. I suddenly remembered that the whole time we lived and worked at the factory in Dresden, the windows had always been barred and the glass taped and painted out: we never saw the sky. It looked beautiful to me now.

Back in Theresienstadt, those who knew I had travelled all the way to Dresden to find Sztajer and Szwajcer and perhaps bring them back with me wanted to know whether I had at least managed to see them.

'By the time I got to Oberpoyritz, Sztajer and Szwajcer were gone,' I told everyone, including Moniek's woman who was still sick and in the infirmary.

She took one look at me as I entered the room and said, 'He's dead, isn't he.'

'He was gone by the time I got there,' I lied. I don't know why I said this to her.

I was tired and hungry, and saddened by my trip to

Oberpoyritz. All I wanted was to eat something and then sleep, sleep, sleep. I made my way to the soup kitchen. The cook gave me three helpings. She asked where I was living and when I told her I had no place to live at present she told me to try the Children's Home. I ate the soup and went to find the Home. There, the man in the office spoke Polish. When he asked my age, I told him I would be eighteen soon and he replied that I was too old for the Home where the oldest children in care were sixteen. I went away in a daze, so tired my brain wasn't working. I sat outside and rested against the wall, wondering what to do next.

I felt defeated. I had liked the look of the place. Then I remembered Dr Kleszczelski's words about lying: 'Lying in our circumstances is not a crime, if we do it to save lives, our own or others', or to avoid suffering.'

I got up and went to the man in the office and said I had made a mistake, that I had actually been born in 1929, which made me sixteen years old. He smiled at me and said that I certainly looked sixteen. There was another man with him and they asked me to wait outside while they talked something over. When they called me in again, the man I had spoken to first said he was glad I had returned because the Home was intended for young people exactly like myself who had lost their families. In fact, he had been about to send some boys out to look for me and bring me back. What would I like to do now? he asked. I told him that I wanted to wash my face and go to sleep because I was very tired.

The man smiled. He handed me a tin with a powder inside called Ovaltine, a present from the Red Cross, he said. Then he showed me where the toilets and showers were and led me to a room full of bunk beds.

'Here you are,' he said, pointing to the top bunk that was going to be mine, a real bed with a mattress, pillow and blanket.

I washed my face and hands and before I could put my head down I was fast asleep.

Next thing I knew I was being shaken awake by a youth sitting on top of me. He was a boy about my age, naked from the waist up, holding a knife and yelling first in Polish and then in Yiddish to get off his bunk this minute. It was still light outside. I heard his voice as if through a haze because he had woken me out of such a profound sleep. I asked him to get off me please, that I would move to a different bunk later but that now I had to sleep. And then I rolled over with the boy still sitting on me and fell fast asleep again.

Izzy, Menachem, Moniek, Cygan, Pomerance, Harry Balsam and others from the home in Theresienstadt became my friends. We would walk around with our tins of Ovaltine under our arms, and chew the powder of fortified barley, powdered egg and malted milk – eating the dry powder instead of mixing it with liquid and drinking it. A spoonful of Ovaltine glues up the mouth for a while.

One day Cygan told me about some tins of meat that he had heard rumoured were buried just outside of Theresienstadt. We went to investigate the site, which looked like a mound, or an archaeological Tel, a site where city upon city is buried under the same spot, with a barbed-wire fence around it. Cygan said the Germans had buried the tins there some time in 1944 and it was said that those who ate that meat got typhoid and died. The Russians had prohibited anyone from digging for the tins.

But Harry Balsam nudged me and when Cygan wasn't listening, whispered that he could tell which tins had good meat inside and which ones would make you sick. He was an expert, he said. He ate the good meat all the time. Every morning he would dig for meat in the mound, and in fact, he was planning on going there tomorrow, if I cared to come along. I said I would.

The following day Harry woke me at dawn. We tiptoed out of the house and made our way to the mound. Harry was always laughing. He called me Rom. He liked to shorten people's names like that. Pomerance was Pom. We had our tins of Ovaltine with us and stopped for a mouthful of the dry powder. A silence of several minutes followed as we stirred the Ovaltine around in our mouths and tried to moisten it with our saliva.

We crawled under the barbed wire and then climbed to the top of the mound and began to dig. We uncovered the first tin. Harry pointed to the convex lid and when he pierced it, a foul-smelling gas came out. Only the flat-lidded tins contain edible meat, he explained. Then he found a good tin. He opened it and it smelled fine. He ate a few chunks that he cut with a penknife and passed the tin to me. I helped myself to a few chunks too, and then we put the half-finished tin in a safe place and began to search for more. But the rest of the tins were spoiled, it seemed, with bulging lids the size of inverted saucers.

I was tired of digging by then and went down to wait near the barbed wire. Soon Harry joined me. He thought it was wise to leave quickly before the Russians caught us. We crawled out from under the wire with our improvized shovel and our Ovaltine and the half-eaten tin of meat and found a place nearby to rest and chat.

'Ever been with a woman?' Harry asked. The question surprised me because at home before the war no one ever talked about sex, or even alluded to it.

'Why do you ask?' I answered with a question and Harry replied that for the price of the leftover meat in the tin we could both have sex with a 'smashing' woman he knew in one of the barracks. He had started as a shoeshine boy and graduated to master of the household for an SS commander named Müller, so he had found plenty of opportunities to have sex, he explained. Though it went against what my mother had always told me – 'Girls and boys should stay pure until they fall in love and get married' – the vision of sex with a 'smashing' woman was rather appealing.

'Let's go right now and make a date,' I said.

Harry gave a little laugh at the thought of making a date with Miss Rutka. We walked through the barracks to the first floor where Miss Rutka lived. Harry knocked on the door.

'Who's there?' asked a squeaky voice inside.

'Harry Balsam with a friend,' he answered.

'So early in the morning?' asked the voice, and then added, 'Wait.'

One day a Czech doctor arrived at the Home. He had a connection with the Jewish Refugee Committee in London, an organization set up by a number of well-to-do Jewish families in the UK. The idea was to send Jewish children who had lost their families during the war over to England where they would help us to start new lives and act as financial guarantors. They had permission to bring over a thousand children, but I later learned that only 735 could be found. One and a half million Jewish children were murdered, were killed or were starved to death.

One by one, the doctor called us into his temporary surgery, asked us various questions, talked to us at length about this and that, and only then carried out the examination.

He told me that although I was skinny, I seemed in excellent health. What sport was I keen on before the war? he asked. I told him that there was a lake in our town where my brother had taught me to swim at an early age. 'Then you should do as much swimming as possible here in Theresienstadt,' he said, and sent his assistant to show me where the pool was. I found it in the middle of a park lined with horse chestnut trees, except that it looked more like a pit than a pool, full of leaves and rubbish.

The doctor received permission from the Russian officer at

Theresienstadt to clean and fill the pool. He called the boys together and told them about the project. I said I would start emptying it the following day but that I would need volunteers to help me. Everyone laughed. I had forgotten that in the Lodz ghetto sometimes, volunteers were promised extra rations. 'Just go with the escort and dig some pits,' they were told, but the volunteers never came back. When they finished digging they were the first ones to be shot. Now everyone knew that only simpletons and fools volunteer. Why work, the boys thought, if you can spend your time doing nothing? And anyway, they were not really keen on swimming.

The following day I began to empty the pool all on my own. I was given two large old buckets and a spade. I made myself a yoke and began to fill the buckets and empty them out. I figured that the work would take about five days to complete. It was warm and sunny, the air was fresh and clean and as I didn't have to hurry, I found it rather pleasurable. I remembered how Podlawski used to come over to load manure once a year and take it out to our fields where someone else would spread it. I wished I had Podlawski here with me – together we could have finished the job in a couple of days. And I was bringing up a lot of compost too that would have been good for the fields and gardens back home.

Several of the boys came out to watch me, mostly out of curiosity; they didn't offer to help. I worked my way methodically from one end to the other. The doctor showed up with some sandwiches for me, part of his lunch, he said, because I was working so hard I needed good nourishing food. When I was taking my lunch break I saw a curious dead chestnut tree whose shape intrigued me greatly.

Mrs Wisniewska had once taken the whole class out to sketch trees. It was a lovely spring day and I chose a dead horse chestnut tree and she gave me a high mark for it. I was nine years old at the time and my drawing was pinned up on the wall of our class for a whole week, a great artistic achievement for me. Tomorrow, I thought, I will ask the helpful doctor for a pencil and some paper and come and draw this tree.

The boys who watched me working must have thought I was having a great time, because the same day, late in the afternoon, a boy my age called Yoyne Fuchs came out to help me. We worked, talked and laughed together and became fast friends. His younger brother, a perky boy who kept jabbering and giving us advice, marred our enjoyment somewhat, but only for a little while.

Next day two other boys came to lend a hand, so there were now four of us working. The doctor visited us again and sent special food out to us. After lunch I took time off to sketch the tree. I signed the finished drawing and gave it to him as a gift.

It took us longer to empty and clean the pool than I had originally estimated. But none of us worried about it. We had plenty of time. It was enough that we felt safe. No more guards, no more SS, no more fear of being murdered. Those days were gone. Now we felt playful and free.

When we eventually filled the pool from a nearby hydrant,

the water looked a little murky, and to some of the boys, uninviting. Not so to me. I plunged in immediately and swam a few lengths. The water was cold but I enjoyed it.

In the days to come others who knew how to swim joined me in the pool. The pool became our meeting point, the centre of our activities. Here we sunbathed, splashed and swam. As both ends were deep, those who could not swim would carefully lower themselves into the water and pull themselves along the railing.

We went on swimming all the time during those sunny and carefree days of July 1945. Some time later, the doctor called me into his office. In return for the sketch of the chestnut tree, he said, and for my hard work emptying the pool and cleaning it, he wished to present me with a small gift. He handed me a little packet. In it I found an old penknife, two pencils, a rubber and a barely-used sketchbook. I was overjoyed. These gifts meant a lot to someone who had absolutely nothing.

The doctor also said that he understood from the man in the office that every day I asked if there was a letter for me. I told him I was hoping to hear from Chodecz, and from my aunt in Switzerland. He asked me to let him have all the details. He would follow up on them, he said, and do his best to help me.

During my time in Theresienstadt I received no letters from Chodecz or from my aunt in Switzerland. I longed for news and this became a bit of an obsession with me. Every day at the office of the Children's Home the man would say, 'Still no letter for you, sorry.'

Whenever the doctor came he would greet me warmly, find out how I was and tell me feelingly that so far no letter had arrived from Chodecz or Switzerland.

'But don't give up hope... I have a feeling that one of these days it is going to come.'

I would never give up hope. I had seen what happened to the people in the Lodz ghetto when they gave up hope. Their eyes would lose a certain clarity and cloud over, they would cease to care about most things, about life itself, and within two or three days they would be dead. In the concentration camps the process was quicker still: death struck within hours when a person ceased to hope. Now that I was free and safe at last and there was so much to live for, how could I lose hope?

I wrote to Chodecz and to my aunt and gave my letters to the man in the office to post. I would write the letters either on my bunk bed or in the park by the pool. All the while I kept thinking about my family, about my future. I could not conceive of the days and weeks and months ahead without my family. It suddenly seemed unreal to me that I was alone. I needed my family. Why? I didn't know. I just did. My letters to Chodecz always ended, 'If I don't hear from you I will take it that Zosia, Iccio and the others have not arrived yet.'

I wrote this because I didn't want to get a letter from Mr and Mrs Podlawski saying bluntly that they must be dead because they hadn't shown up in Chodecz. *So dear Romek, you must accept the fact...* I just didn't want to get a letter like that. And I never did.

•

On 7 July 1945, my eighteenth birthday, some of my newly-acquired friends and I walked out of the Theresienstadt compound – we no longer referred to it as the ghetto – and went down to the river. There we undressed and splashed about in the shallow water. I was the only one who could swim, and when I grew bored with splashing, I dived into the deep water and swam with the current. I was thoroughly enjoying myself but suddenly I turned and saw my friends waving their arms at me, shouting, 'Come back!' When I reached the shore I offered to give them all swimming lessons, but there were no takers. It would not have been a smart thing to try in any case, with the current so strong.

Then, after we had dried off in the warm sun and dressed again, we wandered through the countryside till we came to a field where the strawberries had been picked. Still remaining after the harvesting were the very small berries, which had ripened in the meanwhile. We sprawled among the strawberries and basked in the sun. The war was over, and we were free. We ate our fill of the tiny, overripe berries.

Postscript

In the autumn of 1945, we youths who had survived the ghettos, concentration camps and working as slave labour were brought over from Theresienstadt to England by the Jewish Refugee Committee. We were flown in Lancaster bombers to Carlisle in northern England. There, army trucks were waiting to transport us to the Lake District for a short recuperation period at a camp by Lake Windermere. Later, we would be split up into groups of thirty or so and placed in hostels on the outskirts of cities all over the UK.

Our camp was between Windermere and Ambleside – the address was Troutbeck Bridge. It was a makeshift complex of wooden structures and huts that had been erected for hydroplane workers during the war on the edge of Lake Windermere. The Jewish Refugee Committee (JRC) had decided to bring us there to recuperate in the natural beauty of the Lake District, where the air was clean, fresh and healthy.

The JRC sent people to observe, study us and ask questions. All Jewish, the majority of these people had come over from Germany in 1936 or 1937, and were interested in child psychology. They wanted to ascertain how physically and mentally damaged we were after such a long time in ghettos and concentration camps, and the effect that the loss of our families had had on us teenagers.

A few weeks after my arrival in Windermere, I was called into the office and handed a typed postcard from Aunt Wiener in Lausanne. It had been sent to the Red Cross in Prague, and then re-directed by the nice lady there to Windermere. I found a person who knew English and Polish who could translate it for me. It read: 'We are happy that you are alive. Please let us know who else from the family has survived. Tell us how is your health.'

I wrote back in Polish, telling her that I was ready to come to Lausanne and live with her, her husband and all the cousins. Could she please send me the tickets for the train and the boat and a little money. I then added a rather long P.S: 'I feel very good within myself and the doctor here has told me that I am healthy. I grieve for all the members of my family – Mother, Father, Grandfather, brothers and sisters, who have died. I do this mostly when I go to bed or in the middle of the night, as I don't want others to see me doing it. They would think me weak. The woman doctor who examined us, told me that if I want to put some meat and muscles on my bones, I should eat everything that they give us here and swim in the lake twice a day. That this will make me fit and strong. My parents may have written to you before the war that at the age of nine I swam across the lake in Chodecz. Please don't worry about me, for soon I shall be with you all in Lausanne.'

In due course a letter in Polish arrived back from my aunt. Inside the letter was a five pound note. My aunt wrote: 'Coming to Switzerland cannot be rushed. It is not so easy. We are not yet Swiss citizens although we have lived here for twenty years. We shall do all we can and will let you know how things progress.'

I was shattered by this news. I had been so completely, so absolutely certain that they would have me as soon as they received news that I was alive. I was in such need of family love, and I had got it into my head that I would be going to my aunt in Switzerland. I read Aunt Sarah's reply over and over, feeling bitterly disappointed; it was not the reply I had expected. That night I wept for a long time.

This deeply hurtful news from Lausanne came at the time when the full loss of my family was really dawning on me; I felt it harder then than at any time since the end of the war. I so much needed the warmth, the caring, the closeness of my extended family – now that my own close family were no longer alive. Though some of my friends had developed close friend-ships with one another, I kept everyone at arm's length and treated them all as acquaintances. I wanted my family; I didn't want any close friendships. My aunt's letter left me in a con-fused state of mind for days.

•

I missed Mrs Lewandowska as well. When I had returned to Chodecz in May 1945 and found it so empty of all the Jewish people, she was the one who cared; she was warm and kind towards me. I needed that kindness and warmth. I told myself: 'Well, this is natural, after all, she breastfed me and she knew me from the day I was born until the age of thirteen, when I was sent to the Lodz ghetto.' But I am sure that her kindness and warmth was intermingled with a great amount of love. She was a natural and spontaneous person and I wrote a long letter to her. My letter was returned unopened. On the envelope were the words scribbled in pencil: *Left Chodecz*.

I wrote to her sister, Mrs Podlawska, with a small gift of soap. At the hostel we were given a very small amount of pocket money and I could only, and with difficulty, buy a small gift. I asked her to send me Mrs Lewandowska's new address. Gienia, the youngest of Mrs Podlawska's three daughters, replied to my letter. She told me that her aunt had left a number of weeks ago, and that they hadn't heard from her since and had no for-warding address. There was a P.S. to the note: 'Stasiek [her father] would like you to send him some tobacco.'

Poland at the time was a communist government under the thumb of the Soviet Union. In 1947 I went to the Polish Embassy in London. I asked whether the embassy could help me find family Lewandowski from Chodecz, who had gone to settle in the Western Territories of Poland. I received a very short, negative reply: 'No, we can *not* help you.'

Twenty years later, in 1967, I visited Chodecz. Mr Podlawski was no longer alive, and neither was my former teacher, Mrs Wisniewska. Mrs Podlawska was then seventy-two years old. I knew this because my mother had been born in 1897 and Mrs Podlawska two years earlier, in 1895. When we embraced, I realized what a diminutive person I was holding in my arms. Her blue-grey eyes still had that alert sparkling look but her face was all wrinkled. To me she looked about eighty-five. She was thrilled with the gifts that I had brought her. Her hands trembled as she was opening the packets. I told her that I had also brought some gifts for her sister, Mrs Lewandowska.

'Oh,' she said, 'you might just as well give them to me, I haven't heard from her in years, not so much as a squeak, not since they left Chodecz all those years and years ago.'

She told me the latest town gossip – mainly about who had died. Our former neighbour, Mrs Eszner, had died... and indeed, none of her sons had ever come back from the war. Mr and Mrs Giewis, the butcher and his wife, were also no longer alive. Then she told me about who now lived in my parents' home and that only one of her own daughters was married.

I went to visit Marysia Giewis, and to express my condolences on the death of her parents. She introduced me to her husband and their three children. Her husband was also a butcher and had worked for Marysia's father. I said that I had been sorry to learn from Mrs Podlawska that both Mr and Mrs Giewis were no longer alive, but Marysia's husband cut in with a remark that surprised me: 'When father-in-law was told that he had only hours to live, he asked for a bottle of vodka, but the poor blighter never finished it, he died spilling the liquid all over himself.'

I asked Marysia about Mrs Lewandowska and her daughter Jadwiga, whom Marysia had known well. 'Not a word from them since they left for the new Polish Territories. If I were you, I would go first to the post office, as they may be re-addressing Lewandowska's letters, and then, if that fails, to the town hall.'

At the town hall, I spoke to an official who seemed optimistic that he might be able to help me find the address of Mr and Mrs Lewandowski. He said that he knew them well, and that his hunch was that they must have settled in a place in the new Polish Territories where there was a lake for Mr Lewandowski, since he could not exist without fishing. This made sense to me, and to encourage the official, I gave him a tip of a few pounds. He thanked me, pocketed the money and warmly pumped my hand. 'By the time you get back to England, Mr Architect, there will be a letter awaiting you from me, with the precise details of the Lewandowski family, how they are and where they live.'

About a week later, a letter arrived from this town hall official saying in a round-about way that tracing the Lewandowskis was proving a difficult, costly and time-consuming undertaking... and that one required funds to complete the task. I understood the kind of person I was dealing with, and wrote back that I would reward him generously when he sent me their address. But I never did manage to find lovely Mrs Lewandowska and her family.

In autumn 1946, a group of us were now living in a hostel on the edge of Epping Forest, and there I received two letters. One was from Mr and Mrs Podlawski, written, of course, in Polish on their behalf by someone in Chodecz.

'Szanowny Panie Romku', *our sow which we bought with some of the things your father and mother left with us, had eight piglets. We had to register them with the authorities which we have now done. The girls* [their three daughters] *are in the cities. No Jews have come back to Chodecz. We grew potatoes on your father's land – the plot near Przedecz which you assigned to us. Stasiek would like you to send him tobacco and some English money with which we could buy many things here. Fond greetings...* followed by a squiggle from each of them.

The other letter was from my Cousin Izaak from Izbica Kujawska, who had now returned from the Soviet Union. (Izaak went there with my half-brother Iccio in 1939.) Iccio was shot by Stalin's men because he was a communist and a Jew and knew too much about Trotsky. Stalin did away with such people. Cousin Izaak, who was not a communist, got only four years hard labour. He married a non-Jewish nurse called Marusia, and they had a daughter, Ilana, who was born in 1944.

In 1945, Cousin Izaak and his wife and daughter returned to Poland to Wloclawek. (All the Jewish people from Izbica Kujawska, 1500 of them, including Cousin Izaak's mother, brothers, sisters, aunts, uncles and cousins, were murdered in Chelmno. Cousin Izaak's father died before 1939.) Now he wrote to me:

Marusia had a son, and now little Ilana has a brother. We have named him David after my father. Both Marusia and David are well and so am I and Ilana. I went and collected Danusia [the daughter of his brother, Szlamek, who had been killed in the Lodz ghetto, and had been hidden with a Polish family]. *Danusia thought that the Polish woman and her husband were her parents and cried, and so did this woman. When I came there, I found Danusia barefoot, looking after geese. It was not easy for me to take her away. Then this woman came one day to Wloclawek and stole Danusia back. It took me, with the help of the police, over two weeks to find her. And again screams and tears from them both. Now I have given her to a Zionist organization who will take her, together with other Jewish children whom they have collected in Poland, to France, and from there to Palestine. We will all be going to settle in Palestine too, but a little later, when the new baby is a bit bigger and stronger. We have received a small parcel from Aunt Sarah in Switzerland. If you could send me these things for the baby, it would be much appreciated…*

There followed a list of what he wanted.

•

Of the fate of others I came across during the war, Mr Braun, the civilian manager of the armaments factory in Dresden, became a deputy mayor of the city after the war. Later, he, his wife and their two sons were murdered by the Russian Stasi during the Communist period. Apparently, before the war, Braun had denounced some Communist comrades, and the killing of him and his family was intended as revenge for this.

Czarnulla, whom I first came across in the Lodz ghetto and who, with Braun, had placed me with the Fuchses, was a kind of Schindler figure. It was in fact Czarnulla who obtained Himmler's consent for us 500 metalworkers to be sent to Dresden on 23 November 1944. Czarnulla was captured when the war ended and was taken to Poland and sentenced to death. Mrs Fuchs told me this in the early 1980s, when I visited her. She had liked Czarnulla very much, and saved the letters that he wrote to her from a Polish prison. Czarnulla must have been in his late forties when Mrs Fuchs was about thirty-seven, around the same age as her husband. Czarnulla had a dual personality. On the one hand, he was responsible for terrible things in the Lodz ghetto, such as fleecing the Jews of Luxembourg etc, channelling the booty through the metal factory: on the other hand, on a personal level, capable of doing some good to a few individual Jews.

Leibel, who had been in the Lodz ghetto and whom I encountered just after the war, I didn't see again until 1968. I visited

Leibel in Toronto, where he worked as a butcher in a meat-processing plant. He came to collect my wife and I in his huge car, and then proudly showed us around his large bungalow, which had a television in every room. His wife was sensitive and nice and terrified of him; apparently he often shouted at her, one day so much so that the police were called in. He had a little seven-year-old boy who loved reading, and I took him to a shopping mall to buy him some books. He sat on the floor of the shop and became so absorbed that for a while I couldn't find him. This son of Leibel's is now a doctor. Leibel is no longer alive.

My son Ardyn, who lives in Israel, found that Sztajer (who, like me, had been helped by the Fuchses) was living there too. In 1991, when I heard the news, I flew to Israel and together with my son, went to visit him. He told us what happened that May in 1945. This is his story.

The day before the shootings, he and Szwajcer had gone to Dresden. There they met a high-ranking Soviet Jewish officer who was in charge of a group of sappers repairing bridges along the River Elbe. This Jewish officer needed a house close to the river for his headquarters. Sztajer and Szwajcer found him such a place and the officer agreed that they could both live in the basement of this house and thus be under his protection. They returned to Oberpoyritz and the Fuchses' house to collect their belongings but the following day was the day they were rounded up and taken to a field by three local ex-SS men.

Fuchs and Szwajcer were shot, but just as Sztajer was about to get a bullet in the back of his head, he told the killers that he had something important to tell them. He told them that after the bombing of Dresden, together with others, he had been assigned to collecting the dead, when he had come across a box filled with gold, foreign money and precious stones. He said that he had buried it in a spot which he had marked. He told them he was willing to take them to this spot in return for them sparing his life.

He led the three men to the high-ranking Soviet Jewish officer's garden, and he began digging in the ground for the fictitious box. The Soviet officer was at home and with a number of his soldiers. They came out of the house to see what all the commotion was about, and Sztajer ran up to him and said in Yiddish that the men who had brought him were armed and were killers. The Soviet officer told his soldiers to go and give the three men a .9 in the back of the head. The killers were shot.

Sztajer stayed in Dresden with this Soviet officer and in 1947, made his way to Italy and then to Palestine. He and his wife had one daughter, who became a lawyer. Sztajer became an industrialist and when Mrs Fuchs reached the age of eighty-five, he and I and his daughter went to Dresden to celebrate her birthday. Mrs Herta Fuchs lived out her life in Oberpoyritz, on the outskirts of Dresden, where I visited her several times. She was honoured as a Righteous Gentile by *Yad Vashem*, Israel's Holocaust Martyrs' and Heroes' Remembrance

Authority and she passed away in December 2003, at the age of ninety-four.

In 1950 I was chosen to swim and play water-polo for Great Britain in the Maccabiah games in Israel. A cousin had told me that my maternal grandmother was still alive and living in Haifa. By this time, she was 94 years old, completely blind and very frail. In the company of Susie Nador, an ex-Olympic swimmer and my wife-to-be, I made my way to my grandmother's place, an old age home on Mount Carmel. We entered a fairly spacious and attractive garden with tall palm trees. The buildings were single-storey, constructed of wood.

It was a pleasantly warm afternoon with a light breeze blowing from the sea. The nurse on duty told us that all the residents were having a siesta, including my grandmother, Mrs Makower.

We sat down to wait on a bench outside in the shade and the nurse promised that she would bring Mrs Makower out to meet us when she woke up.

'Who is it who is visiting her?'

I told her that I was her grandson, Romek, from Chodecz.

After about half an hour a small figure in a black dressing gown was led towards us. We stood up. She sensed our presence and stopped.

'Romek, *Reuven fin Hotz.*'

She said in Yiddish. Her voice quivered.

'Romek, *Reuven fin Hotz*,' she repeated.

The nurse sat her on the bench between Susie and me. I was on her left and she half-turned towards me and raised her right arm searching in space for my face. Her hand landed by my mouth. With her fingers she traced my lips, nose and eyes and now she called me Romoosh.

She didn't ask me who Susie was and we sat in silence. Her bony fingers moved around my lips again and I kissed them.

Now her left hand rested on my head and her right one on Susie's.

She began murmuring prayers... blessing us.

After three or four minutes, she fell silent again. And then, in a trembling voice, she asked if my mother, her daughter, was still alive.

'No,' I replied. 'She was murdered.'

'And your sister Zeesa, Zosia, alive?'

'No,' I replied. 'Murdered.'

'Your father Mordechi?'

'He died of starvation in the Lodz ghetto and so did my grandfather, your husband.'

'What about Sabina, Ignac and little Meshulam, Misio?'

'They were shot, shot at Babi-Yar.'

'Babi-Yar?' she questioned.

'Babi-Yar...?'

She then asked about Shlamek.

'No.'

'Peccio?'

'No.'

'Iccio?'

'No.'

'Sala?'

'No.'

Her head drooped and tears fell onto the black lap of her dressing gown.

We sat there in the shade for almost an hour without speaking, holding hands, the sea breeze rising up the Carmel carried through the pines and the palms.